Single Adult Ministry:
The Next Step

Single Adult Ministry:
The Next Step

Douglas L. Fagerstrom, Editor

A DIVISION OF SCRIPTURE PRESS PUBLICATIONS INC.
USA CANADA ENGLAND

Copyediting: Carole Streeter and Barbara Williams
Cover Design: Scott Rattray

Library of Congress Cataloging-in-Publication Data

Single adult ministry: the next step / Douglas L. Fagerstrom, editor.
    p.   cm.
    Includes bibliographical references.
    ISBN 1-56476-066-9
    1. Church work with single people — Handbooks, manuals, etc.
I. Fagerstrom, Douglas L.
BV639.S5S554   1993
259'.08'652 — dc20   92-37344
                                                          CIP

CONTENTS

89534

FOREWORD

In 1971 I inherited a small, struggling single adult ministry as a part of my work. At that time only a few had a prophetic vision of the need for reaching out to single men and women. Just a tiny handful were beginning to understand the emerging phenomena of the vast growing army of single adults in America. As the 1970s began, you could have counted the single adult ministries in local churches across the country on the fingers of both hands.

Through the next few years, leaders began to develop and share ideas. By the mid-'70s, a few conferences and publications were available. But not until the early 1980s did a national network come into being. You hold in your hands a book that is one of those valuable materials. A focused ministry with single people has now come of age in the church, and the tools to accomplish it are now available. Those of us who have specialized in this area for a long time are privileged to share with newer leaders some of the principles, methods, and ideas that we have learned.

I am deeply appreciative and thankful to the men and women in single adult ministry whose expertise, effort, and creativity are reflected on these pages. Continued power and blessings to these colleagues and partners in ministry who are taking single adult ministry to a new and higher level of sophistication and excellence. Power and prayers, also, to those who read and apply the content of these pages into Christ-centered ministries with single people across America and beyond.

Bill Flanagan
Minister to Single Adults
Newport Beach, California

PREFACE

In the early 1970s Single Adult Ministry was born in the life of church ministries across our nation. Indeed, single adults have always been a part of the body of Christ. However, the twentieth-century phenomenon of an exploding single adult population caused many Christian leaders to respond to a plethora of needs. Single adult ministry was defined. It was modeled. It produced leaders, resources, and "how-to" seminars. The infant ministry began to grow.

It is now the 1990s. Single adult ministry has changed. It has grown. It has stabilized. It has matured. Certain standards have been accepted and established. A wealth of books, articles, periodicals, journals, tapes, and videos are available to those beginning in ministry and seasoned veterans. Much is available through publishers, church models, and the Network of Single Adult Leaders (NSL). So where do we go from here?

We must keep on keeping on! Single adult ministry leaders must never lose sight of the biblical mandate to fulfill the Great Commission and "win some" (Matt. 28:19-20; 1 Cor. 9:19-22). We are here to bring single adults to a saving knowledge of Jesus Christ as Lord. We are here to encourage single adults to grow as godly men and women. We are here to unify and build the body of Christ by equipping single adults to use their spiritual gifts. We are here to comfort and bind up their wounds.

Single Adult Ministry: The Next Step is designed to encourage and help single adult leaders take the next steps in ministry. This book goes a step beyond the *Singles Ministry Handbook,* Victor Books, 1988. It offers additional insight and introduces areas of ministry that often demand the leader's attention.

This manual of monographs is not meant to be the "final word" on any

9

of the topics introduced. It is an encyclopedia of general knowledge written by those who have wrestled with the issues and "earned their stripes" by personal sacrifice and involvement as ministry leaders. The reader will be encouraged to begin new areas of ministry. The reader will be stimulated to gather more information from the wealth of resources suggested and will gain a new confidence to lead and affect a biblically based ministry. The leader will be able to make new choices based on years of experience and research from the authors.

Special thanks goes to the authors of this book, all of whom have given their work to the development of single adult ministry. All proceeds of this book go to the Network of Single Adult Leaders (NSL) to continue developing training conferences both nationally and locally.

My prayer is that the single adult ministry will continue to grow and reach single adults around the world with the good news of Jesus Christ. Thank you for sharing that prayer with me and many others. Welcome to the team of single adult ministry leaders.

Yours and His servant,
Doug Fagerstrom

(For more information on the Network of Single Adult Leaders, contact Doug Fagerstrom, NSL, P.O. Box 1600, Grand Rapids, Michigan 49501, 616-956-9377.)

A SINGLE PASTOR'S PRAYER
Rev. Frederick G. Cain

How good life is in Your love, dear God.
How good life is when surrounded by Your love for all people,
    Jew and Greek,
    male and female,
    white and black,
    rich and poor,
    slave and free,
    married and single.
How delightful the world would be if all Your people
would love as You love.

Why, O Lord, do my so-called brothers in the ministry
not love me as You love me?
Why do they say to me:
    Where is your wife?
    When are you going to get married?
    We're going to have to marry you off.
    You must have serious emotional problems—
    there is no other reason to be single!
When will those who name themselves as Your servants
love as You love?

Amen.

DEVELOPING LEADERSHIP

1. DEVELOPING A MINISTRY VISION

"The first guarantee the church must make to people is to always love them, under every circumstance, with no exception."

David Savage

Recent magazine and newspaper articles are declaring that the traditional family is dead, that the American people have become a nation of friendless adults, and that marriage is an outdated institution. While some journalists have exaggerated the state of affairs regarding family and friendship in America, they have captured the spirit of likely changes in the next decade.

George Barna, president of Barna Research Group, believes that the reported disintegration of the family is not an accurate portrayal. What has happened is that the traditional family unit — the working father and a mother who stays home to care for the two children — has been replaced by a different type of household. In 1960, this stereotypical family represented 60 percent of all households; today, it reflects just 7 percent of our households.[1]

The average American family in 1990 consists of a married couple with one child; both parents are employed. At least one of the parents is likely to have been, or will be, divorced. Parents are having fewer children and having them later in life. Increasing numbers of households are "blended families" — homes in which the children from two or more marriages are combined as a result of remarriage. There is also a growing trend for partners to have children without being married. In 1990, it was estimated that one out of every fifteen children would be born out of wedlock.[2]

In his book *The Baby Boomerang,* Doug Murren states that the singles population in the United States may be in excess of 50 percent of all adults above the age of 18 before the year 2000. Such figures mean that the church is faced with the "singling" of its communities.[3]

15

The attitude of society toward marriage and the traditional family and the rising divorce rate impact the growing singles population. The church for the 1990s will have to redefine its role to single adults if it intends to minister to them. The new realities of the single life must force the church to be fresh and creative when planning outreach and overall ministry.[4]

An Inward Look—Look Out, Church! Here Come the Single Adults

Divorce, a largely unthought-of and unplanned-for event in the lives of well over a million Americans every year, can drastically affect the lives of children, in-laws, families, social networks, and communities.[5]

In the late 1960s and early 1970s, as the divorce rate among Christians skyrocketed, and as disillusioned wives left the house to find work and greater fulfillment, concerned Christians began to look for a solution. Linda Raney Wright in *A Cord of Three Strands* stated that the church could have entertained a number of options at that time. It could have examined the root problems of dissatisfaction in marriage and their solutions; it might have seen each marriage as unique unto itself and dealt with each accordingly; it might have assessed total needs and considerations before drawing a conclusion; it might have encouraged communication between husbands and wives; or it might have observed what was happening between secular couples to determine whether Christian couples could learn anything constructive.[6]

Many churches took the challenge and began to develop ministries to meet the needs of the family and bring healing to marriages, while not neglecting the single adults and their multiple needs. However, the majority of churches did little or nothing in either area.

The recent growth of the single adult population in America has been a great shock to many in church leadership. In many churches couples with children no longer dominate the membership rolls. The boomer generation is such a large one that any statistical slant will have large ramifications for those seeking to serve them.[7]

Not to be forgotten is the "Buster" generation. These "post-boomers" have been referred to as the "postponed generation." Our ministries will need to adjust and adapt in the present and for the future to this issues-oriented, conservative subculture.

The church must be aware that the singles population in America will impact the function of the church. When a church undertakes programming, staffing, preaching, sharing illustrations or anecdotes, and addressing needs from the pulpit, that leadership should keep in mind that possibly half of the congregation is single.

Therefore, the church cannot be blind to the fact that singleness is a very complex and difficult issue because it represents numerous age categories and life situations: teenagers who have moved out of their parents' homes; never married, young single moms; divorcées with children; a growing number of single fathers; the never-marrieds of various ages; the elderly—both widows and widowers; and a generation of single-parent children.

This reality of singleness is forcing the church to face new issues when planning outreach and ministry. Each age-group and life situation copes with different concerns and challenges. Each one requires a different setting for fellowship and pastoral care.[8] Before a church starts a ministry to single adults, it must have an inward look into two basic issues—the divorce and remarriage issue, and the single bias issue.

• Possibly the most difficult issue the church will face is divorce and remarriage. Since there is so much controversy over this issue, it will be dealt with as a relationship issue first.

Balswick, in *The Family—A Christian Perspective on the Contemporary Home,* deals with divorce and remarriage from a relational position. He states that wherever Jesus talks about divorce (Matthew 5:31-32; 19:3-9; Mark 10:2-12; Luke 16:18), the clear thrust is that marriage is of the Lord and is not to be broken. Christ is calling couples to a lifelong commitment. However, He does not have in view a marriage of legalism and law which involves a commitment only to the institution and not to the relationship. Balswick states:

> This perspective that the well-being of the people involved is more important than the structure of marriage has shaped our view of simple parenthood and remarriage. The Christian message is that out of brokenness can come forgiveness and restoration.
>
> Some divorced persons with children will choose to remain single and shoulder the responsibility of being the head of a one-parent family. We must not deny them or their families the encouragement and support that are necessary for them to thrive. These members of the church body are to be accepted and welcomed into the church as legitimate parts of God's family.
>
> Some divorced persons will find restoration through remarriage. The church must resist the temptation to develop a legal-

istic rationale which would deny them the opportunity to find wholeness and hope through remarriage. Remarried persons who live in reconstituted families have much to offer to our community in Christ. When our theology of relationships is practical, the restoration and renewal of the remarried will be a blessing and strength to the whole community of believers.[9]

Many church groups do not accept Balswick's relational position on divorce and remarriage. They believe that the doctrinal position is the only way to deal with the divorce and remarriage issue.

Since the issue of divorce and remarriage will continue to be a doctrinal issue for the church in the 1990s, a recent book that gives four Christian views is helpful. This book, edited by H. Wayne House, includes four standard arguments on divorce and remarriage as well as refutations from each of the other three. The four standard arguments are:

1. no divorce and no remarriage;
2. divorce, but no remarriage;
3. divorce and remarriage for adultery or desertion;
4. divorce and remarriage under a variety of circumstances.

There is considerable controversy over the meaning of certain Hebrew and Greek words, and often the meaning of a Scripture passage will turn on the correct understanding of these words. The contributors to this book come to different conclusions because of the different weight they give to the various passages.

To develop a ministry, bold questions need to be asked and answers need to be sought. What is the meaning of one flesh? Does it refer to blood relation? What is the meaning of marriage? Is it inherently indissoluble? How does one explain the divorcing of foreign wives in Ezra and Malachi? Is Jesus speaking of fornication in the betrothal period in Matthew 19:9, or is this a reference to an incestuous act? Does Jesus offer new teaching that sets aside the teaching of Moses in Deuteronomy? Is only divorce in view in Matthew 19:9 and not remarriage? Or is remarriage inherent in the understanding of divorce? If fornication includes adultery as well as other sexual sins, does it refer to a single act, or does it refer to a continual state? Does Paul introduce another exception besides fornication or sexual immorality in 1 Corinthians 7, namely, desertion by an unbelieving spouse? Does this require the believing spouse to remain unmarried or does it allow a new marriage to be contracted?[10]

Although there are varying interpretations of the divorce and remarriage issue, church leaders need to reflect on this statement: "While the

18

church must uphold the importance of marriage, the church cannot reject people who are divorced, or who struggle with the need to extricate themselves from a destructive marriage."[11] The church that ministers to singles will be able to love the divorced and the remarried, and truly care for the needs of their families without feeling that this ministry contradicts their doctrinal views of divorce and remarriage.

• The second major area where the church needs godly wisdom is in dealing with the biases it may have against single adults. For some time the church has looked at singleness as an oddity. This subtly suggests that if you are not married, you are either out of the will of God or your love is still on the way to rescue you.

The "swinging single" image has fostered a stereotype that may create a bias in many church groups. A national questionnaire given to both married and single adults dealt with problem areas for singles. The results indicated that married people perceived that the number-one problem singles face was related to sexual frustrations and expressions. Given the same questionnaire, singles rated sexual frustration fifth, their biggest frustration having to do with "being left out" or "not being included, especially in couples or family events." The second greatest frustration was finances and being the sole breadwinner. Third was the finding of meaningful and rewarding friendships.[12]

Because single adults do have trouble with the whole issue of sexuality, they are regarded as living "loose" lives. "But anyone who has pastored for any length of time knows that . . . married people struggle with their sexuality just as much, if not more, than the singles."[13]

The church that envisions the tremendous potential of a single adult ministry, and prepares both the leadership and congregation for evangelism ministry to the single adult population, will be a mighty church in the 1990s. The single adult population is searching for answers to their questions and for meaning to fulfill their lives. The church of Jesus Christ has the answers they are searching for. Help is available if they are made to feel welcome into the fellowship of believers and are taught the Word of God and the love of Jesus Christ.

The alternatives available for single adults are very limited and, in most cases, reinforce or compound the problems rather than help solve them. For example, the bars and singles clubs are materialistic and encourage immoral values. Special interest social organizations such as health clubs, spas, and sports clubs, do not offer the kind of nurturing needed to help people reach their God-given potential. The church can provide hope, understanding, personal feedback, role models, interpersonal learning, and belonging within the context of teaching people about the Lord.

The church that chooses to minister to singles will reap the results in many areas of the fellowship. As single adults learn and grow, they become responsible leaders committed to serving God and the needs of the church. A single adult ministry can also be a very effective method for a church to reach out into its community and provide community service. For the church with enough vision to reach out and touch the lives of single adults in the community, there will be benefits in all areas of ministry.

An Upward Look — Look Up, Church! Here Comes the Answer

In defining the church's role to singles, there must be a clarification of the church's overall role in relation to the family structure designed by God. The church needs to educate people about the benefits of permanent monogamy and intense family relations. It also needs to provide more extensive premarital counseling to individuals seeking to marry.[14] The church ought to consider celebrating successful marriages instead of just wailing over the demise of relationships. Americans learn best by behavorial modeling. Showing that marriage can work is part of persuading people to rethink the place of divorce and "serial monogamy."

While the church must uphold the importance of marriage, people who are divorced or who struggle with the need to extricate themselves from a destructive marriage cannot be rejected. Postmarital counseling must be available to help people through the rocky times. Churches must offer counseling programs, support groups, recreational opportunities for single parents and for their children; it is important to help them become the kind of people they want to be.[15]

Some churches are providing counseling and support groups for single adults. Jim Smoke, in *Growing in Remarriage,* states that many churches have classes for those entering first marriages. They cover the various facets of building a healthy marriage. But few churches have classes for those entering a second marriage. Generally, these couples are left to fend for themselves when, in truth, they need far more help and instruction than those entering first marriages.[16]

A marriage preparation manual prepared by Wes Roberts and H. Norman Wright, *Before You Say I Do,* should be considered a requirement in counseling a couple planning remarriage. This manual can help any couple to understand that "marriage is a refining process that God will use to have us become the man or woman He wants us to be."[17] If children are involved in this newly formed family, Wright suggests that counseling is essential.

> Can the person who may never have been married before accept the experience of the other's love life with someone else in years gone by? If there are children still in the home, can the new partner accept and love them? Will the children accept someone else in Mother's or Father's place? If one has never married before, can he or she suddenly take on a ready-made family and adjust to them?[18]

The new parent may fail to understand the psychological problems of the stepchild and retaliate by rejecting the child or showing favoritism, if his children are involved. Older children can oppose the marriage and, even from the beginning of courtship, show hostility toward the new partner.

David and Bonnie Juroe, in *Successful Stepparenting,* emphasize that church leadership and Christian counselors need to see the great importance of reaching out redemptively to children of the divorced. There is a great rise in the number of people waiting for help because of the staggering problems encountered in step-families. Many parents really do care about their children's needs and sincerely want to help them through the pain of a divorce or remarriage, but they do not know how. As people in church leadership become familiar with the reasons behind the stresses they have to cope with, the quality and durability of their new relationships will be greatly enhanced.[19]

David and Bonnie Juroe encourage churches to develop counseling services as well as support groups for their single adult community. They also suggest that churches desiring to have an effective ministry to blended families need to consider having Stepparents Day. "The neighborhood church that celebrates Stepparents Day builds a bridge of friendship and acceptance to families who need support and love but have not been sure that their participation is welcome."[20] A special day would give worthy recognition to a growing host of individuals in the church and society who rightly should be honored for their great sacrifices of caring. A Stepparents Day would allow stepchildren a special opportunity to express appreciation without feeling uncomfortable over a divided loyalty between a stepparent and the absent, natural parent.[21]

If a church does not have a specialized program for single-parent families, Jim and Barbara Dycus have suggested some ways a church can

21

adapt its current church program to meet the needs in the single-parent family. Church leadership can train teachers to include in their lessons illustrations and Bible stories about one-parent homes. Visits can be made to single-parent homes to express a more caring, empathetic relationship with members of these families.

Church leadership must make sure that children of divorce are not excluded from church activities just because parental visitation schedules keep them from achieving perfect attendance, because they lack transportation or funds, or because the "right" parent is unavailable (as in a father/son dinner). Every teacher in the church should make a commitment to unconditionally love and accept each single-parent family in their church and community.

It is also essential that the church exercise the belief that God can heal the hurt of divorce, by focusing on the wholeness of families in crisis, rather than treating them as second-class citizens or "emotional basket cases." The emphasis in ministry should be to lead children of divorce and their parents to adapt positively to the changes they face.[22]

If a church serves a number of teens from broken homes, it may wish to form an ongoing support group for them. However, the teens should also be encouraged to stay with the established youth group. A support group led by a youth worker with counseling experience can be valuable for teenage divorce victims on the road to recovery.

Such groups will not work if the church leadership does not have genuine love. The "don't touch" syndrome is a part of a Victorian attitude about sex and the human body. However, not all the blame can be placed there, for among men, this rule about not touching is related to deep fears of possible homosexual tendencies. Is it not interesting that in our society the bumper sticker appeared, "Have you hugged your kid today?" Why should such a question ever be asked? Because there is a hang-up about hugging on the part of many parents.[23] Churches that reach the single adult population will express love in a genuine, healthy, and caring way.

One of the most important ministries to the single adult community is the Divorce Recovery Support Group. The purpose of divorce recovery is to help people work through the issues which impact life because of marital disruption. Divorce recovery serves as a bridge between the divorce crisis and life as a single-again adult. A divorce recovery program must integrate the truth of the Gospel into a program mix which meets the felt needs of the participants. Such a mix will include crisis intervention and grief management within a framework designed to understand the past, cope with the present, and prepare for the future. Divorce recovery provides an excellent opportunity for outreach and evangelism, since participants are attracted to fellowship within the singles ministry of the sponsoring church.[24]

Harold Ivan Smith, in *I Wish Someone Understood My Divorce*, gives three reasons why a divorce support group is essential for a church. First, such groups are emergency rooms for the newly separated or divorced, providing the care needed to heal hurts and help to reenter the world of singleness. Many people attribute their survival to the nurture of a support group.

Second, these groups are stabilizers because they provide structure, friendship, social activities, and leadership opportunities. Third, the groups help the newly divorced to learn the ropes of their singlehood. They serve a valuable cultural role because divorce has not been recognized as a rite of passage. Such support groups are not pity parties but rather cheerleaders who help individuals to function more effectively.[25]

Support groups, seminars, and retreats can be used to educate or reeducate the single in enhancing communication skills, restoring self-esteem, and learning personality traits.

An Outward Look—Look Out, Singles! Here Comes the Church

The church of the 1990s needs to meet single adults where they are. This means presenting them in a positive light. The church that is effectively reaching single adults knows that the secret of successful single living is not self-sufficiency, but sufficiency in Christ Jesus. The season of singleness must be understood as an opportunity to discover and become all that God dreams for one to be.

Single adults must come to realize that they can lead productive lives, contradictory to the stereotype of the swinging single. Single adults generally have more time to invest in careers, and business rewards such commitment with raises, bonuses, and promotions. Single adults must be taught to alert themselves to the danger of "unproductive spiritual lives."[26] The church that teaches that God calls all of His children, married or single, to ministry and endows all of His children with ministry gifts, will be a church with the outward look.

The church with the outward look is the church that has a goal to minister salvation to all. The word *salvation* in its broadest sense means "to bring to wholeness," and is interchangeable with the word *healing*. In James 5:15 we read, "And the prayer of faith shall save the sick" (KJV). The same Greek word rendered "save" here is translated "heal" elsewhere; the NIV version says, "will make the sick person well."

Within the community of the gathered church, married and single adults need to be saved, healed, and brought to wholeness in every sense of their lives. But before there can be a coming to wholeness, certain guarantees must be made to people. Otherwise, they will not risk themselves to be open with the church leadership to receive this healing.

The first guarantee the church must make to people is to always love them, under every circumstance, with no exception. The second guarantee is to totally accept them, without reservation. The third guarantee is that the church will reach out to them, no matter how miserably they fail or how blatantly they sin. Unreserved forgiveness is theirs for the asking, without a bitter taste left in anybody's mouth. The final guarantee is the absolute faithfulness of God and truthfulness of the Bible. If singles are not given these guarantees, they will never allow the church the marvelous privilege of bringing wholeness to them.[27]

The aggressive outreaching church of the 1990s will also look for alternative church service times. The Barna Research Group has found many reasons why single adults do not attend church. According to this research, Murren believes that the most common reasons for not attending church are problems of time and priority. Most single adults say they have to work on Sunday or that it is their only day off. They also say that other issues in their lives take precedence over church attendance. The typical all-American single adult claims she or he also needs Sunday for doing other activities to keep life and limb together.[28] New paradigms for ministry are needed.

The aggressive outreaching church will present singleness in a positive light, will recognize the potential spiritual leadership single adults can provide, will give themselves to the challenge to guarantee to love, accept, and forgive, and will provide alternative worship times and new ministries appropriate for single adults.

Conclusion

In a survey of unchurched single adults, Barna Research Group found that almost four out of ten said they had a positive disposition toward attending church in the future. This finding may mean that at least four out of every ten single people in your community would be happy to attend the church if someone would reach out to them in a friendly, accommodating manner.[29]

The role of the successful church in the 1990s will be in relationship— friendly and single-sensitive. Once this church has had an inward look and is truly prepared to minister to the single community, then an upward look will give that church a vision as to what they can do to reach out to and meet the multiple needs of the single adult community. Then their focused outward look will be followed by an aggressive mission to bring in the harvest.

David Savage
Minister with Single Adults
Trinity Church
7002 Canton Avenue
Lubbock, Texas 79413-6399

Notes

1. George Barna, *The Frog in the Kettle* (Ventura, California: Regal Books, 1990), 67.
2. Ibid., 67.
3. Doug Murren, *The Baby Boomerang* (Ventura, California: Regal Books, 1990), 76.
4. Barna, 77.
5. Jim Smoke, *Turning Points* (Eugene, Oregon: Harvest House, 1985), 115.
6. Linda Raney Wright, *A Cord of Three Strands* (Old Tappan, New Jersey: Fleming H. Revell, 1987), 11.
7. Murren, 76.
8. Ibid., 77.
9. Jack O. and Judith K. Balswick, *The Family—A Christian Perspective on the Contemporary Home* (Grand Rapids: Baker Book House, 1989), 271–72.
10. H. Wayne House, ed., *Divorce and Remarriage—Four Christian Views* (Downers Grove, Illinois: InterVarsity Press, 1990), 10–11.
11. Douglas L. Fagerstrom, ed., *Singles Ministry Handbook* (Wheaton, Illinois: Victor Books, 1988), 28–29.
12. Ibid.
13. Murren, 76.
14. Gerald L. Dahl, *How Can We Keep Christian Marriages from Falling Apart?* (Nashville: Thomas Nelson, 1988), 168–69.
15. Barna, 77–78.
16. Jim Smoke, *Growing in Remarriage* (Old Tappan, New Jersey: Fleming H. Revell, 1990), 43.
17. Wes Roberts and H. Norman Wright, *Before You Say I Do* (Eugene,

Oregon: Harvest House, 1978), 6.

18. H. Norman Wright, *Communication* (Ventura, California: Regal Books, 1984), 138.

19. David J. and Bonnie B. Juroe, *Successful Stepparenting* (Old Tappan, New Jersey: Fleming H. Revell, 1983), 12.

20. Ibid., 177.

21. Ibid.

22. Guy Greenfield, *We Need Each Other* (Grand Rapids: Baker Book House, 1984), 24.

23. Ibid.

24. Fagerstrom, 158.

25. Harold Ivan Smith, *I Wish Someone Understood My Divorce* (Minneapolis: Augsburg Publishing House, 1986), 146–47.

26. Harold Ivan Smith, *Positively Single* (Wheaton, Illinois: Victor Books, 1989), 22.

27. Jerry Cook, *Love, Acceptance, and Forgiveness* (Ventura, California: Regal Books, 1978), 11–12.

28. Murren, 91.

29. Ibid.

2. DEVELOPING
SPIRITUAL LEADERSHIP

"The inward journey will provide the motivation, discipline, and staying power needed to love, care for, and heal those who are broken."

Robert Duffet

The term *spiritual leadership* has been much discussed and debated during the last thirty years. Books, sermons, and seminars on the subject have tried to define it and encourage its development. All agree that effectiveness in ministry and world evangelization will be determined by the quality of spiritual leadership in the church.

All institutions in our society are searching for ways to raise the quality of leadership. It is almost a universal principle that the success and effectiveness of any endeavor will depend on the quality of leadership. In a general way, leadership may be defined as influencing people in a certain direction. President Dwight Eisenhower defined leadership as the ability to get people to do what you want them to do. In his excellent book, *Leadership,* James Burns calls leadership "the ability to induce followers to act toward certain goals that are important to both the leader and followers."

These definitions are applicable to almost any leadership situation—politics, educational administration, business management. But at issue for ministry is the similarity and difference between the above definitions and spiritual leadership. At first glance, single adult leaders would affirm these definitions. They certainly are influencing people, at times getting others to do what they don't want to do, and they firmly believe followers in single adult ministry need to be committed to the goals of the ministry. However, the difference between leadership in general and spiritual leadership is the means and ends. Spiritual leadership is concerned with influencing followers by the *right* means toward the *right* ends (goal). The Christian single adult leader demands a more comprehensive definition of

27

leadership that emphasizes means and ends. To find such a definition of leadership, we need to consult the Bible.

A Biblical Definition of Spiritual Leadership
Spiritual leadership may be defined as the increasing personal acquisition of world vision, ministry skills, and character development, all grounded in a commitment of faith and obedience to the Gospel of Jesus Christ.

• World vision is the ability to see the world in all its complexity and diversity. It is the opposite of ethnocentrism, racism, and provincialism. It encompasses the whole world in response to Christ's mandate to preach the Gospel to every person and to the recognition that God loves all people. Specifically, world vision means a personal grasp of the principle of spiritual multiplication, personal involvement in world need, and understanding of the infinite worth of the individual.

• Ministry skills are required to be an effective servant of Jesus Christ. The single adult leader recognizes the priesthood of all believers and the fact that the Holy Spirit gives ministerial gifts to all. These skills include the abilities to share one's faith, to encourage other people, to apply the results of Bible study to one's life and behavior, to work with those who disagree with one's point of view, to practice the spiritual disciplines, to be flexible, and to understand one's spiritual gifts.

• Character development is the cultivating and evidencing of the fruit of the Spirit (Gal. 5:22-23). This includes love, honesty, obedience, faithfulness, a servant heart, generosity, openness, humility, patience, confidence, hospitality, gentleness, stability, kindness, and self-control.

The above definition of spiritual leadership, with its emphasis on world vision, ministry skills, and character development, attempts to balance the *being* and *doing* of the Christian life. Balance is important. In her book *Journey Inward, Journey Outward,* Elizabeth O'Connor observed that those who overemphasize the outward journey (doing) of spiritual leadership (social change, evangelism) often run out of the necessary spiritual power to make the desired and needed changes. Similarly, those who overemphasize the inward journey (being) discover that their spiritual experience is stunted, self-centered, and devoid of meaning.

Without the other, each is shallow and lacks substance. Being (inward journey) without doing (outward journey) is idolatrous and the worst sort of putrid piety. Doing (outward journey) with being (inward journey) will ultimately collapse under its own weight, since being provides the spiritual strength and power to persevere. Unless the inward journey is cultivated, individuals and the Christian community will not be able to stand

28

up to the oppressive powers of the world and, hence, will either capitulate or become status quo. The inward journey will provide the motivation, discipline, and staying power needed to love, care for, and heal those who are broken. The goal, then, of spiritual leadership is to open our lives to God in such a way (inward journey) that we may be used to help heal a world of pain (outward journey).

A Theology of Spiritual Leadership

Any discussion of spiritual leadership must begin with the Gospel, the Good News. By definition the Gospel is the proclamation or announcement of a new reality of living for individuals and communities that has come to pass due to the death and resurrection of Jesus Christ. This is not just a new possibility but a new reality of living. The Apostle Paul speaks about this new way of living as being "in Christ." Being "in Christ" gives individuals and communities the inclination toward responsibility and obedience. This inclination comes from a moral transformation of life through faith. Hence, the Gospel is both indicative and imperative—we personally experience the power of Christ through faith (what God does for us) and then live out a moral and obedient lifestyle based on our experience of faith (what God expects from us). Through this Gospel, salvation is experienced by the people of God.

Salvation implies a twofold commitment of faith: to God through Jesus and to the community of believers. True spirituality manifests itself in community. Spiritual leadership must go beyond the privatization of faith to a growing demonstration of the presence of God's kingdom in our midst. The power of the kingdom is demonstrated by relationships based on humility, responsible living, forgiveness, compassion, bearing each other's burdens, and obedience.

At the heart of spiritual leadership for single adult leaders is the need to provide programmatic and personal means to encourage other single adults to choose—in every event of life—to act obediently and responsibly before God. As this happens, both individuals and ministry will experience the power of Christ. In our life together, the Gospel calls us to do for others what God has done for us. Since God is giving, merciful, and forgiving, we may be giving, merciful, and forgiving to each other based on Christ's acceptance of us (Rom. 15:7).

The Necessity of Spiritual Leadership

Why is spiritual leadership important? Why should single adult leaders aspire to spiritual leadership or bother to train others to be spiritual leaders? The answers to these questions come from the Bible and also from contemporary needs. The first book of the Bible clearly explains the problem of humanity; the present brokenness of our society cries out for some type of leadership to heal our land (2 Chron. 7:14).

The story of Adam and Eve (Gen. 1–3) is fodder for advertisements, jokes, and sermons. But the event itself describes humanity's problem in such clarity that it sounds like it occurred yesterday. Through their choice to disobey God (3:1-7) and overstep the limitations God placed on them, the harmony and joy of creation was shattered and fragmented. Adam and Eve experienced fragmentation of their lives in four ways.

First, there was relational fragmentation between them. They were created to have open and trusting relationships with each other. Once they were "naked and not ashamed" (2:25); now they were naked, ashamed, and they hid from each other (3:7). The perfect relationship was now shame-based and fractured.

Second, the relationship between God and humanity was fractured. Not only did Adam and Eve hide from each other, but they also hid from God (3:8). After experiencing all of God's gifts in an astonishing environment, they chose to overstep their bounds and jeopardize their relationship with the One who gave them beauty and joy.

Third, the story of Adam and Eve demonstrates intrapersonal fragmentation. Both explained their actions to God by blaming. Eve blamed the snake and Adam blamed Eve (3:12-13). Blaming another for one's actions indicates the presence of an inner war—the essence of intrapersonal fragmentation.

Fourth, the removal of the first couple from the Garden produced the world's first ecological disaster and environmental fragmentation (3:20-24). Gone were the beautiful surroundings, and basic life functions (work, childbearing) were painfully altered (3:16-19).

The first three chapters of the Bible offer perspective on the pain and brokenness of our lives. Humanity *did not* and *does not* accept the limitations placed on us by God. As a result, we live in the midst of fragmentation and brokenness. Although all ministries attempt to deal with human brokenness, few see that more clearly than the single adult leader. Much of the single adult leader's time is given to personal and programmatic ministries dealing with broken relationships.

Stan and Debby promised to live together and love each other ". . . till death us do part." But one day Stan walked out for another woman. Devastated, Debby turned to the single adult ministry in her church. Many other women there had gone through a similar experience. For several months, members of the group and single adult leaders helped pick up the shattered pieces of Debby's life. The betrayal still hurts, but by her own admission life is getting better.

Bill wanted to marry and have children, but the right woman never appeared, and he is lonely. Now in his mid-forties, he sees some of his college friends' children having children, and he often feels left out. He loves his nieces and nephews, but his family takes little interest in his life. Everyone is so preoccupied—his parents with the grandchildren and his brothers and sisters with their homes, children, and lives. Bill often wonders who loves and cares about him.

A few years ago a single adult leader took an interest in Bill. A bit shy at first, Bill wanted no part of a single adult ministry. But now he feels a sense of belonging. His sense of fragmentation due to loneliness is lessened through the single adult ministry in his church.

Susan and Ray were the perfect couple. Two years ago Ray went out for a morning jog and never returned. He was found on a running path in a nearby woods. While running he suffered a massive heart attack and died within minutes. Susan's grief was unbearable, but a single adult leader encouraged her to participate in a grief recovery group. She still misses Ray, and her life at times feels broken, but she is growing stronger and more confident each day. Her radiant smile, so much a part of her demeanor but missing since Ray's death, is now back. She tells all who will listen how the single adult group was there when her world fell apart.

Why is spiritual leadership important? Only spiritual leaders put in place ministries that enable people to hear and respond to a God who will put the shattered fragments of their lives together through faith in Jesus Christ.

Criteria for Spiritual Leadership
The Bible offers five criteria for spiritual leaders:

 • Personal integrity. Single adult ministry is rooted in the ministry of Jesus. As Jesus sought those whom society at times shunted aside, so single adult ministry works with those who often feel marginalized by the church. Jesus demanded followers to "follow Him." Single adult leaders must hear the call of the Master as well. The call to follow Jesus demands obedience and an ethical lifestyle.

Let it be said firmly and clearly that there is no spiritual leadership where there is no personal integrity! First Timothy 3:1-7 and Titus 1:5-9 not only spell out the moral criteria for spiritual leadership but also define the nature of personal integrity. Based on these passages, a spiritual leader must be reliable, an effective mother/father, wife/husband, an able teacher, competent, experienced, and blameless from scandal. In a day when the juiciest scandals and stories come not from Hollywood but from high profile ministries, personal integrity for spiritual leadership must be reemphasized. Moral words without a moral life are hypocritical and hollow.

• Self-awareness. American culture and high-power ministries encourage and thrive on action. Some ministries are so fast-paced there is hardly time to catch a breath. If their leaders do slow down to reflect on life, ministry, interpersonal pain, or the future, they can feel bewildered about their motivations.

It is essential that spiritual leaders periodically set aside time to think about why and how ministry is done, and about the impact the spiritual single adult leader has on his/her followers. The result of this exercise is increased self-awareness.

They not only need to reflect on their impact, behavior, and ministry, but also to develop a small group of trusted peers who will honestly provide feedback on their strengths, weaknesses, gifts, limitations, and on how they are being perceived by others. Without an accountability group, a single adult leader's ministry will be limited, if not hampered. The individuals who constitute this group must be "safe." That is, they must be individuals outside the ministry with whom single adult leaders feel free to open their hearts without fear of condemnation or job reprisal.

There is a link between personal integrity and self-awareness. No one is so spiritual that he/she no longer possesses character defects that could undermine ministry. However, awareness of these defects and a small group of supporters who allow the leader to talk about them will enable him/her to gain increasing sense of victory over the problems. Defects, sins, and temptations named and discussed with others often cease to have power to harm.

Bob was the recognized spiritual leader of one of America's largest single adult ministries. A gifted communicator and able minister, he was asked to speak all over the country. When he traveled, the urge was overwhelming—he simply could not pass by adult book stores and x-rated pay-per-view films in his hotel room. What started as merely sensual curiosity led to a literary, pictorial, and video obsession. He even paid in cash for his pay-per-view movies so they would not appear on his hotel bill. Bob confessed to the Lord time after time in city after city that he would never look at that material again, but he simply could not stop.

Healing came when Bob told his small support group about his behavior. As he talked through his feelings of guilt, pain, and disappointment, he began to feel healed. They did not judge but prayed for and encouraged him. Although still tempted, the craving within subsided. In Bob's case, his honesty and confession and the support of his group gave him freedom.

• Building on strengths and seeking balance. Single adult ministry is a high-touch, people-oriented concern for individuals. Single adult ministries start with the needs of people, but they do not end there. The biblical goal (or task) is to develop ministries that enable some single adults to come to faith in Jesus, some to grow in faith, and others to become spiritual leaders. However, a tension exists between concern for human need and programmatic ministry. If the single adult leader becomes so preoccupied with needs, the numerical growth of ministry will be stunted. One person is able to effectively minister to about eighty people. In time a ministry fixated on interpersonal need will become little more than a therapy group. Key biblical mandates — outreach, inclusion, expansion of ministry — will be subverted.

On the other hand, a single adult minister who is a great programmer, visionary leader, first-class marketer, and inspiring teacher may be perceived as aloof, cold, or uncaring. The programs and attendance may be great, but the commitment to the task may thwart other biblical mandates like compassion, joy, and peace. Often ministries like this subtly reinforce the notion that single adults must look good and appear successful.

A ministry takes on the characteristics of its spiritual leader. No one is so perfect as to consistently balance what leadership theorists call people orientation and task orientation. Both task and people orientation are needed in single adult ministry. One is not better than the other, and effective spiritual leadership may be either task or people-oriented. Most people lean to one side or the other. Self-awareness and feedback from those who observe one's leadership are the best sources to determine one's leadership style.

Since few of us are both people- and task-oriented, and since single adult ministry needs both styles to be effective, the goal of spiritual leadership development is to surround yourself with people of a different style. For instance, a hard-charging task-oriented person should build a leadership team of those who are people-oriented. Likewise, a warm, loving, caring person, one who is able to "key into" individual hurt, should build a leadership team from task-oriented people.

The Apostle Paul's teaching on spiritual gifts is helpful (1 Cor. 12–14). All have some gifts, but no one has all the gifts. When all use their gifts, ministry is dynamic and effective. One key criteria of single adult spiritual leadership is to follow Paul's pattern of understanding the gifts, allow the utilization of the gifts, and build a leadership team that balances task and people orientation.

● Bouncing back from failure. How happy it would be if God never let us fail, if all efforts ended in success. The Bible offers no such guarantees. We will fail—sometimes miserably, despite our best efforts!

Single adult ministry is often about failure. Death, divorce, bankruptcy, job termination, and sickness make us *feel* like failures. Even if they are not our fault, our goals are thwarted and the future seems bleak. To be a spiritual leader means dealing with failure—either in the past, present, or future. For most, the real question is not failure, but whether they will bounce back.

I live in Chicago. Michael Jordan, a player for the Chicago Bulls, is considered by many to be *the* best basketball player ever! But Jordan was cut from his high school basketball team. Only he knows his feelings and how he dealt with this setback. It must have been difficult. I am sure he felt like a failure; nevertheless, he continued to play and today he is at the top.

There is no easy way to get cut or fail. It is not a pleasant experience to be dismissed from a church staff. There is no medicine for the emotional pain and no road map leading to success. However, if the world's best basketball player gets cut and bounces back, there is hope for you.

The Apostle Peter had a similar experience of failure. During Jesus' most difficult days, Peter promised to stand by Him, regardless of the consequences. But when Jesus was seized and taken to Pontius Pilate, and Peter was recognized several times as one of the groupies, in a fit of anger, cursing and swearing, he insisted to an inquirer he did not even know Jesus (Mark 14:71-72). Is there a more egregious example of failure in all history? A close confidant of Jesus denied even knowing Him when He was being falsely accused!

There is an interesting twist to this story. When the women went to Jesus' tomb on Easter morning and found He had risen, the angel told them to tell the disciples *and Peter* that He would see them later (Mark 16:7). Peter was singled out because Jesus wanted to make sure that he was not cast aside. He was not washed up. He had a future with Jesus.

On the surface spiritual leadership can appear to be risky business. All will not go smoothly. However, in the midst of failure, the promises of

God shine brighter. Peter's life, ministry, and failure show that Jesus grants all a second chance, a new beginning, another opportunity.

Spiritual single adult leaders will fail. However, the story of Peter is a reminder that failure is not the last word. We have a God of the second chance.

• Hanging tough when times are tough. The biblical word for this is steadfastness or perseverance. Some would call it guts. It is the ability to hang in there when times are tough. The single adult spiritual leader knows how tough it gets—people's needs, demands, and crises never end. Add to this the constant complaints, and it is no mystery why the single adult leader wants to quit. Wanting to quit is a natural and logical feeling. Other spiritual leaders have wanted to throw in the towel too. Since perseverance and steadfastness are such important qualities in the New Testament, it would seem that many spiritual leaders of the first century were tempted to quit as well. Scripture gives three reasons not to quit.

First, God is with you, particularly when times are tough. At low points God is especially close to you. Throughout Scripture, God delighted to work in and through those who were at the end of the rope.

Second, spiritual leaders face a spiritual adversary. It should come as no surprise that the spiritual nature of leadership will come into conflict with the demonic. The ministry of Jesus was one of conflict with Satan and the demonic. Ministry today follows in the same pattern. As spiritual leaders seek to heal the brokenness of people's lives, they should expect conflict from the source of the brokenness! Conflict is never easy. Warfare is always taxing. In the midst of spiritual warfare it is easy to become discouraged. However, the conflict and pain may in actuality be a sign that you and your ministry are successfully causing Satan to fall.

Third, quitting now may foreclose on a future victory. No one quits at halftime, regardless of the score. With time left to play, anything may happen. Often dramatic events and unforeseen happenings occur, and all of a sudden the losing team wins!

The moral of the story is—don't quit! There yet may be a dramatic turnaround from the Lord.

Robert G. Duffet
Director of Doctoral Studies and Assistant Professor of Ministry
Northern Baptist Theological Seminary
660 East Butterfield Road
Lombard, Illinois 60148-5698

3. DEVELOPING VOLUNTEERS

"Your goal is not to have everyone think what a wonderful encourager you are. Your goal is to have encouraged leaders."

Rob McCleland

My first recruiting experience as a minister with single adults was a dismal failure. I asked about ten gifted and capable young adults if they would consider serving on our leadership team. Eight of them said yes, so I took them on our first leadership retreat. During our first session, I had each of them write down what role they desired to fulfill. A few of them had specific answers, but most said, "I'll do whatever you want me to do." There was only one problem — I didn't know what I wanted them to do. I had no vision, no direction, and no goals for our ministry. Since I didn't know where we were going, I couldn't tell our volunteers how to get there. By God's grace and hard work, I've come a long way since then. I want to share with you a few of the things I've learned along the way.

Your success in singles ministry will be directly proportional to your ability to recruit, equip, and encourage volunteers. That's a strong statement. You may be a paid singles ministry professional, or you may be a lay person who desires to lead. Either way, in singles ministry volunteers are everything.

The goal of this chapter is not to enable you to double your group in the next year or even to lessen your workload. The goal is to help you to build people. No singles ministry will fulfill its potential unless lay volunteers are actively involved in meeting the group's objectives. Therefore it is essential to continually find new volunteers, train them in ministry skills, and encourage them to continue developing in their effectiveness for the kingdom of God.

I've worked with many people who feel competent in completing assigned tasks, but feel very uncomfortable trying to involve other people in the completion of the tasks. Don't get me wrong, they have great excuses—"I'm not a people person," "It's easier to just do it myself," "I don't have the time to train other people." They need to be reminded that training lay leaders is top priority. Recruiting and equipping volunteers is challenging, but without them our ministry cannot reach its full potential. Since I am completely committed to this concept, I believe our work with volunteers is the most important work we do.

Recruiting

Many single adult leaders recruit and work with more volunteers in their first year of service than most people do in a lifetime. It is essential to recruit with excellence if you want to have a solid leadership team. There are several prerequisites that must precede actual recruitment. Applying these four biblical principles will give you a head start in recruiting volunteers.

• Pray (Luke 6:12-13). Our tendency is to say, "Of course I would pray," and go on to step two. I'm not talking about the kind of prayer which says, "God, please bless our recruiting efforts." The text cited records the only instance where Jesus stayed up all night praying. Why? "When morning came, He called His disciples to Him and chose twelve of them, whom He also designated apostles." Earnestly pray. Ask your pastor and your elders to pray for your selection process. Ask the single adult group to seek God's guidance for the group's leadership. Put your request on the church prayer chain, or ask that it be noted in the Sunday morning worship folder. Please don't overlook this step. Prayer is your first priority in the recruiting process.

• Seek advice from people you trust (Prov. 12:15; 15:22). You may be tempted to choose your friends to serve with you on the ministry team. Friendship is very poor recruiting criteria. If you recruit only your friends, you will have a difficult time reaching those with whom you do not have a natural affinity. Ask for advice from a well-balanced group of people whom you respect. Be certain to include many opinions from the opposite sex. I've had the privilege of working with many outstanding individuals whom I personally would have never chosen for a position of leadership. Their service on our leadership team is due to answered prayer and wise counsel.

• Recruit to specific tasks (Acts 6:2-4). After reading my earlier comments, you can tell I've learned this lesson from experience. It is fine to give a new leader options for his or her leadership role, but the options must be defined by those areas you see as essential to your group's purpose. It is paramount that your group have an overall vision, and that you know how each role contributes toward that goal.

• Set standards (Titus 1:7-8). A call to leadership is a call to a high standard. This theme runs throughout the Bible. As I develop standards with each new Core Team at the beginning of their term, I have found that the group tends to set higher standards for themselves than if I made up the standards. The requirements are fairly consistent from one core group to the next. Our current leaders adhere to the following:

1. They attend all weekly meetings when they are in town.
2. They attend church on Sundays.
3. They tithe.
4. They attend at least half of our group's social events.
5. They meet half an hour before the weekly meeting for prayer.
6. They attend one Core Group meeting per month.
7. They greet new people before socializing with their friends.

The issue here is not the above seven criteria of a leadership in one church, but the point of developing biblically based standards for commitment, modeling, and growth.

Now you are ready for the actual recruitment contact. I personally meet with each person we invite to be on our leadership team. The meeting usually takes place over a meal. I say that we have been praying and seeking guidance for selecting our new leaders, and that their name has come up on several occasions, and I would like to discuss the possibilities of their making a commitment to our group. I talk to them about the specific options available, and do my best to listen well.

Two common fears I hear during a recruiting contact are fear of failure and fear of time constraints. These two reservations might be stated in any number of ways. When I hear people saying they are not sure that they could do a good job, or they lack experience in singles ministry, I realize that they probably have a fear of failure. To counteract this, I take two steps. First, I assure them they will be given every opportunity to use the strengths and abilities God has given them. I also commit to assisting them in acquiring any needed skills. (See "Equipping" section.) The second step is to inform them that they will have significant input in their job description. They will be encouraged to use their personal gifts and creativity to accomplish established goals. The fear of time constraints seems to be an ever-increasing burden to single adults. During my recruiting contact, I show them a copy of the current standards set by our Core Team. I point out that they are meeting most of the criteria already. I don't belittle the fact that I will be asking them to invest about three additional hours per week in the ministry. Most individuals with leadership capabilities understand this necessity.

Volunteers should always be recruited for a specific time period; they must be given an ending date. Your recruiting efforts will be more successful if you say, "Will you organize our greeters from January until July?" instead of, "Will you lead our greeters ministry?" We have found seven months to be a very effective leadership term. These seven-month periods begin in January and July. The first period begins January 1 and ends August 1. The second period begins July 1 and ends January 31. These overlapping terms allow new leaders to learn their job for one month, perform their job for five months, and teach their job to the next leader for one month. We have found it necessary to have two leadership meetings during the transitional months of January and July. This system has enabled many individuals to serve in leadership capacity for one term, while most serve two terms (one year), and several serve three terms or more. This system also allows leaders to take a term off and then return to leadership, often in a different role.

Before leaving the area of recruiting, let's note one more principle for finding volunteers. What if a visitor comes along who has great potential to hold a future leadership position? I believe these highly motivated individuals are going to plug in somewhere, and I would prefer it to be in our singles ministry. Individuals with great leadership capability need to be challenged as quickly as possible. I have three suggestions that have worked well in the past. First, meet them as soon as possible for a meal or a cup of coffee. Taking this personal interest means a great deal. Second, inform them of a ministry area that needs assistance and ask if they would consider helping out. Third, invite them to come to your meetings for three to five weeks and to note what they observe. Is your group friendly? Do they see areas that could use improvement? Tell them that you would like their fresh perspective. By making simple observations they will assist your group a great deal. Involving capable people early will greatly enhance the retention rate.

Each time we recruit a new Core Team there is a great sense of excitement about the possibilities that lie ahead. New personalities, high energy, fresh creativity, and renewed commitment are wonderful, but the most challenging work lies just ahead. It's one thing to talk about what you are going to do, but now it's time to do it. Equipping your volunteers for service is where the rubber meets the road. In addition to being the most challenging area, it also holds the greatest potential rewards.

Equipping

Beginning with my first years in ministry, I've never had a problem getting people to volunteer for ministry. I recruited dozens of volunteers, and I needed every single one because I lost them as fast as I found them. They were not enjoying completing tasks that brought no rewards or fulfillment. I had not considered how personalities, gifts, and abilities fit into the picture. Now I find *equipping* volunteers to be most challenging . . . and most essential.

Believe it or not, there are still some who say, "Why are you getting others to do all the work? That's why we hired you!" That statement is unbiblical and also disregards sound management principles. We are told in Ephesians 4:12 that we have a responsibility to "prepare God's people for works of service." But why? The rest of the verse holds the answer, "so the body of Christ may be built up." John MacArthur's commentary on this verse expands this line of thinking:

> No pastor [singles leader], or even a large group of pastors can do everything a church [singles ministries] needs to do. No matter how gifted, talented and dedicated a pastor may be, the work to be done where he is called to minister will always vastly exceed his time and abilities. His purpose in God's plan is not to try to meet all those needs himself but to equip the people given into his care to meet those needs. Obviously the leaders share in serving, and many of the congregation share in equipping, but God's basic design for the church is for the equipping to be done so that the saints can serve each other effectively. The entire church [singles ministry] is to be aggressively involved in the work of the Lord.[1] [Additions mine]

Your group's vision or purpose statement should point the direction that you want to take. Then you equip your people for the journey.

Just prior to some practical application steps for equipping, I want to share two foundational principles. First, we do not do all the work just so others can come to a singles club. Second, we do not try to meet everyone's needs. One we do try to meet is the single's need to serve God in a tangible way. This necessitates our being willing to make new contacts and continually include nonleaders.

The second principle is that if we don't have the leadership, we don't have the ministry. I learned this from Don Cousins, Administration Pastor at Willow Creek Community Church, who writes:

Ask most leaders on what basis they start a ministry and they'll say, "We see a need, and we try to meet it."

That need is undoubtedly the seed that plants a ministry idea, but we found need alone is an insufficient foundation upon which to build a ministry. We need to start with leadership. Any endeavor that works seems to require a strong leader.

Yet what do we often do in our churches? Well, we have a need, so we round up a committee and . . .

We went four years without a Junior High Ministry—no youth meetings, no Sunday School, nothing. Parents asked us what we were doing for junior high kids and we had to gulp and say, "We're looking for a leader, but right now we can't meet your needs."

We looked high and low for qualified junior high leaders— volunteer or paid. The man who eventually became our key leader had proven himself as a lay leader in a high school ministry. Eventually he developed such a zeal for junior highers that he quit his job and joined our staff. He has since built a tremendous junior high ministry.

We could have begun with three or four untried volunteers. But we're convinced it was worth the wait to find the right person and build the ministry properly. It's a lot harder to undo and redo a weak program than to build a quality program from scratch.[2]

In our ministry we stopped having a praise time when we couldn't locate a new leader. Our music had been one of our highlights each week. After the first meeting without music, I got home late and had several messages on my answering machine. Two of them were "volunteering to lead the worship team." It's amazing how God supplies!

To practically equip leaders, we must insure that they have the opportunity to gain skills necessary to accomplish their ministry task. Since people enjoy participating in things they do well, we help our leaders discover their spiritual gifts and then allow them to minister accordingly. One of my favorite Bible passages on this subject is from Exodus.

Then the Lord said to Moses, "See, I have chosen Bezalel son of Uri, the son of Hur, of the tribe of Judah, and I have filled him with the Spirit of God, with skill, ability and knowledge in all kinds of crafts—to make artistic designs for work in gold, silver and bronze, to cut and set stones, to work in wood, and to engage in all kinds of craftsmanship." . . .

And He [God] has given both him [Bezalel] and Oholiab son of Ahisamach, of the tribe of Dan, the ability to teach others. He has filled them with skill to do all kinds of work as craftsmen, designers, embroiderers in blue, purple and scarlet yarn and fine linen, and weavers — all of them master craftsmen and designers (31:1-5; 35:34).

God blesses every group with uniquely talented individuals, but none of us has the ability to equip every volunteer. God has gifted me with leadership skills and the ability to communicate effectively. I attempt to prepare our volunteers in those areas, but I can't equip them to lead our small groups. You might have to locate someone in your church or in the larger Christian community, but God will supply a person, a resource seminar, or another means to guide someone in their gift and skills development. Another practical step is to have each person on your current leadership team equip a leader for his or her position. As you read earlier, we have a one-month overlap between leadership teams specifically designed for this purpose. Another way I equip volunteers is to prepare a practical lesson for each month's Core Group meeting. I got this idea from Pastor John Maxwell at Skyline Wesleyan Church in San Diego. Each month he records a teaching lesson from his staff meeting and makes it available to leaders throughout the country.[3] I'll take one of his *Injoy* lessons, or one that I develop on my own, and teach a ministry principle to our leaders each month. The past few months I have concentrated on teaching them how to reach out to new people in our group. Other topics have included mentoring, giving, and teaching someone to pray.

Encouraging
Recruiting and equipping have us well on the way, but encouraging volunteers is what keeps them there for the long haul.

By nature, I'm a self-starter. While there are probably some strengths to this personality trait, I've discovered several weaknesses. Primarily, I don't tend to include others in what I'm doing. Since I don't need others to come along and give me a pat on the back, I don't naturally encourage others. But I've found volunteers respond more to encouragement than to any other form of motivation. I believe encouragement deals with attitude. Pastors, leaders, volunteers, janitors, and garbage collectors who have a good attitude greatly enhance their work environment. Each of us should do everything possible to see that good attitudes abound in our ministries. A leadership team characterized by many encouragers, and therefore much encouragement, will be infectious to the entire group.

There is too little encouragement in the world. To encourage simply means to "give courage." Single adults have fewer possible sources of encouragement than married people, and we have the opportunity to play a very positive and important role in their lives. Be an encourager; give courage to your volunteers!

I challenge you to come up with many creative ways to involve your volunteer leaders in the encouraging process. Your goal is not to have everyone think what a wonderful encourager you are. Your goal is to have encouraged leaders. Practical ways in which our volunteer team encourages each other include:

• Celebrate volunteers' birthdays. Surveys continue to show that a person's birthday is their most important day of the year. Yet most singles go home to an empty house and no presents. Do everything you can to encourage your group to make this a special day.

• Core group date night. One night per month our core team goes out on a group date. We've gone out to fancy restaurants, to baseball games, or to someone's home for Domino's pizza and a video. On our date night we don't discuss any group business, we just enjoy each other's company. We plan all of our date nights at the beginning of the leadership term, so everyone will be able to attend.

• Handwritten notes. When you get your mail, what's the first thing you look for? . . . an envelope that is not computer generated. Personal mail always brightens the day. Each week, jot a note to a different person on your volunteer team.

• Meet for lunch or breakfast. If possible, meet your volunteers where they work. This will enable you to better understand their work culture, and it will communicate your personal interest in their well-being.

• Publicly acknowledging their efforts. Express your thankfulness in front of the rest of your group. Cite specific instances where a volunteer has gone "above and beyond."

• Appreciation time. Before a meeting, challenge each leader to talk to at least two people and say, "I appreciate you because," and let them fill in the blanks. Encourage them to approach individuals who might not have received much encouragement lately. Note the effect this simple step will seem to have on the rest of your group. People respond to encouragement.

- Rewarding faithful servants. At the end of each leadership term, make sure to recognize those who are leaving your volunteer staff. Give them a token of your appreciation (we give a gift worth about $10 for every six months of leadership service). Prepare some personal comments as you recognize each person.

Recruiting, equipping, and encouraging volunteers is extremely challenging but worth every ounce of effort. Volunteers will look forward to working with those they believe have their best interest at heart. The most gratifying experience I have is to see our volunteers' spiritual gifts and ministry skills blossoming. I'm thrilled when they realize they are being used by God in the lives of other people. Yes, it takes a lot of time, but it's top priority. If you are effective in developing volunteers, you will be effective in ministry. Working with volunteers does not *prepare* for real ministry. Working with volunteers *is* real ministry.

Rob McCleland
Minister of Singles and Administration
Long Hill Chapel
525 Shunpike Road
Chatham, New Jersey 07928

Notes
1. John MacArthur, *Ephesians* (Chicago: Moody Press, 1986), 155.
2. Don Cousins, Leith Anderson, and Arthur DeKruyter, *Mastering Church Management* (Portland: Multnomah Press, 1990), 75.
3. *Injoy Life Tapes*. INJOY, 1530 Jamacha Road, Suite D, El Cajon, CA 92019, 1/800/333-6506.

4. DEVELOPING MINISTRY THROUGH SPIRITUAL GIFTS

"The small group context may well be the most powerful setting for spiritual gifts discovery."

Paul R. Ford

The orchestration of the Body is something beautiful to behold. Christ himself selects who will play each instrument. As the conductor, he determines the sections and then decides which parts each will play. Because he is also the composer, the music he writes is perfectly designed to impact the world as well as encourage the members of the orchestra. It's a phenomenon duplicated nowhere else. . . .[1]

Singles who claim to be followers of Jesus Christ are a part of a grand scheme that stretches from the whole of the universe down to every individual Christian. "And God placed all things under His [Jesus'] feet and appointed Him to be head over everything for the church, which is His body, the fullness of Him who fills everything in every way" (Eph. 1:22-23). We are a part of the church, an organic body which is being built together as a place where God lives by His Spirit (Eph. 2:22). Single Christians are instrumental to God's purpose — not because they are single but because they are Christians, crucial players in this phenomenon called the church!

There is more. God is in the process of reconciling the world to Himself through Jesus Christ and granting the forgiveness of sins in Him (2 Cor. 5:19). Who carries out this incredible ministry of reconciliation? He has chosen Christians. "All this is from God, who reconciled us to Himself through Christ and gave us the ministry of reconciliation. . . . We are therefore Christ's ambassadors, as though God were making His appeal through us" (2 Cor. 5:18, 20). Christian single adults, are you ready for your role of reconciliation?

There is still more. Single adults are very much a part of the church, *the body of Christ, where God lives by His Spirit.* They are His ambassadors, those carrying the responsibility to bring Christ to the world. How can this plan involve every Christian on earth? It comes back to that remarkable phrase—the body of Christ. "The body is a unit, though it is made up of many parts; and though all its parts are many, they form one body. So it is with Christ. . . . Now you are the body of Christ, and each one of you is a part of it" (1 Cor. 12:12, 27). There are no exceptions. Single adults have no special exemption!

How do you and I play our parts in this body, in this ministry of reconciliation, in this world scheme where everything will be filled up with the fullness of Jesus Christ? It is through the gifts of the Holy Spirit, spiritual gifts exercised by each Christian. Listen to God's grand strategy as expressed in these words of the Apostle Peter: "Each one should use whatever gift [*charisma*] he [she] has received to serve others, faithfully administering God's grace [*charis*] in its various forms" (1 Peter 4:10). In His amazing design, the Lord of the universe has chosen to manifest His free gift of grace by empowering us with supernatural gifts of grace.

It is time that we take seriously the task of enabling Christian single adults to discover and use these supernatural gifts of grace. What a broad and forceful impact these Spirit-empowered gifts would have in maturing, building up, and unifying the body of Christ in its mission of reconciliation to the world!

Biblical Background on Spiritual Gifts

God has done a marvelous work in our lives. By His free grace we have been saved: "For it is by grace you have been saved, through faith—and this not from yourselves, it is the gift of God—not by works, so that no one can boast" (Eph. 2:8-9). We have not only been saved, but also creatively prepared to do God's work. "For we are God's workmanship, created in Christ Jesus to do good works" (v. 10). As God's workmanship, we have been equipped with Holy Spirit-empowered spiritual gifts. God calls us out, saves us, and then equips us—all with His grace! "Grace comes from God, [and] takes hold in humans. . . ."[2]

● A spiritual gift defined. What, then, is a spiritual gift? In a basic definition, a spiritual gift is a supernatural endowment of God's grace given to every member of the body of Christ, to glorify Jesus Christ, to equip the body for ministry, and to build the body to unity and maturity in Christ.

Jesus established a plan on how the world would be reached. His followers were empowered and gifted by the Holy Spirit to be part of an organism, the body of Christ; with each part of the body doing its work, that body would multiply throughout the world. Thus Paul commands us, "We have different gifts, according to the grace given us . . . *let him [her] use it . . .* prophesying . . . serving . . . teaching . . . encouraging . . . contributing . . . leadership . . . showing mercy" (Rom. 12:6-8). The issue is clear: get moving, body of Christ! Every Christian single adult: go after it! Spiritual gifts are already in place to be used by each and every Christian.

It seems that service was always on Paul's heart when talking spiritual giftedness, and for good reason. "Every service . . . finds its meaning in the organic unity of the body of Christ."[3] A spiritual gift for the individual Christian ". . . sets him in a concrete place and equips him for specific service."[4] Do you know any Christian singles who are searching for identity and meaning in the midst of life's crises? The process of discovering and using spiritual gifts will bring concrete meaning to the life of the Christian single adult. A new sense of place and a purpose will invade any person who gets serious about the use of spiritual gifts.

Christian church "body life" now has opportunity to develop itself organically:

> Gifts are awakened, identified, and channeled as believers are intimately tied into the community life of the church. Further, as the range of gifts is awakened and begins to function, these gifts quicken other aspects of the church's life and mission. . . . The functioning of gifts provides much of the dynamism of the church's witness and worship, as well as building community. If we trust God and His working in the body, we will find that the Spirit raises up people with the necessary gifts to make the full ecology of the church function.[5]

Discovering one's spiritual gift focuses each Christian on his or her task in the larger body, and initiates the expression of the gift. Everyone ends up fitting in *and* playing a crucial role, designed by God with *His* best interests in mind!

When I came to the realization that my primary gifts were exhortation and leadership, I suddenly found myself able to focus in ministry like never before. It helped to clarify what areas of service I could be most effective in, and I found that I bore much more fruit there as well. Ministry involvement was most certainly still a challenge, but my joy in

49

doing God's work grew tremendously. I was playing my part in the ministry of the body of Christ! I did and do have personalized equipment for ministry, given to me by the Spirit of God Himself.

If all members of the body of Christ began to experience what I have in spiritual gift discovery and usage, a remarkable thing would begin to happen in the church. "Many people [would] begin to demonstrate the multiplicity of ministries which He [Christ] longs to perform through their united efforts."[6] We would indeed begin to understand that each of us has an instrumental role to play in the ministry of the body of Christ — created, motivated, and empowered by God Himself!

Do not overlook one critical element in the giving of gifts by God: spiritual gifts were given to the individual for the common good. The sum total of the individuals makes up the common good. If you have any question about this, try going to a symphony concert and listening to a flute solo for two hours! It is the sum total of all parts of the orchestra that produces a unified, joyful sound. It is teamwork all the way, rather than a bunch of individuals doing their own thing.

This interdependent functioning of the members of the body of Christ is the way God orchestrates it, "The body is a unit, though it is made up of many parts; and though all its parts are many, they form one body. So it is with Christ" (1 Cor. 12:12).

Do We Use Our Spiritual Gifts? What Are Our Options?

> The identifying of gifts brings to the fore . . . the issue of commitment. Somehow if I name my gift, I cannot "hang loose" in the same way. I would much rather be committed to God in the abstract than be committed to Him at the point of my gifts. . . . Life is not the smorgasbord I have made it, sampling and tasting here and there. My commitment will give me an identity.[7]

Many Christian singles simply do not exercise their spiritual gifts, for a variety of reasons. Some do not recognize they have gifts, and most often their leadership does not encourage them to discover their gifts. Others refuse to recognize that they are called to the work of ministry. Still others are lazy in carrying out their Christian body life responsibility. But after the overview we have just been through, what options are there for empowered Christian single adults who have been purposefully prepared by their Maker to play their part? The call is clear and the preparation is done. It is now our choice — our chance — to act!

Shall we get serious about body life, the context for a ministry of spiritual gifts? "An active congregation, given the liberty to do so, readily develops the necessary gifts among her members."[8] Single adults responding out of their own spiritual giftedness are an important segment of that natural, organic growth in the larger church.

George Patterson gives us a glimpse of just exactly what this reality looks like. Feel free to substitute the words Christian or single adult for elder or deacon in the following text:

> An elder with the gift of teaching interests himself in the details of biblical doctrine. Another with the gift of prophecy is more concerned about the long range implications of theological truth for men [and women] in today's world. . . . Another with the gift of exhortation just wants to get the job done. . . . A deacon with the gift of serving wants better worship facilities. . . . God's Spirit coordinates different people, interests and truths in the one combined ministry of the body of Christ.[9]

How are people prepared to play their part? Go back briefly to Ephesians 4:11-12 to again catch God's strategy for every member ministry preparation. "It was He [Christ] who gave some to be apostles, some to be prophets, some to be evangelists, and some to be pastors and teachers, to prepare God's people for works of service." Certain Christians in the body have been empowered to function as primary equippers. They have been prepared by God to call out, equip, and encourage the rest of the church to fulfill their ministry roles.

It is important, then, that those in church leadership, both paid staff persons and laypersons, have at least one equipping gift. Scripture acknowledges that equipping giftedness is the key ingredient in leadership in the local church. The preparation for ministry starts with those whom God has designed to equip and train the rest of us!

Step One: Develop Leadership Which Releases Authority with Responsibility

Those in primary leadership, often paid staff persons, are the key to a gifts-based ministry for single adults. They must do more than just say they support single adults in ministry. Such leaders must be willing to free single adults to do ministry, without seeking to overly control their actions.

Approaching leadership as a parent rather than an equipper — the more dominant model practiced in the American church—will greatly limit the ministry of singles in the local church in fulfilling its discipling objectives. Equipping leaders are compelled to lead by calling out, training, and releasing adults for their God-anointed ministry, rather than by functioning in a parent-child relationship with single adults who "probably don't know enough to minister meaningfully." Yet adult singles' calling and ministry preparedness is from God first, found through abiding in Christ and being available to the Spirit and His gifts. In the church, each person is empowered for a certain role with supernatural spiritual giftings. These gifts will not be found and exercised unless equippers allow enough freedom in ministry for gifts to be confirmed and used.

A gifts-based ministry means growth. In a living organism there will be spontaneous movement, change, growth, and multiplication in the church. "Under His [Jesus'] sole command, the Church grows and multiplies in a manner natural to herself."[10] This is not a church growth principle pulled from some marketing manual. Listen again to Paul on growth:

> Instead, speaking the truth in love, we will in all things grow up into Him who is the Head, that is, Christ. From Him the whole body, joined and held together by every supporting ligament, *grows and builds itself up* in love, as each part does its work (Eph. 4:15-16, emphasis mine).

Some Christian leaders fear that if the body of Christ did indeed begin to expand in amazing ways spiritually and numerically, they could not handle it. But it is the Lord who established a ministry of spiritual giftedness, so that the Holy Spirit can provide a balance of shared ministry in the body expressed through spiritual gifts.

Yes, leaders still lead, and submission to that leadership is still essential in any local church ministry. Teachers still teach truth, and pastors protect and guide. But we must acknowledge that the organic process going on is much more complex than any Christian leader can control and direct. God has created an order that grows out of the ministry of the body, as each part does its work. Many called to equip and lead out of their giftedness, thereby enabling others to play their God-ordained part in the serving, administration, leadership, teaching, and discipline of the local church. Consider what could happen in your ministry to and through single adults with such a biblical mind-set!

We are seized with terror, as Roland Allen says, for fear of disorder.[11]

52

But body life is not so called for nothing! With Christ the Head, we will in all things grow up [together] into Him, as *each part does its work,* and as *each supporting ligament strengthens the church* (Eph. 4:15-16). When you consider the number of spiritually active, growing single adults available to such grace-empowered work of the Lord, the potential is staggering.

Step Two: Develop Lay Ministry Job Descriptions

If everyone is supposed to play a part, how do we begin to work out that "fitting" process? As part of the local body, each active participant is responsible for his or her part of the work of that local ministry. Every single adult has a place to fit in the carrying out of God's call in the church. Perhaps a "ministry prospectus" showing possible ministry opportunities would help people prayerfully determine how they might fit into body life. Make special note in the following suggestions to see whether they can be best carried out just within your single adult ministry or as an overall ministry to the church, of which adult singles would be active players. Neither is better; wisdom on which direction to take is the issue.

What better way to provide specific information about specific ministry roles in the church than to develop a Lay Ministry Job Description Notebook! On a half or full page, develop basic information on every church ministry position presently available. Include these particular aspects of the role:

1. Area of ministry (if needed)
2. Job title
3. Three or four sentence summary of the position
4. Time commitment (weekly)
5. Length of service desired or required
6. Who responsible to (ministry leader)
7. Who responsible for (group, individuals, if anyone)
8. Special qualifications
9. Helpful spiritual gifts

How does one determine the helpful spiritual gifts for any one particular ministry role? It takes a great deal of study on the individual spiritual gifts, for which many resources are available.[12] Put together a team from your church, including spiritually gifted teachers, to study the gifts and determine several qualities about the function of each gift in action.

Secondly, go over each ministry role and list from two to five gifts which could be very helpful in carrying out the responsibilities for the position. Anticipate some margin of error, since this is not intended to be

53

a scientific procedure. The intent of providing *potentially* helpful gifts will have been met.

As new ministry positions are created according to need, a new job description should be provided and immediately put into the Lay Ministry Job Description Notebook. New ministries and positions will indeed begin to appear, especially as a process is provided for people to learn to discover and use their spiritual gifts.

After the job descriptions have been assembled into a notebook by category most helpful to your ministry, the gifts can be presented in a simple fashion. In addition to listing gifts as a part of the job description, develop a comprehensive list of ministries by spiritual gift categories. Each ministry would be listed in as many places as gifts listed for that position. For example:

Ministries Listed by Helpful Spiritual Gifts

Administration
Senior High Youth Coordinator
Vacation Bible School Coordinator

Helps
Information Booth Worker
Youth Club Cook

Leadership
Director of Youth Choirs
Singles Lay Coordinator

Pastoring
Small Group Leader
Stephen Minister (lay pastoral counselor)

Notice one very important factor in the ministry possibilities listed: many of them are in areas other than single adult ministry. It is absolutely essential that single adults be encouraged to use their gifts beyond the area of single adult ministry! The larger church body needs the vision, the understanding, the availability, and the perspective that single adults can bring to various ministries. If you want your single adult ministry to truly impact your church, then infiltrate the trenches from every angle!

Once this Lay Ministry Job Description Notebook is prepared, who will oversee its use and updating? Equally important, what process can be established to assist people to find out their potential gifts and then gain access to the Lay Ministry Job Description Notebook?

Step Three: Develop a Gifts Discovery Class

As you develop several program tools to assist single adults in gift discovery and usage, make certain that you know what you are really helping them to do. Two elements of identity are central in the gift discovery process.

The first is obvious: *spiritual giftedness,* as God Himself has arranged (1 Cor. 12:18). This defines much of how we will function in any ministry position, because it is who we are and not just what we do. Our identity as Christians is *who we are in Christ,* and our gifts are clearly a part of our spiritual identity.

The second important area of identity is *burden for ministry.* This is the context, the "where" and "who" that God so often places on your heart and mind with great conviction. You might also call this spiritual want-to. Burden is not just something you ought to do, but something (or someone) that you really have a desire to pursue or encourage. Though this is not always clearly discernable at first, through prayer, the counsel of godly friends, and your own heart sense from Scripture, it is clarified. This sense of calling may be to:

1. A certain group of people or individual(s):
   a. Muslims in Egypt
   b. Young Christians in the first few months of their spiritual growth
   c. Unwed mothers
   d. Other single-again men and women in the workplace
2. A particular or timely need:
   a. Responding to a crisis situation: i.e., flood, etc.
   b. Caring for persons with AIDS
   c. Assisting children with learning disabilities
   d. Sharing Christ with anyone in crisis
   e. Helping a newly divorced single get through the "crazies" period
3. A specific type of situation or interest:
   a. Teaching church history
   b. Discipling someone on a one-to-one basis
   c. Assisting single moms with childcare needs
   d. Serving through medical missions in poor countries

Throughout one's lifetime, the particular burden for ministry or service can change a number of times, but to identify one's burden *now* can be strategically helpful to ministry focus. After all, it is a part of *who we are* in Christ, a response to God's specific call on our lives. We become more who we are intrinsically as children of God with a profound sense of His call in our lives.

What happens when we clearly define our burden and our gifts? We become organic! That is the fancy way of saying that we become fully available to the Holy Spirit in our ministry focus, and He has free reign to work mightily in and through us. We stop doing Christian things and start being Christians, living in the Spirit. Beyond conversion, there is no more important discovery than clarifying these identity issues.

I am free to be me, to find tremendous joy exercising my gifts in the primary contexts for which God has burdened me! I am functioning *as* God wants *where and/or with whom* God wants. The Apostle Paul did suggest staying single to more freely serve the Lord. What could be more exciting than sold-out, focused, Christian single adults with a clear sense of ministry identity?

One of the easiest and most effective ways to help individuals discover and use their spiritual gifts is to provide a learning context that has concrete points of application in ministry placement. People may be drawn to the process to learn about their gifts, when in reality the true result will be the actual testing of gifts in a ministry setting.

With a team of laypersons I have had the opportunity of developing a spiritual gifts process called *Discovering and Using Your Spiritual Gifts,* effective for use in a classroom setting or in small groups. Hundreds of people have gone through the process over the past five years, and the results are fascinating:

• 35 percent of the people found confirmation of ministries in which they were already involved.

• 35 percent either got out of ministries in which they did not fit and into new areas by gifts, or entered ministry roles for the first time through the gifts process.

• 30 percent took no action following their spiritual gifts interview.

The two biggest pluses of the process were, first, the discovery that No is a spiritual word, that they did not have to participate in every ministry role they are asked to consider, and second, a discovery of greater joy, fulfillment, and fruit with the accurate ministry placements. Their ministry identities are now in place.[13]

The purpose of such a class is to move individual Christians from a basic understanding of the Holy Spirit into a biblical rationale for discovering and using one's spiritual gifts. The six weeks of spiritual gifts presentations are done by students to model body life in the very process of the class. The class is taught by both pastoral staff and laypersons — again for the purpose of modeling body life in the process. Pastors are not the only gifted ones.

Although the class can be taught in fewer than twelve weeks, one value of a ten or twelve-week class is that it demands high commitment over an extended period of time. Commitment to a gifts discovery process may connect to commitment in a future ministry role where one seeks confirmation of his or her gift(s).

Each of the nine assignments included in this gift discovery process is personally focused on an individual's spiritual background, ministry experience, potential gifts, and burdens for ministry, among other tools. The nine tools are invaluable resources both in preparation for and during the actual interview with the adviser. No student may go through the class without an interview with an adviser at the end of the process, nor can anyone be interviewed without completion of all the assignments.

This material (with leader's guide) is available through the Charles Fuller Institute in Pasadena, California under the title, *Discovering Your Spiritual Gifts in Small Groups* by Paul Ford. A second excellent set of materials, geared especially for larger churches, is called *Networking*, by Bruce Bugbee of Willow Creek Community Church in Chicago. It is also available through the Fuller Institute.[14]

Step Four: Develop a Gifts Discovery Small Group

While the classroom process is aimed at helping the individual find his or her role in the larger body, the small group context provides a totally different dynamic for spiritual gift discovery. In fact, the small group context may well be the most powerful setting for spiritual gifts discovery. The established group has its own dynamics:

• The group is a place where one studies God's Word and functions in accountable relationships with others (two-thirds of discipleship triangle).

• Because of the already established relationships, the small group is a "safe" place for testing gifts.

• Who would be better qualified to affirm potential gifts than a small group leader with whom a solid relationship has already been established?

• The small group is an organic cell, a living unit of the larger body of Christ. People not only have a safe, natural context in which to discover their gifts, but they also have the dynamic of the Holy Spirit already present in the group, seeking to bring unity and build the body. Want to get into a prime context to discover your gifts? Get into a small group.

The small group can establish its own gifts discovery process in its group context, or can go through the classroom process as a group and focus on class issues on their meeting night as well. When it comes to confirming gifts, the small group may use its own structure to enable some to find their gifts. Here are some sample ministry roles which provide contexts in which giftedness could be discerned:

1. Assistant leader (potential gifts of leadership, pastoring, exhortation)
2. Prayer logkeeper (intercession, service, helps)
3. Teacher (teaching, knowledge)
4. Hospitality host (hospitality, service)
5. Pastoral supports (pastoring, mercy)

The small group leader may function as an enabler for placing people in ministries in the group itself (with counsel from the group), in the larger church body, or beyond.

Step Five: Develop a Spiritual Gifts Ministry Team

Spiritual gifts and specific ministries need to be brought together. The Spiritual Gifts Ministry Team helps coordinate the Job Description Notebook and an understanding of the ministries of the local church. They serve individual Christians who are searching for their ministry identity out of the gifts discovery class or small group process.

Team members are the specialists: the consultants for small groups, the class facilitators for discussions on the individual spiritual gifts, and the team that provides spiritual gift interviews for those involved with either type of gift discovery ministry (classroom or small group). Note that different advisers need varying gifts to effectively function in one or more of the potential advising roles.

Since your team may need training, I want to suggest some resources for this. Both *Networking* and a tool called *Spiritual Gifts Implementation,* by Robert and Janet Logan, provide solid models for training spiritual gift advisers or consultants.

Because the miracle of computers has touched the ministry of spiritual gifts mobilization, I suggest *The Spiritual Gifts Data Base,* an invaluable resource for both ministry leaders and spiritual gift advisers. It makes available to ministry leaders and advisers the following:

- Information on individual's giftedness, ministry interests, and history of involvement.

- Information on all church lay ministry job descriptions.
- Ease of entering data and maintaining information by laypersons, through menu-driven software.
- Timely processing and printing of sorts and searches.
- A design for matching individual giftedness with gifts associated with lay ministry job descriptions.

The availability of this data base program streamlines the recruitment of laypersons for ministry. Data gathered has shown that people who are asked to consider a ministry because of giftedness respond positively at twice the rate of those asked through arbitrary contact. Since gifts are a part of ministry identity, such high results make sense. This gift discovery approach to ministry provides church leadership the opportunity to invite people to serve out of giftedness rather than from guilt or pressure. This means that body life is given a better chance to function from healthy motivation.

Develop a Gifts Mobilizing Focus

- Educational ministries. The Discovering and Using Your Spiritual Gifts class can be a core class in your singles educational curriculum, or a part of the larger church. Other classes which can be developed along this same focus include a series of classes called "A Deeper Look at. . . ." The content focus would cover definition, key biblical passages, characteristics, liabilities, and context for use of each gift.

Another course to consider is Discovering and Using Your Spiritual Gifts, Part 2. The purpose of this class would be to provide a follow-up process on some of the class assignments for Part 1, a honing in on burden for ministry issues, continuing education on all the gifts, and an in-depth interview with a spiritual gifts adviser.

- Small groups. Group ministry projects designed by each group would represent how the Lord had burdened them as a whole for ministry or service. Again, the Spiritual Gifts Adviser could come alongside in a consultant role.
- General ministry possibilities. Specific ministries could be developed from a focus on individual spiritual gifts. For example, a ministry of evangelism could grow up in a singles ministry where several had the gift of preaching/teaching. The discipling of new adult education teachers would most certainly be done by teachers and exhorters presently involved in that ministry. Our church is developing a specialized ministry for those with the gift of discernment of spirits. The possibilities are endless!

• New ministries. When singles have the chance and freedom to respond to the burden and gifts that God has laid on their hearts, a door to new opportunities opens wide. One can expect that new ministry ideas will come out of spiritual gifts interviews, out of the ministry identity that the Lord has placed in some individuals. In our church, over a five-year period with over 400 people interviewed, four new ministries were developed by people with distinctly different burdens and gifts.

• Outreach possibilities. Here are some ways to allow the Great Commission to affect your thinking and application while people seek to discover and use their spiritual gifts.

1. Be particularly sensitive to those going through the gifts discovery process who have a ministry burden to develop a program that has tremendous evangelistic implications.

2. Encourage the development of ministries targeted to reach unbelievers and new Christians, such as a specialized ministry to mothers with young children, or a Christian big brother/big sister program, especially considering the overwhelming needs of children from single-parent families today.

3. Team up a gifted evangelist with a person who has the gift of hospitality for a short-term evangelistic Bible study. The combination will bear fruit in conversions.

4. Effectively train gifted exhorters to share their faith, as they invest in the lives of unbelievers. Exhorters are proving to be particularly effective witnesses for Christ in their verbal sharing.

5. Help people whose dominant gifts are more service-oriented to realize that their most effective form of life investment in unbelievers will often be with their hands and hearts in serving, rather than with a profound verbal witness. Finding who they are in Christ by ministry identity means that their nonverbal witness will be filled with the Holy Spirit. They will indeed *be* witnesses!

"A church that faithfully uses its gifts in the Spirit's power experiences the joy of great unity, love and fellowship in ways that no amount of human ability, planning or effort can produce."[15] This sounds like a plan of action for single adult ministries today!

Paul Richard Ford
Director of Discipleship
Heights Cumberland Presbyterian Church
8600 Academy NE
Albuquerque, New Mexico 87111

Notes

1. Charles Swindoll, *Spiritual Gifts* (Fullerton, California: Insight for Living, 1986), Introduction.

2. John Koenig, *Charismata: God's Gifts for God's People* (Philadelphia: Westminster, 1978), 59.

3. Colin Brown, ed., *Dictionary of New Testament Theology,* vol. 3 (Grand Rapids: Zondervan, 1975), 546.

4. Siegfried Schatzmann, *A Pauline Theology of Charismata* (Peabody, Massachusetts: Hendrickson Publishers, 1987), 67.

5. Howard Snyder, *Liberating the Church* (Downers Grove, Illinois: InterVarsity Press, 1983), 89.

6. Stuart Briscoe, *Romans* (Waco, Texas: Word, 1982), 219.

7. Elizabeth O'Connor, *Eighth Day of Creation: Discovering Your Spiritual Gifts and Using Them* (Waco, Texas: Word, 1971), 42–43.

8. Ibid.

9. George Patterson, *Obedience-Oriented Education* (Cucamonga, California: Church Planting International), 1.

10. Ibid., 15.

11. Roland Allen, *The Spontaneous Expansion of the Church* (Grand Rapids: Eerdmans, 1962), 13.

12. Good starter volumes include *Your Spiritual Gifts Can Help Your Church Grow* by C. Peter Wagner and *Discovering Your Spiritual Gifts in Small Groups* by Paul R. Ford.

13. Rick Blose, Heights Cumberland Presbyterian Spiritual Gifts Lay Coordinator's data results, summer 1989.

14. The toll-free number for the Fuller Institute of Evangelism and Church Growth is (800) C. Fuller.

15. John MacArthur, *The MacArthur New Testament Commentary: 1 Corinthians* (Chicago: Moody Press, 1984), 295.

5. DEVELOPING MINISTRY WITH WOMEN

"When we understand that the church was designed by God to be an equipping agency, as opposed to a programming agency, we will be more likely to include women in all aspects of service within the church. In fact, it will be hard to exclude them, because all gifts will be needed to complete the task."

Pamela Dodge

Because many churches all across the country are now aware of the great need to reach out and minister to single adults, such ministries are increasingly a part of church life. One recent survey of forty-seven senior pastors with a membership of 500 or more shows that 67 percent place a higher priority now than five years ago on the importance of a need for single adult ministry in their churches. Church pastors, elders, deacons, and members within the church are increasingly sensitive to single adults. But many churches have failed to take into account the lives of single adult women and their changing roles in our society. Therefore, they have been slow in adapting and adjusting ministries and programs to include this large segment of our society.

A survey of women in the American society today shows an interesting number of changes in their lives. First, there is an increasing number of single women in our population. According to the U.S. Census Bureau, there are 43 million unmarried women, as compared with 36 million unmarried men, out of a total population of 250 million. The proportion of unmarried women between thirty and thirty-four was 6 percent of our population in 1970 but had increased to 16 percent by 1990.

Recent surveys also show that women are waiting longer to get married. First-time brides are older today than at any other time in the past 100 years. In 1990 women were typically just under twenty-four years old when they first married.

Another significant change that must be taken into account is that today approximately 50 percent of all American women are gainfully employed. Only 21 percent of women consider themselves full-time homemakers. With close to a 50 percent divorce rate in America, the majority of single mothers find themselves working outside the home as a necessity.

There is also an increased number of women with college and graduate degrees. Women are more educated today than ever before in our history. In 1970 41 percent of college graduates in America were women, but by 1982 that percentage had climbed to 52 percent.

These statistics mean that churches which fail to take them into account and adapt their ministries to the changing role of women in our society, and to single adult women in particular, will miss out on the opportunity to minister to a growing segment of our population. If the church is insensitive to the changing lives of women, it will lose its ability to minister to women who are interested in a growing relationship with Jesus Christ and in fellowship with other believers.

Insensitivity will also lead to a disregard of a large segment of the church's own human resources — women who can meet the many needs within the church community as well as fulfill the Great Commission. This task is large enough in itself to involve every member of the church for a lifetime.

While the church's message should never change, the methods and strategies for reaching out must take into account our societal needs. Many women are justifiably becoming frustrated because many churches ignore the ministry of women at any level.

A few examples of women who have experienced recent frustrations within the church should help in our understanding. Stephanie has never married and is in her early thirties. After attending a church for almost a year, she decided it was time to get involved. A corporate executive in a large company, and holding a Ph.D. in business administration, she is a gifted manager and possesses special people skills. But when she approached one of her pastors about getting involved, he directed her to the church nursery. She served there for about six months but found that she was not especially suited to this task and so she quietly resigned. She never volunteered to serve again.

Mary was a young Christian and divorced mother to two small children, who was forced to work in order to provide for her family. She desired very much to grow in her relationship to Christ and to enjoy the fellowship of other young mothers. But when she tried to get involved in a small group study within her church, she found that all such events were held during the day while she was working. As a result, Mary was never able to get involved.

These sad but true stories illustrate the urgency for churches to grow in their awareness of the changing roles and needs of women. Church ministries designed for the traditional family of the 1960s, with Mom as a homemaker and single women remaining in the home until they married, will not work in the 1990s. In fact, church programs oriented only to traditional families often overlook or neglect the needs of single women and married women who work outside the home.

Churches must stop ignoring the spiritual giftedness of women. Today's highly educated, working, single woman wants to serve in ways that offer her the chance to make a significant contribution.

Women represent a valuable resource for ministry and should be given greater opportunities to serve within the church. No issue in the church seems to raise more questions and tempers than that of women and Christian ministry. It is not my purpose to argue a particular theological viewpoint. Questions concerning the ordination of women and limitations on women in the area of teaching are beyond the scope of this chapter. My purpose is to show that the church must increase its sensitivity and adapt its programming in order to meet the changing needs of today's woman. Churches need to actively explore ways to involve women, and particularly single women, on a more meaningful level.

Three Points of Agreement about Women
If the church as a whole is to progress in this area of women and ministry, it must acknowledge that differences do exist and will continue to exist in the future, and then help people to respect one another in those differences. The church also needs to look for solutions at common points of agreement. What are some of these common points? It seems appropriate to highlight briefly three common biblical teachings on which most churches do agree.

• The first is that men and women are of equal value from God's perspective. Galatians 3:28 says, "There is neither Jew nor Greek, slave nor free, male nor female, for you are all one in Christ Jesus." When we make single adult women feel that they are misfits in the church, we have failed to accept them as created in God's image. Genesis 1:27 tells us: "God created man in His own image, in the image of God He created him; male and female He created them." Applying this passage practically means that there is a sense in which both the male and the female working together as a team reflect God's image completely. A church that encourages only male involvement in specific areas does not fully reflect His image.

• The second point of agreement is that men and women are interdependent. First Corinthians 11:11 states: "In the Lord, however, woman is not independent of man, nor is man independent of woman." That means we need each other. Studies have shown that men and women often think and view situations differently. Neither is right or wrong in itself, just different. But when both perspectives are brought together, a more complete picture is likely to appear. Men and women need to minister together in order to achieve a truly balanced perspective.

• The final point of agreement is that God has equipped every believer, both male and female, with spiritual gifts according to 1 Corinthians 12:7-11 and Ephesians 4:11-16. In 1 Peter 4:10 we read: "Each one should use whatever gift he has received to serve others, faithfully administering God's grace in its various forms." Spiritual gifts are not given just to men. The use of spiritual gifts is essential to one's completion in Christ. When women are not allowed to use their gifts, they fail to grow as they should. In the past, being denied opportunities to serve, many women sought to use their gifts outside of the local church. Also, women have been drawn to the mission field to be able to serve the Lord with their unique capacities.

Meeting the Ministry Needs of Single Women
Many churches today have tried diligently to understand and develop new marketing strategies in order to meet the needs of people within their communities. Yet often these same churches have failed to understand the feelings, needs, and strengths of single women who are within their ministries.

Just what are the needs of the single woman? First of all, they have a strong need to feel significant. They need to understand their identity as Christians, and to see how they fit into the body of Christ. The lack of a family is not going to keep a single woman from a promotion in her profession. When the church offers few opportunities for women to be involved, it is not uncommon for the career-oriented single woman to seek that feeling of significance and value in the workplace rather than the church.

Single women also have the need to discover and utilize their spiritual gifts and God-given abilities. Understanding and using their gifts helps them answer the question of who they are and how they fit into the body of Christ. Gifts are given to be used, and when these gifts lie dormant, whether in men or women, the entire church suffers. Women are struggling just as much as men to adapt to the changes within our society. They need to be accepted and valued just as God accepts and values them. We dare not ignore the immense potential of the spiritual gifts that women possess; we must encourage them in the exercise of these gifts and abilities. As a result, the church as a whole will profit.

When women are confined to the traditional domestic roles (kitchen and nursery) when God has gifted them for other ministries, and even for leadership positions, the Spirit is actually quenched.

What are some practical suggestions and possibilities for single women to be more involved in the church? There are many creative ways they may serve within the church, no matter what your theological persuasion. Ephesians 4:11-13 reveals God's purpose for the church: "It was He who gave some to be apostles, some to be prophets, some to be evangelists, and some to be pastors and teachers, to prepare God's people for works of service, so that the body of Christ may be built up until we all reach unity in the faith and in the knowledge of the Son of God and become mature, attaining to the whole measure of the fullness of Christ." When we understand that the church was designed by God to be an equipping agency, as opposed to a programming agency, we will be more likely to include women in all aspects of service within the church. In fact, it will be hard to exclude them, because all gifts will be needed in order to complete the task.

Women are able to serve effectively in any area on various committees or action groups within the church as well as in the single adult ministry. Often women are quicker to volunteer and are more willing to serve than men. Those with administrative gifts and people skills will be an addition to any committee or ministry. Women often have a different perspective, and this allows for a greater insight and perhaps new approaches to tasks.

Many women have the gift of teaching, and there are varied ways of allowing them to exercise this gift. They can lead or co-lead small group studies. They can teach Sunday School classes. Workshops and seminars that utilize their own particular background and strengths are another way to involve them. For example, if a woman works as a personnel manager in a business, she could teach a seminar on writing résumés or how to interview for a job. Training and skills seminars for various jobs within the church also allow women to use their gift of teaching. Many people do not volunteer to take on a task because they feel that they are not adequately trained. Allowing women to lead training seminars lets them utilize their spiritual gift of teaching. A woman who is a school-teacher by profession might be willing to lead a one-day training seminar for potential Sunday School teachers on teaching skills.

Many women have the gift of hospitality. They enjoy entertaining and reaching out to others, including strangers. They would love to be asked to greet newcomers at the door or to host a dinner during the week for these people. Holidays can be lonely times for many, and some women enjoy overseeing holiday programs such as Christmas or Thanksgiving dinners. Fellowship activities within most churches are usually delegated to women. Many women are very relational and love to be involved in this capacity. But they also need encouragement; their hard work should be acknowledged and not taken for granted. They are connecting to the larger picture of ministry—not just hosting a dinner, but reaching out and ministering to newcomers.

For those who have writing skills, developing curriculum for Sunday School, plays, dramas, etc. offers an opportunity to use this gift. Many churches put out newsletters or bulletins, and women can find satisfaction helping out in these areas.

For those with the gift of evangelism, opportunities abound. With over 50 percent of women in the work force, there are many ways they can reach out to their fellow employees who, by the way, have a 50 percent chance of being male. They can invite these people to Bible studies, seminars, concerts, etc. within the church.

Mission opportunities are another way women may be involved. Many churches are beginning to send out summer mission teams. In many urban centers of the world, as well as in most Muslim and other patriarchal cultures, women and men live in separate worlds. The only way the women of that culture will be reached is by other women.

Every area of the church needs to utilize women who possess the gift of leadership. They should be present on long-range planning committees, heading up task forces, giving overall direction to any number of programs based on their particular areas of giftedness. A woman manager who gives direction to a group of employees at her job could also lead people within the church, perhaps on the single adult council, or in taking charge of a retreat.

Counseling is another area where women are gifted and can be included in ministry opportunities. Many churches are not large enough to support their own counseling center, but they can utilize those with a degree and background in counseling to help meet individual crisis needs. Many churches offer telephone ministries where people may call day or night. Single women could help in this area.

A number of women today have financial and accounting skills and gifts. They should be included in this area of ministry as well.

This list of ways to utilize the gifts of women is not intended to be complete. We could add prayer ministries, community service opportunities, discipleship, driving the church bus, and many others. I hope it has stimulated your thinking on creative ways to involve women more meaningfully within the life of the church.

Women are greatly needed now in these crucial days when our world cries out for every believer to participate in the great harvest. Jesus illustrates this truth in the Parable of the Vineyard (Matt. 20:1-16). In this parable a landowner went out five different times to hire workers for the vineyard. He asked those in the last group, "Why have you been standing there all day long doing nothing?"

They responded, "Because no one has hired us." They were then invited to join in the harvest, and they were given the same wages as all those who had worked all day. We are not told why these workers had not been hired. Some have speculated that perhaps they were women.

For women, the hour is indeed late and the Lord is calling them to serve. Jesus' concern is reaping the harvest. And the time is now for women to join the work.

Pamela Dodge
Director of Young Adult Ministries
Ward Evangelical Presbyterian Church
17000 Farmington Road
Livonia, Michigan 48154

Notes
For an overview of various perspectives see *Women in Ministry: Four Views*. Eds. Bonnidell Clouse and Robert Clouse. InterVarsity Press, 1989.

6. DEVELOPING A LEADERSHIP TEAM

"Throughout the Old and New Testaments, we repeatedly find models of team leadership. They are the norm, not the exception."

Jeffrey R. King

In his book *Holy Sweat*, Tim Hansel began his chapter on teamwork with a terrific anecdote from the life of Jimmy Durante, one of the great entertainers of a generation ago. As the story goes, Durante was asked to be a part of a show for World War II veterans, and he agreed on one condition. Since his schedule was so busy he would be able to do only a short monologue, after which he would need to leave for his next engagement. The show's director happily agreed.

When Jimmy appeared on stage, he went through his monologue, but then stayed on. As the applause grew louder with each succeeding joke, he stayed longer and longer. After thirty minutes he took a last bow and left the stage. The director stopped him and said, "I thought you had to leave after a few minutes. What happened?"

Jimmy replied, "Yes, I did need to go, but let me show you the reason that I stayed. You can see for yourself. Look down there." In the front row there were two men, each of whom had lost an arm in the war — one his right arm and the other his left. But together they were able to clap, and that's exactly what they were doing, as they were thrilled to see and hear Jimmy Durante perform.

That's teamwork! By definition it only takes two to make a team! The principle that two people effectively working together can achieve greater results is emphasized in Ecclesiastes, "Two can accomplish more than twice as much as one, for the results can be much better. If one falls, the other pulls him up; but if a man falls when he is alone, he's in trouble . . . three is even better, for a triple-braided cord is not easily broken" (4:9-12, TLB).

The creative genius Buckminster Fuller explains in his book *Synergetics* that it is very possible for "one plus one to equal four if we put our efforts together in the same direction." The word *synergy* means "the sum total is greater than the total of the separate parts." It is derived from the two Greek words *erg* and *syn* meaning "work" and "together" and implies that a team can be far more powerful and effective than any of the separate members working individually. It has been estimated that if we could get all the muscles in our bodies to pull in one direction, we could lift over twenty-five tons!

The business sector has also caught on to the team concept. Although many people think the use of self-directed workteams is a recent import from Japan, the fact is, they were pioneered in Britain and Sweden during the 1950s. Volvo is now so advanced that in their new Uddevalla plant, workteams assemble entire cars. In the United States Proctor & Gamble, along with other forward-thinking companies, implemented workteams in the early 1960s with very profitable results. The list of major companies using self-directed workteams includes Boeing, Caterpillar, Champion International, Cummins Engine, Digital Equipment, Ford, General Electric, General Motors, LTV Steel, and Tektronix, to name just a few.[1]

When we turn to the Bible for examples of team leadership, we find no shortage. In Exodus 3 God told Moses to talk to the elders of Israel. These men were a team set apart by God for judicial and governing purposes, to rule His people in the context of a body. Hundreds of years later Boaz, in his action as the kinsman redeemer, went to the elders in order to have them witness a land transaction.

Jesus Christ clearly believed in the principles of teamwork when He chose twelve men to follow Him closely in a Rabbi-disciple relationship. He subsequently divided that twelve-member team into six two-member teams for a specific task (Mark 6:7-13). And then James, John, and Peter emerged as a kind of executive team within that apostolic band.

This same theme of team leadership permeates the pages of the Book of Acts—the apostles in Jerusalem, the various missionary teams consisting of Paul, Barnabas, Mark, Silas, Timothy, and Luke, the appointment of elder teams with the establishment of every new church. Throughout the Old and New Testaments, we repeatedly find models of team leadership. They are the norm, not the exception.

The Benefits of Team Leadership
Rod Wilson of Ontario Theological Seminary has outlined five key reasons for a team leadership approach in ministry endeavors.[2]

- Team leadership allows for the contribution of varied individual gifts. Every team has players of differing traits, strengths, talents, and abilities. When the team is working well together, there is a certain chemistry and magic about it. Each member knows where he fits and why. But this presupposes team members who complement each other's strengths. One of the most subtle dangers is a leadership team comprised of similarly gifted people who are merely echoes of each other. They may double their strengths, but they also double their weaknesses. Leadership teams must be very careful to round out and complete their team, rather than simply extend themselves.

- Team leadership allows for the sharing of wisdom. Our contemporary culture tends to exalt individuals, isolated and autonomous, who have expertise and skill in a certain field. This is a different notion than we see in the Scriptures. The Bible places more emphasis on the principle given in Proverbs 11:14: "For lack of guidance a nation falls, but many advisers make victory sure." Team leadership allows for the blending of unique backgrounds, experience, and approaches to creative problem-solving.

- Team leadership allows for mutuality. Much has been written about the inherent faults of pyramidal management structures. In this system, power resides at the top in one person. The sense of mutuality and reciprocity is lost since one person has control. This style of leadership risks arrogance, power, pride, and poor decision-making. In team leadership, however, mutual decision-making allows for a solid base of unity. Group decisions arise out of respect and a shared struggle for truth as the best course of action instead of domination and power.

- Team leadership allows for representation. A team approach to leadership creates a healthy environment for the representation of many ideas and concerns. Team members will undoubtedly have different circles of constituents. As each listens carefully and reports back to the leadership team, a free flow of open communication is encouraged. People will feel that their needs are "heard" and the leadership team will be able to respond to those legitimate needs.

- Team leadership allows for accountability. Almost without exception, the Christian leaders who have fallen in recent years had no real accountability to a team, nor challenge from someone close. Many people do not like or understand the concept of accountability and seek to avoid it. However, individuals, and consequently teams, do their best work under clear terms of accountability. A team built on mutual trust, respect, and a passion for the mission at hand will hold each other accountable for group and individual achievement. They will interrelate in such a way so as to sharpen and encourage one another to greater heights. Teams that take accountability seriously are always winners!

The Principles of Team-Building

Like most things in life, leadership teams don't just happen. They are the direct result of people who believe in the values of the team concept, and deliberately organize their leadership structures this way. Team-building is an on-going process and is never really completed. Healthy teams keep on changing, maturing, and adapting. While the process is fluid and dynamic, it is based on certain principles.

● The selection principle. By far the most common question is, "How do we form a team and then replace its members over time?" Leadership teams can be put together many different ways, and some are better than others.

First, single adult ministries need gender-balanced leadership; male *and* female representation brings greater insight, integrity, and complementarity. An even balance of men and women is the optimum.

Second, it's a maxim that leaders are the ones most capable of choosing other leaders. Although this idea flies in the face of our culturally created democratic bias, sheep never choose their shepherds. Current leaders need to be on the constant lookout for potential new leaders. They need to be assessing the gifts and leadership abilities of others, evaluating the team's weaknesses and needs, and nudging people toward leadership responsibilities on a regular basis. Whatever the selection methodology chosen, current leaders need significant input. In a very true sense the future of any ministry depends directly on the leadership selection process, whether it be a formal nominating committee or an informal network. The success or failure of the group rides on its leadership.

Third, leadership selection must be based on qualification, not simply on availability or personality. Unfortunately, many churches create leadership "committees" with a certain number of "slots" to fill. Then, one of two things happens: either the ballot becomes a popularity contest with a winner and loser for each open seat; or worse, the first person to volunteer is offered the position, regardless of qualification. Both compromise the integrity of a true leadership team. The New Testament sets high standards for those who seek to lead (1 Tim. 3, Titus 1). Leaders must be chosen thoughtfully and deliberately. Their Christian character, conduct, and abilities need to be evaluated. Only after careful examination should a

74

person be asked to serve in a leadership capacity.

Fourth, we must recognize that most single adult ministries are fast moving and rapidly changing, with a high turnover of people. Instead of despairing, we need to accept this phenomenon and capitalize on its strengths. This means a constant flow of potential leaders. In some ministries, leadership may change as often as every six months by design or natural movement, and that's OK. The challenge is to continually discover and develop new leadership.

• The niche principle. Great teams are made up of players who understand themselves and their own unique role on the team, and also the functions and roles of their teammates. Teams break down when team members misunderstand roles and responsibilities. Teams are comprised of individuals who occupy a special place and perform in a special way, in a kind of niche. Each is in the right "spot" for the benefit of the enterprise. It is like saying, "You do what nobody else could do." Members are neither independent nor codependent, but *interdependent!* Understanding those personal niches humanizes the work and makes participants feel special. People need to feel needed, and a philosophy of team leadership capitalizes on that basic need.

Teams are as different as snowflakes, but many of the niche roles on the team are similar. Here are some of the more common ones:

1. The Sparkplug—the one who makes things happen
2. The Analyst—the rational deliberator
3. The Dreamer—the optimistic idealist
4. The Peacemaker—the conflict resolver
5. The Engineer—the project organizer
6. The Traffic Cop—the project controller
7. The Friend—the developer of social interactions
8. The Helper—the cooperative supporter
9. The Maverick—the nontraditionalist
10. The Bridge-builder—the one who reaches out to other team members

This is not to say that every team must have each niche, but that people tend to fill these general roles. Perhaps you identified your basic role or immediately placed names beside each niche as you read the list. That's fine. The purpose is not to create a psychological personality test, but for everyone to be aware, accept and affirm each member's unique and valuable contribution.

• The mission principle. What transforms a group of people into a team is *a sustained commitment to a common goal with a purpose*. This is usually called a mission, a dream, a vision, or a master plan. It needs to be simple, memorable, inspirational, biblical, and profound, and must be capable of energizing and motivating because it is the flag around which the troops rally. Each person on the leadership team must know, understand, and embrace the mission since the mission statement sets the overall direction and tone for the ministry. The formation of this statement should be the first order of business of a newly formed ministry or leadership team; later, it becomes the baton that is handed off to each succeeding leadership team.

Specific and measurable objectives grow out of the vision at regular intervals, but the controlling mission rarely changes. It is the stabilizing, unifying factor characteristic of successful long-term ministries. The statement must be repeated often, both verbally and in print, so as to be indelibly impressed on the minds of all. Recently, at a very large community church in the Southwest, the senior pastor asked the members at a congregational meeting, "What is the mission of our church?" With no prompting whatsoever, 500 people responded in unison, "To bring people to maturity in Christ." That's a clear, concise, memorable mission statement.

• The ownership principle. Closely associated to the mission principle is the ownership principle. The more team members participate in setting the practical objectives that operationalize the mission, the more they will personally own and commit to the dream and its goals. Team members feel a sense of accomplishment when they participate in the goal-setting process and become firmly cemented as a goal-sharing team.

• The coach principle. Who can imagine a team without a coach? Actually, every team has someone who functions as the coach or player-coach, whether recognized or not. In single adult ministries that person may be the president of the singles group, the director of singles ministries, the pastor to singles, an associate pastor, or even the senior pastor.

What do coaches do? Well, they don't usually play in the game now, but they have played the game before. Their purpose is to teach others to play. Coaches demonstrate the skills, develop team spirit, recruit team personnel, design team strategy, motivate, discipline, and do whatever is necessary to prepare the team to play the game. Coaches discover hidden potential and put it to use, create a winning environment, and deploy the team to the field in order to win the battle! In short, coaches teach the basics, are the keepers of the vision, give inspiring pep talks, encourage teamwork, develop talent, give credit for success, and take responsibility for failure.

Elton Trueblood, one of the foremost evangelical theologians and intellectuals of this century, in commenting about the analogy of coaching and the equipping ministry of the pastor in Ephesians 4:11-13, wrote: "The glory of the coach is that of being the discoverer, the developer, and the trainer of the powers of other men. But this is exactly what we mean when we use the biblical terminology about the equipping ministry."[3]

Tom Landry, the coach of the Dallas Cowboys football team for twenty-nine years, is often quoted as saying: "I have a job to do that is not very complicated, but is often difficult: to get a group of men to do what they don't want to do so they can achieve the one thing they have wanted all their lives."

Another legendary coach, Paul "Bear" Bryant, of the University of Alabama, reportedly said:

I'm just a plowhand from Arkansas, but I have learned how to hold
a team together, how to lift some men up, how to calm down
others, until finally they've got one heartbeat together, as a team.
There's just three things I'd ever say:
   "If anything goes bad, I did it.
   If anything goes semi-good, then we did it.
   If anything goes real good, then you did it."
That's all it takes to get people to win football games for you.

A successful single adult leadership team must have a coach who knows how to coach.

• The trust principle. Team members who share a common vision, who personalize the ministry process through ownership, and who accept one another in biblical agape love, come to deeply trust one another. Trust is the *glue* that binds the team through thick and thin. A member cannot effectively contribute, even in a small way, if animosity and distrust prevail, for it will create further rifts and the formation of cliques. Each team member must come to trust the role abilities of fellow teammates.

• The interaction principle. Teams have all the characteristics and interpersonal dynamics of a small group. They move through predictable phases and cycles, from formation to dissolution. The same team, with virtually the same personnel, may be extremely effective at one time and in disarray at a later date. Much of the success or failure of a team can be attributed to the quantity and quality of interaction between team members. Teams just can't function well when they don't meet to practice.

There must be regular face-to-face exposure between team members. The more they see and get to know one another, the more they bond. Bonded people share deep needs and dream great dreams together.

Bonding is one of the most important and yet least prioritized needs of solid team building. Some single adult ministries devote up to 60 percent of their operational budget to leadership development retreats and seminars. Getting the leadership team away for an intensive half day, day, weekend, or even week, is not only one of the greatest experiences they will ever have, but one that will yield the greatest long-term return in the ministry.

• The submission principle. People who submit to one another in a servant-leadership style elevate the goals and good of the team above the individual. This puts the ministry's vision and goals at the forefront, where it can capture the team's attention and energy. Deep loyalty to the team fosters respect and appreciation for the other team members, confidence in the team and its abilities as a whole, and also personal fulfillment and enjoyment. Team members enthusiastically claim, "I get to play on the greatest team in the world, and play the position I want to play!"

Teams are very fragile and can break apart for minor reasons. Petty rivalries can grow to immense proportion and trouble if left unchecked. Although it may be a communication problem, more often the root issue is a lack of genuine humility. An attitude of mutual submission keeps one person from taking the credit when the *team* deserves recognition.

• The Spirit principle. Up to this point in our discussion nearly everything that's been said could be true of a leadership team in almost any setting. The social sciences have done extensive research into these leadership issues and have provided us with a solid base of understanding. But Christian ministry adds another dimension—a spiritual one. Leadership teams engaged in ministry endeavors to God's glory are supernaturally empowered by the Holy Spirit. His power generates a new level of vision, unity, and sacrifice.

The third Person of the Trinity not only indwells each team member but offers divine guidance. We have to realize that God is more concerned about the success of the single adult ministry in our location than we are! It's His glory and reputation that are at stake! When leadership team members get hold of this principle, they are both freed to minister effectively and filled with the power necessary to accomplish the task at hand. Then love flows, giving testimony to the world of Christ's love as they love one another (John 13:34-35).

Gauging Team Health

In *The Well-Managed Ministry: Discovering and Developing the Strengths of Your Team,* Philip Van Auken offers some insightful observations about the health of teams. Health is much more than merely the absence of sickness; team health rarely stagnates; it is either improving or deteriorating over time. Teamwork is based on interpersonal relationships—the ability of people to interact productively and harmoniously. Therefore, when interpersonal relationships deteriorate, so does team health. Team coaches and leaders must constantly be sensitive to the warning signals or "handwriting on the wall" of interpersonal problems developing on a team. The five most common warning signals are:

- Poor communication—the result of the failure of team members to understand one another; focus is on talking rather than listening; verbal hostility, etc.
- Sloppy implementation—"the right hand doesn't know what the left hand is doing" syndrome.
- Avoidance—members show a pattern of avoiding disagreement, avoiding accountability, or avoiding one another.
- Chronic dissatisfaction—occurs when certain members acquire a negative, pessimistic, or critical spirit that casts a shadow of gloom over team activities.
- Loss of trust—team members doubt one another's motives, submerge agendas, and begin to question the ministry vision.

These five items do not actually cause team problems; they are merely the symptoms of the disease at work—spiritual immaturity. "Spiritually immature people inevitably encounter difficulties working together, because they often act and move out of self-interest and pride."[4] This, of course, brings us back to the principle of submission.

Van Auken's penetrating analysis continues as he suggests seven key ingredients of team health which move in unison, either undergirding teamwork or unraveling it. He says that team health may be gauged by the team's capacity to:

- Set and internalize goals. When team vision excites members, they readily "buy into" ministry goals they help set.
- Make decisions. Consensus in the decision-making process is easily reached because the goals are so firmly shared.
- Implement decisions. Smooth implementation of goals results from their ownership.
- Resolve conflict. Because trust runs high on healthy teams, conflict is easily resolved.

- Change. Change is seen as an opportunity for progress, since members want what is best.
- Maintain accountability. Accountability is seen as positive.
- Satisfy team members. Healthy teams have satisfied members who feel needed, unique, productive, and appreciated.[5]

Team Renewal: Some Practical Suggestions

By this point you may be greatly encouraged about the strength of your leadership team, mildly upset, or just plain "blown away." Assuming that you have some kind of leadership team currently in place, let's turn our attention to practical suggestions for its renewal.

- If the coach of your single adult ministry leadership team is not yet identified or recognized, start there. Using the proper channels and decision-making processes of your particular church, recruit and recognize the team coach. It may mean going to a pastor, a board, or the singles themselves. If *you* are the recognized coach already, then begin coaching!

- Go back to basics. Have the leadership team spend a great deal of time defining and clarifying the team mission and operational goals. Current research indicates that *unity of purpose* is the chief distinguishing feature of an outstanding team. Try a one-day strategic planning retreat format at a nice location in order to spur creative juices. Encourage leaders to dream great dreams; nothing is too big for God! Ask yourselves:

1. If God absolutely assured us of success in this singles ministry, what would it look like?

2. What hinders us from seeing that success come true?

3. What do we need to do this month, this year, the next three years to bring this about? Seek unity and pray about your vision. Word the mission in concise terms, put it in print for everyone to see, and keep it in front of you at all times. It is your biblically based purpose; treat it as such.

- Begin the process of role clarification within your leadership team. Find and utilize some good role clarification exercises. Have each person think through and then verbalize, "Who am I in this team?" Each person could draw a personal lifeline (my history, my background, my spiritual pilgrimage — perhaps charted in decades), marking significant peaks and valleys. Take plenty of time to hear, interpret, and affirm these autobiographies. The important questions are: "How did I get here? What do I bring to this team? What are my strengths — personal, skills, styles? What are my weaknesses — where do I need to develop; where could I potentially block the work of this leadership team?"

- Make conscious, deliberate attempts to enhance the bonding process of the team. Plan annual retreats together, if finances permit. Schedule regular recreation or eat a weekly meal together. Have more frequent but less lengthy work meetings and pray in twos or threes. Whatever the method, increase the time spent together. Emotional bonding is directly proportional to time. Don't expect team bonding to just occur naturally at business meetings. Plan for it!

- Mutually decide on a leadership development plan of action for the year. Find a good book on leadership—there are scores of them available—and read it together, taking the first half-hour of your regular meeting to discuss a chapter and its implications for your team. Try keeping personal leadership journals with insights about yourself and the team. Have an outside consultant objectively evaluate your single adult ministry . . . but be prepared to receive the report. Attend leadership conferences together or begin a single adult leadership breakfast on a monthly basis to integrate with other churches in your locale. Take leadership responsibilities seriously, and seek to develop skills just as you would for your job or career.

- Renew your regular business meetings: arrange the agenda items in order of importance; listen to all the strong points of a new idea before discussing any of its drawbacks; establish a written list of criteria by which to evaluate new ideas or proposals; provide team members with adequate information before meetings to facilitate advance "homework" in preparation for the meeting; compose the minutes of the meetings around what was beneficially accomplished rather than around what agenda items were discussed.[6]

Jeffrey R. King
Minister of Adults
Bethany Community Church
6240 S. Price
Tempe, Arizona 85283

Notes

1. Jack D. Orsburn, Linda Moran, Ed Musselwhite, John H. Zenger, Craig Perrin, *Self-Directed Work Teams: The New American Challenge* (Homewood, Illinois: Business One Irwin, 1990), 13–14.
2. Rod Wilson, "Team Players," *Interest* Magazine, March 1990, 16–17.
3. Elton Trueblood, *The Incendiary Fellowship* (New York: Harper & Row, 1967), 43.

4. Philip Van Auken, *The Well-Managed Ministry: Discovering and Developing the Strengths of Your Team* (Wheaton, Illinois: Victor Books, 1989), 168.

5. Ibid., 163.

6. Ibid., 159–60.

DEVELOPING THE MINISTRY

7. LET'S BEGIN AT CHURCH

"Perhaps the greatest need of single adults is to feel a sense of belonging."

Paul M. Petersen

The tip-offs are everywhere, from the grocery store to the newsstand. Stouffers alone makes eighty-six different foods designed to feed just one person. Want-ads in search of relationships are so pervasive they have reached the august *New York Review of Books* and dating services have proliferated to the point that they are targeted to such subgroups as the physically handicapped and the astrologically inclined.

The U.S. Census Bureau confirms that singleness is the highest it has been since the early part of the century. According to Steve Rawlings, a Census Bureau family demographer, about 41 percent of all adults of marriageable age (fifteen and older) are now single. That includes the never-married, the divorced and the widowed. Demographers call it a "glacial" trend—one that creeps up on us.

The rise of singlehood in recent years, particularly among people in their twenties and thirties, has led Rawlings and others to predict that the percentage of people who will never marry— now about 5 percent—is likely to double by the end of the century.[1]

Are Single Adults Welcome in the Church?
There appears to be a rising consciousness in the church of a new demographic trend in the land, yet that consciousness seems to be barely a sliver of light on the total landscape of the church. Some churches are taking note, implementing fledgling ministries to single adults; networking is beginning to happen, with interdenominational organiza-

tions being created such as the National Association of Single Adult Leaders; authors and publishers are beginning to take note as well.

In the book *Lost in the Land of Oz: The Search for Identity and Community in American Life,* Madonna Kolbenschlag says:

> The Celtic myth of Macha is an awesome metaphor for the wound in our contemporary civilization: a divided consciousness that abuses power and breathes all sorts of social ills, while denying the life-giving "feminine" experience and values in human society. This wound in our consciousness, in our culture, has made orphans of us all . . . and is it not easy to see in the story of Macha and her children . . . the *divorced single parent,* struggling to work, support, and raise her children in a society that is hostile to her in the role of provider?[2] (italics added)

Kolbenschlag's observation of hostility is a valid one concerning the oppression not only of divorced single parents, but indeed of single adults in general in Western and American culture.

This seems to be a case where what is true of American culture is many times more true of the American church. The instances of alienation of single adults in the church are rife. The church is well known to be a couple-oriented society where memberships are measured in families. High stress is laid on nurseries and child care. A common question is, "When are you going to get married?" The underlying thought is that you are not complete, not whole, until you have a spouse. The church has an Ark Mentality — salvation is found in twos, rather than the Kingdom of God motif — salvation is found in an *individual's* faith response to God's grace. "A recent study of parish life in the United States indicates several groups who might be perceived as not really included: traditionalists, *singles,* newcomers, cliques that formerly dominated church life but no longer do, *those alienated by church response to divorce,* and ethnic or racial minorities."[3] (italics added)

This result is probably encouraged in the Roman Catholic Church by the Pope's own teaching and dictums. "The affectivity of the young Christian must be molded by a process of primary socialization such as occurs, ideally, in the family. Following several texts of Vatican II, Pope John Paul II has expatriated on the family as 'church in miniature.' "[4] Such teaching as this is bound to have an effect on the church's lack of acceptance and encouragement toward single adults.

Another author has observed, "Ironically, . . . singles may feel alienated because they are surrounded by a church that constantly uses family metaphors in both theology and parish life; are located in parishes that often list membership by family units; worship in liturgies whose hymns, responses and sermons reinforce family images; and observe that great disproportion in parish programs and activities directed to people in some stage of family life rather than to singles."[5] (It should be noted that Harris is using only a nuclear family definition in this quote, and only partially addresses alternative forms of family later. She never indicates that never-married, childless single adults can be family as well.)

Even as society has begun to take note of the boom in the unmarried population, so there is also a crack in the door of the church as some local congregations take seriously Christ's admonition to care for all with a cup of cold water. However, even as these ministries begin to flourish and attract large numbers of single adults of all ages, so questions are also raised as to why single adults should be set apart from other adults in the church, how can single adults be ministered to, and what are dangers to be avoided?

As I talked with a senior minister at a medium-sized church, he asked what area of specialization I was involved in. When I responded Single Adult Ministry, and asked if his church had such a ministry, his response was, "No way! Those single people only take and never give. They don't go to church and they don't pledge. Besides, they're all promiscuous and will cause our counseling load to increase too much."

Such unsubstantiated rumor is circulating widely throughout churches and denominations. I have received calls from singles ministers in despair, as churches obscure and famous have reconsidered their commitment to Single Adult Ministry.

As the single adult population flourishes and grows, many questions are raised concerning proper ministry methods and programming ideas. This is due to the relative newness of Single Adult Ministry as a valid and needed area. The experience of one pastor is a good example of the silent treatment that single adults are apt to get in churches.

> As a pastor of a United Presbyterian Church congregation in Tacoma, Washington, I was more aware of the nuclear family and its needs. Our congregation, like so many others, aimed its primary ministry toward families and couples. We had family retreats, family nights, a couples club, and sermons on the family and marriage. Our language, in church newsletters and worship, expressed the same focus. We were little aware of the subtle

ways that single adults in our midst were made to feel excluded. We weren't sure why so many singles never came to church.[6]

Why Does the Church Not Accept Single Adults?

At a recent Christian Education conference held by one denomination, two workshops were offered to participants. One workshop was designed for those in positions of pastoral care to assist them in helping adults suffering through a divorce to deal with their practical, emotional, and theological issues. The second workshop had to do with developing a lay team of single adults to minister to single adults in the church. The first workshop was not subscribed and had to be canceled, even though over 200 churches were in attendance, and in excess of 800 people were registered. The second workshop was held with four attendees. Apparently, the crack in the door of the church is a mere sliver!

Why are our churches "asleep at the wheel"? To some churches single adults are either the lepers or the Samaritans, or both! There are probably as many reasons for this oppressive mentality as there are churches. A brief survey might reveal theological discomfort with divorce and remarriage, or a sense that those who are not married must be socially inept, unable to make commitments, or emotionally unstable (not the sort of persons we want in our church). However, being single does not presuppose irresponsibility; and Christ wants us to accept even those who have suffered and do suffer through physical, cultural, and personal disabilities. Other reasons may hinge on the conservatism of the local church: "We've never done it that way." There may be fears of various unknowns—change in status quo, threat to those "in power," the singles' reputed promiscuity, financial and time drains.

> When I began to explore the ministry with single adults, there were persons within the congregation who questioned whether it was "worth the effort to go after singles." . . . In pursuing the concern, I began to realize what was really being said. It was that they were "poor prospects" for church membership. Like so many local congregations, we were falling into the subtle "numbers game" which overlooks the unique needs of persons.[7]

Widows are the "safest" of single adults, and even they are seen as dangerous. A widowed single adult in her fifties (widowed four years) is extremely thankful for the opportunity that a single adult ministry has given her to find friends on equal footing, as well as to offer her a safe harbor where she can then branch out from to the rest of the church and her married friends. Her experience has been that in her four years of singleness, only four married couples have invited her to their homes for dinner and an evening. One of those four couples was the singles minister and his wife and so (in her words) not necessarily to be counted. Her experience was when she was widowed, she immediately became a threat to her female, married friends.

Why Do We Need Single Adult Ministries?

The above illustration speaks loudly to the validity of Single Adult Ministry. Single adults are a group of people whose needs can be met by the church, the same as families, retirees, and youth, to name a few that do receive attention.

Acts 7 tells us that widows in particular were to be cared for. However, a larger principle of the church is found in Matthew 25:35-36: "For I was hungry and you gave Me something to eat, I was thirsty and you gave Me something to drink, I was a stranger and you invited Me in, I needed clothes and you clothed Me, I was sick and you looked after Me, I was in prison and you came to visit Me." The church should look for opportunities to minister to those in need, bodily, socially, culturally, and spiritually. This certainly fits the description of many single adults. However, this is not to say that every church ought to have a Single Adult Ministry, but rather that every church ought to minister to single adults.

Statistically we know that the segment of society that is missing from our churches the most are single adults in their twenties. They have dropped out of church and are choosing to play Saturday night and sleep Sunday morning.

In the *Philadelphia Inquirer* magazine of Sunday, December 20, 1987, an article addressed the movement of baby boomers back to the church. "R.T. Gribbon of the Alban Institute, a religious think tank in Washington, D.C., has found that churchgoing baby boomers want intellectual challenge, ways to express emotion, opportunities for full participation, a welcoming, responsive minister or rabbi, special services and programs for children, and, for *singles,* chances to meet new companions" (italics added).

Several months ago eight recent "graduates" and three current members of the Highland Park Presbyterian Church Singles Ministry in Dallas went away together for a weekend. The eight "graduates" consisted of four couples that had met in a young singles Sunday School class, had fallen in love and married. The response of the three single adults throughout the weekend was that they felt that they did not fit. In the words of one of the single adults, "The couples did their 'couples' thing and the single adults felt very much out of place and odd."

This in spite of the fact that all eleven adults were longtime close friends. Single adults need a place in the church that does not apply pressure toward marriage, but a place that accepts them for who they are.

I spoke with a singles' pastor in the Pacific Northwest whose church has subsumed Single Adult Ministry under the larger department of Adult Ministry. Highland Park has toyed with this idea as a means of integration, and so I asked him about the results. He stated that placing Single Adult Ministry under Adult Ministry had dried up the Single Adult Ministry visibility, and decreased their "friendliness" to the single adult community. Churches ought to have identifiable ministries.

There are some needs that are shared, and some that are diverse, between single and married adults. Differences include: the need to consciously work on "family" and intimacy needs. Single adults desire a more active social calendar. They must deal with their sexuality in different ways. They must overcome societal and familial biases against single adults.

What Do Single Adults Need?
Statistical surveys of the single adult population of America tell us that there are five predominant concerns that single adults have. They are: Fear of being "left out," Finances, Companionship, Single Parenting issues, and Intimacy. There are many needs that the church can address that lead to positive change in the lives of single adults. In fact, the church may just be the best hidden resource that single adults have, and many of them do not realize it. Some of the needs that the church can meet are:

• Hope. Single adults need hope that, in spite of the failures in their lives, life has meaning. Many single adults have been let down in relationships, family, and work. This is true of single adults of all ages, as older adults realize their life is passing them by and they may not have reached goals that they have set. In younger singles, this lack of hope is often the result of the realization that they may not attain the status or wealth that their parents had; this is in part a result of the large population increase known as the "Baby Boomers." Single adults first need hope in God—that they have not been abandoned; second, in others— that they can have fruitful and productive relationships; and third, in the

90

future—that all is not lost and that tomorrow holds the promise of a new day and new opportunities (Isa. 40:29-31; 1 Thes. 1:3).

• Understanding. Most of the unique needs of single adults result from their marital status. They have no spouse with whom to share ideas, concepts, trials, and troubles. Single adults need someone who will listen. True listening gives value to the person being listened to. It helps to rebuild the self-worth of the single adult. Many single adults are suffering from a lack of understanding because of broken relationships (whether from a divorce, broken engagement, or bad social dynamics), as well as societal and family pressure—"Why aren't you married yet? Are you going to let life pass you by?" Single adults need to know that the sign of adult passages is not marriage but assuming responsibility for their own lives. Single adults also need understanding regarding the opposite sex. Society teaches that anyone still single at age thirty must dislike the opposite sex or "something must be wrong with the single adult." All of this can bring a great deal of confusion. Further understanding can be offered concerning the sharing of problems, temptations, and trials. All people need to know that they are not alone in their struggles (1 Cor. 10:13).

• Belonging. Perhaps the greatest need of single adults is to feel a sense of belonging. Our society teaches that two is a whole number, and if you are not whole you do not belong. Single adults need to recognize their own singular completeness and wholeness. They need to belong— to others, to the church, to society. Along with this need for belonging is the need for *family* and *intimacy*. Family brings much needed stability to individuals. It ideally provides rituals, loyalty, and a nonjudgmental accepting environment. Single adults need to have their isolation broken down. They need proper and healthy contact with people. A few years ago the common rage was that everyone needed between five and forty hugs a day to stay healthy. All people need vital human contact. For a single adult this is difficult, especially in a society such as ours that highly promotes sexually "going all the way," rather than healthy contact through handshakes, hugs, and a slap on the back. There was validity to Ann Landers' survey asking if women preferred hugs or sex; the overwhelming majority voted for hugs.

• Role models. Single adults need to see healthy dating and marriage relationships. Most often single adults see divorce and broken relationships. This leads to a cynical and frustrated view of social skills and relationships. Yet God has made each one of us to live in relationship with one another. Single adults need to observe a healthy Christianity. In

91

a world that seems to revolve around broken promises, broken hopes, and fleeting fantasies, the love that Christ has for each of us can appear to be a myth.

● Information. For a number of reasons, single adults often lack in basic social skills. They may not know how to make a friendship, especially with the opposite sex, and the harder they try the more they seem to drive a wedge between themselves and others. Single adults need information about themselves: who they are and how they are perceived. They need information concerning proper dating skills, sexuality, finances, and their personal spirituality and relationship with God.

● Companionship. Single adults need multiple friendships to take the place of that one spouse, so that their needs are met by a variety of individuals. Then when one individual moves on or lets them down, they are not devastated. Companionship allows for a sharing of ideas, feedback, social activities, belonging, and family.

It is critical that a Single Adult Ministry establish a biblical foundation for their ministry. The Scriptures show a deep concern for widows and the fatherless (James 1:27). Even in biblical times there were those who in their singleness were struggling with broken relationships, pain, and grief. And yet the Apostle Paul (Phil. 4:11-13) said that whatever state we are in, we ought to be content.

Psychologist Lawrence Crabb has said that all people want Deeper Belonging and Deeper Impact or, to put it in another way, *to be accepted* and *to make a difference.* If the church is to meet the needs of *all* its members, including single adults, then these needs must be addressed through all the major ministry areas of the church — preaching, administration, pastoral care, and education.

As these needs are addressed, we also need to work on releasing single adults from the eccelsiastical oppression of the Ark Mentality.

> If the Ecclesial community is centrally concerned with the occurrence of redemption, and if redemption means being set free or released from a binding power, sin, or debt, then we can say with Hedge that Christianity is and always has been the "religion of freedom." . . . For Paul, freedom has both a negative and a positive sense. Negatively, it means liberation from sin, law, death, and the worldly powers. This is the primary sense in which freedom is still understood by most Christians: it means salvation. . . . But freedom also has a positive sense for Paul: it means not only being set free from "bondage to decay" but also

obtaining the glorious liberty of the children of God (Rom. 8:21). . . . The liberation movements have helped us to recover this second, positive sense of Christian freedom and to perceive implications of this historical praxis which escaped Paul since he was thinking primarily in an eschatological context.[8]

Given the earlier research and insights regarding single adults in our culture as well as our church, it is my belief that single adults need liberation from the oppression of prejudice, nonacceptance, and second-class citizenship in the church.

What Can the Church Give to Single Adults?

One of the primary helps that the church can provide to single adults is to help them feel comfortable with their singleness. We should not be challenging people to "make due" until marriage, but to excel in who they are, whether singled or unsingled. The church needs to provide "family" in a nonnuclear sense to single adults as well as to the traditional nuclear family.

"Today, many people seem to be seeking quality and meaning in life. They want a sense of inner direction and forms of community that are inclusive. For the single adults, this means a community that does not put a premium upon being married so much as being whole. To choose the direction that helps persons, whether single or married, to deal with the quality of life is a prime opportunity for the church."[9]

Mark Lee suggests that the church needs to:
1. Recognize that the single status is the appropriate available option to being married.
2. Relate to the interests of singles.
3. Provide full opportunity for singles to act responsibly in the life of the church.
4. Call upon Christians to keep fidelity with biblical principles relative to personal conduct.
5. Adjust the focus of the church's ministry on the nuclear family.
6. Activate programs which will meet the needs of singles.
7. Build the church on Jesus Christ.[10]

The church needs to emphasize to married and single adults that marriage, though valuable, is not the measure of one's worth in the eyes of God or the church. The title of a video series produced by Gospel Films with Harold Ivan Smith as presenter sums up this idea very well: *One Is a Whole Number.*

It is important for the church to rethink its theology of singleness in light of changing cultural norms as well as the light of Scripture. We need to recognize that the Scriptures are inclusive of people, regardless of their marital status. The church needs to develop a theology which affirms singleness as a valid lifestyle. The Scriptures are full of examples of single adults other than Paul and Jesus. The attitude toward divorce and remarriage, as well as forgiveness in these situations, needs to be strengthened and better understood. A concise picture of a successful ministry can be found in Acts 2:41-47:

> Those who accepted his message were baptized, and about three thousand were added to their number that day. They devoted themselves to the apostles' teaching and to the fellowship, to the breaking of bread and to prayer. Everyone was filled with awe, and many wonders and miraculous signs were done by the apostles. All the believers were together and had everything in common. Selling their possessions and goods, they gave to anyone as he had need. Every day they continued to meet together in the temple courts. They broke bread in their homes and ate together with glad and sincere hearts, praising God and enjoying the favor of all the people. And the Lord added to their number daily those who were being saved.

The outline that Dr. Bill Flanagan uses concerning this passage in the *Singles Ministry Handbook*[11] is helpful. He says the ministry ought to grow in numbers, *grow up, grow out,* and *grow together.* Each of these concepts is important in the life of a church. We ought to be examining our ministries to single adults in a similar light. Are we growing in numbers? The national statistic for Single Adult Ministries is that a ministry will have a 50 percent turnover every six months. As I examine our own ministry and travel around the United States, this seems to be accurate. There is the constant need for growth in numbers for the life of a singles ministry. We also need to be growing up or building up our single adults. By this we mean developing spiritual maturity of the people within our ministry. Growing out refers to our mission. While it is true that singles themselves are a mission field, we must also be focusing on mission outside of ourselves. Any ministry that focuses just upon itself will die a quick death. True, we need to reach out to singles, but it is also true that singles need to reach out beyond their own world. Growing together speaks to the issue again of belonging to family. Single adults need the contact of encouragement, accountability, and loyalty. The church of Jesus Christ ought to be offering each of these.

Paul M. Petersen
Minister of College/Single Adult Ministries
Highland Park Presbyterian Church
3821 University Blvd.
Dallas, Texas 75205

Notes

1. *Dallas Times Herald,* June 29, 1988.
2. Madonna Kolbenschlag, *Lost in the Land of Oz: The Search for Identity and Community in American Life* (San Francisco: Harper & Row, 1988), 2–3.
3. *Notre Dame Study of Parish Life,* "The Parish as Community," Report #10 (Notre Dame: Institute for Pastoral and Social Ministry and the Center for the Study of Contemporary Society of the University of Notre Dame, March 1987), 12–13. Quoted in Maria Harris, *Fashion Me a People: Curriculum in the Church* (Louisville: Westminster/John Knox Press, 1989), 82.
4. Avery Dulles, *Models of the Church* (New York: Doubleday, 1987), 218.
5. Maria Harris, *Fashion Me a People: Curriculum in the Church* (Louisville: Westminster/John Knox Press, 1989), 82.
6. Raymond K. Brown, *Reach Out to Singles: A Challenge to Ministry* (Philadelphia: Westminster Press, 1979), 9.
7. Ibid., 19.
8. Peter C. Hodgson, *Revisioning the Church: Ecclesial Freedom in the New Paradigm* (Minneapolis: Fortress Press, 1988), 68–69.
9. Brown, 16.
10. Mark W. Lee, "The Church and the Unmarried," in *It's OK to Be Single* (London: Collins), 50–55.
11. Douglas L. Fagerstrom, ed., *Singles Ministry Handbook* (Wheaton, Illinois: Victor Books, 1988), 31–32.

8. REVITALIZING YOUR SINGLE ADULT MINISTRY

"It is important to design a ministry model around a 'community of family' environment that is nurturing people to spiritual and emotional health. Ministry is much more than programs."

G. Jerry Martin

Environments exert a strong influence on us. When we visit a group, we quickly size up the environment of the ministry. We sense the organization (or lack thereof), the plan for inclusion of new people (or a group that will be hard to break into), and whether or not there is a place where we can be included. *Environment* is defined by *Webster's New World Dictionary* as "all the conditions, circumstances, influences surrounding, and affecting the development of, an organism or group of organisms."

As leaders in Single Adult Ministry, we must expose people to a dynamic, caring ministry environment in which they can develop as disciples of Jesus Christ. This means we begin by meeting their felt needs of friendship, resolving conflicts, and then bringing them along in personal discipleship.

Dr. Bruce Larson, co-pastor of the Crystal Cathedral in California, made a striking comment about developing the environment of acceptance and community: "We must develop a strong sense of acceptance and warmth in our ministry that goes beyond anything a person can get by frequenting the neighborhood bar."

Jesus dealt with people at different levels of commitment to Him. He asked a great deal of the disciples He selected. In fact He asked them to leave their homes and vocations to go with Him everywhere He went. Those who called upon Him with specific problems were asked to trust Him for specific answers. Of course, Christ had a commitment to help His disciples grow spiritually. He took time to teach them, exhort them and correct them, and be a model to them.

Christ created the environment for them to grow spiritually so that they, in turn, would be equipped to train others. Single adults need an environment of love and acceptance where needs can be met within a solid biblically based ministry. Therefore, we need to structure ministry to provide for several levels of commitment to assist people in finding their entry point.

For the past fifteen years as an associate pastor in three different churches, I have had as one of my responsibilities the Single Adult Ministry. I am presently involved in the revitalization of three single adult groups: College-Career, Young Single Adults, and Middle Single Adults.

In each of these churches there was a need to revitalize the ministry to single adults. We needed to refocus, add new structure, breathe some new life into the ministry — or let the present ministry die and begin a new one altogether.

All too often we treat a sick and dying ministry by placing it on life support and treating the symptoms rather than the problems. We may increase the advertising, add new programs, or plan big events in order to boost the program, and yet the ministry continues to be ineffective. We miss the goal of developing ministry and building a community of believers.

There are those in Single Adult Ministry who advocate that single adults should not stay in a singles ministry for a long period of time. They believe a singles ministry should be looked upon as a transition place, a place to stop off on the way to another stage of life. Essentially, a place to find someone and get married.

I believe that being single is a viable lifestyle, one that is acceptable and, in fact, modeled in Scripture. When we take that stand on singleness, we will build the ministry by emphasizing quality relationships and personal growth. For many single adults the people in this ministry may become their "extended family."

We build community by design. It does not happen by chance. Community building tends to happen better in smaller groups, and well-planned events. Community happens on the trip as you travel to retreats, at conferences, "talk-it-over" groups, planning teams, and in a small group ministry in homes.

Select a Task Force
Every singles group I've worked with had some common problems. The leadership of the group was tired, burned out, or their circumstances in life changed (job change, personal problems, or marriage). Therefore,

they were in need of new leadership people to get a new perspective on the ministry.

To begin the process of revitalizing your ministry, develop a Task Force group. A Task Force is a group commissioned for a specific purpose. To establish a Task Force, select a cross section of people that represent long-time attenders, new members, various spiritual growth levels, and a balance of men and women. Ten to twelve people is a good group size.

It's essential to focus the ministry on God, since effective ministry must be based on a devotional life. Then we can have a more effective evaluation of our ministry. The following steps: evaluate, identify needs, write a ministry statement, create simple objectives and goals to relaunch the ministry—this is the plan for the Task Force.

• Evaluate the ministry. In my first Single Adult Ministry experience, I didn't know the right questions to ask. Since then I have used the following questions to keep a ministry on track.

1. Where are the leaders? Have they moved, gotten married, or are they just not available for leadership? In many Single Adult Ministries there will be a significant turnover every six months. In one church ministry we had a significant turnover in the older singles group due to several marriages. The key leaders of the young singles group had career relocations. Some of them had given key leadership for over two years. We came to the realization that new leadership was not adequately developed to take their places in time. Leadership development must be an ongoing process.

2. Have the leaders fallen away from their purpose statement (if they had one)? In one singles group, we reestablished the purpose statement three times in five years because of the turnover in leadership. When there's a significant change in leadership, the new leaders have to "own" the purpose statement.

3. Have leaders served too long and are new ones needed? In my first singles ministry experience, I came into a group that had become tired and stale in their leadership. They needed a new vision for ministry and new leadership.

4. Has the leadership evaluated their ministry recently? Due to the turnover of people, it's essential to have a major evaluation at least every six months.

5. Has the leadership tried to be all things to all people? Select five to seven emphases of ministry and decide to do them well. In one situation, upon my arrival I found a group of singles from twenty to eighty

years old. The planning meeting was spent trying to plan events appropriate to meet the needs of the wide age span. It was necessary to break down the events to meet specific needs of the younger and older adults.

6. Are we more program-oriented than people-oriented? Certainly schedules and programs and plans are essential to organizing a ministry, but we need to make sure that the programs are meeting peoples' needs rather than just perpetuating the program. If a group is more concerned with programming than building relationships, the single adults will stagnate socially as well as spiritually.

• Identify needs. Christ identified people as being "like sheep without a shepherd" (Mark 6:34). You and your leadership team need to discover the needs of your sheep so you can shepherd them. "The effectiveness of our ministry is tied to a clear understanding of the needs of those to whom we are called to minister."[1] A Single Adult Ministry needs to focus on the needs of single adults in four areas.

1. A place to belong. Many single adults are active in a variety of social, church, and community activities. Christian singles desire an alternative to the singles bar and night clubs. A ministry that desires to attract a large number of single adults will need to schedule a diverse number of events. If your church is not large enough to organize many events, find a few other churches in your community to share in the events.

2. A place to be known. One of the big challenges of being single is loneliness. Andrew Greeley says: "There are two kinds of loneliness that afflict human life. The first is the loneliness that comes from the human condition. It can be mitigated and alleviated but it cannot be eliminated. The other is the loneliness that we choose freely. It can always be conquered if we choose to do so."[2]

Building a single adult "family" of believers will help the development of good friendships. We need to find fellow believers who are in the spiritual life journey and travel together.

With each structured meeting or planned activity, there should be some "mixer" time for the development of relationships. A variety of ice-breaker activities or discussion starters can be used as a group gathers to help people get acquainted with each other. When you have your Bible study, plan time for discussion and interaction, as well as for contents delivery.

Many single adults will be dealing with some deep emotional challenges related to difficult decisions they have made or are presently facing. There may be issues of vocation, education, separation, divorce, alimony, single parenthood, financial stress, or the struggle of being single.

3. A place to learn. There is indeed an intellectual concern among single adults. Specially focused seminars for six to seven sessions once a week, or special Friday night and all day Saturdays, are appealing. Some of the seminar topics used in Single Adult Ministries are: Divorce Recovery (for adults, youth, children), Blended Families, Single Parents, Being Single Is OK, Grief Recovery, Intimacy, and Single Adult Sexuality.

4. A place to grow spiritually. It is the spiritual dimension to our ministry that gives what we do an eternal, God-centered focus. God designed us as spiritual beings who desire to explore the spiritual dimension of our lives. There will be those who come to us knowing they hurt, but are unaware that the message of the Gospel of Christ will give them meaning and hope. Some people may have tried many ways to resolve their inner conflict and so discovered their need for spiritual help.

The needs displayed by people searching for spiritual help must be met with loving understanding. Our goal is reconciliation, not condemnation. Bible teaching must not only give information but also focus on the application of God's Word to a person's life. By the end of our teaching session we want to answer the question, "So what? What does God's Word have to do with the issues I face in my life?"

In general, young single adults face issues of education or specialized training, establishing their career, establishing adult relationships with the same and opposite sex, and coming to grips with singleness versus marriage.

Older single adults have a greater focus on "emergency room" ministry. The issues will focus on Divorce Recovery, Widow Support, Single Parenting, and Grief Recovery. "The effectiveness of our ministry is tied to a clear understanding of the needs of those to whom we are called to minister."[3]

● Ministry statement. A ministry statement is a written document that describes the group's direction and values. This document will guide your leaders and participants to know the reason for the group's existence. Defining the basic purpose and the values you hold will help determine the ministries you organize.

After your Single Adult Task Force has compiled a primary list of identified needs, formulate a Ministry Statement which will complete the sentence, "We exist to _____." This statement will need to be broad enough to last for a few years, yet specific enough to provide direction now. Keep your Ministry Statement simple, using one statement or three or four key words or phrases.

A Ministry Statement may be written by first brain-storming what your Task Force considers to be the purpose of your ministry. From what you compile, narrow the list down to five words or phrases that describe your ministry. Then narrow the list to three words or phrases. Using the final words or phrases, write an easily understood statement. One single adult ministry has five key words in their Ministry Statement—Relationships, Spiritual Nourishment, Evangelism, and Involvement.

• Objectives and goals. Once you have settled on your Ministry Statement by answering the question, "Why does this ministry exist?" you should determine the areas of ministry you will provide as you fulfill the Ministry Statement. You may choose broad categories such as Bible Study, Support, Education, and Relationships.

Goals are specific and measurable steps to accomplish the objective you set. Your goals will have a date, number, or time attached to it. Goals need to be specific, obtainable, and measurable, but flexible enough so you can make adjustments as your needs change. Examples of combining the objectives and goals would be:

1. Bible Study. Goal: Begin a 20s and 30s Sunday School class by September 1.

2. Support. Goal: Begin a codependent group by March 1.

3. Education. Goal: Begin a six-week single parent workshop by October 1 with 30 people attending, 10 people from outside our church.

4. Relationships. Goal: By January 1, begin a hospitality team to greet people who attend the Sunday morning adult class. See that everyone has name tags, and follow-up visitors.

Your Ministry Statement, objectives, and goals don't have to be perfect the first time around. Refine them as you go.

Balancing Your Single Adult Ministry

In the process of revitalizing your Single Adult Ministry, you may find out that the ministry is out of balance. You may be overemphasizing your contact with new people, or focusing all your time together in teaching content, or completely focusing on developing an awesome commitment core of spiritual berets.

All too often in ministry we focus our attention on what we tend to know best—such as having a mini-worship service every time we get together. Consequently, we don't intentionally plan for the inclusion of uncommitted Christians or non-Christians. We also don't challenge our people to grow through a deeper commitment to Jesus Christ and to each other; therefore, we lose the great joy of seeing people reproduce themselves in ministry.

The chart which follows contains a three-step plan of *contact, content,* and *commitment.* The plan can be a valuable aid in personal and leadership team planning, so you can communicate with those participating in your ministry.

• Contact. Unless you are seeking to relate to new people who need to know the Good News of the Gospel, you will not have a vital growing ministry. You need to plan nonthreatening events to reach out to the non-Christian person, times when they can come to something enjoyable, such as sporting events, cookouts, and need-related workshops. This kind of contact will help develop a mailing list and lead to follow-up for further involvement. In addition to the event being enjoyable and informative to Christians, it gives them opportunity to invite a friend to something that is positive with a purpose.

• Content. The second level of the balanced ministry is the level where we encourage our people to begin a consistent commitment to the Lord Jesus Christ, to the Single Adult Ministry itself, and to the church body at large. This commitment begins with the regular weekly meetings. The desire is for the person to start with the very basic concepts of the Word of God and move toward a more consistent commitment of time, talents, and treasure.

A concern is that the content level can become the "comfort zone" for a ministry. It easily moves into a ministry to "our people." It can be "safe" to minister at this level because there are few risks. You do not have to contend with very many new relationships or non-Christian people, planning for outreach, and you don't need to stretch yourself in dealing with all those people out there who have problems.

Upon arriving in Dallas, I soon attended my first Single Adult Ministry Steering Committee meeting. This volunteer team of people had developed some good Bible study ministries, held monthly dinners, kept contact with visitors, had a strong Sunday School, conducted some small group Bible studies, had a missions emphasis, and planned some good socials.

However, I was not fully prepared for the response blurted out by one of the ladies when I asked the question, "What are you presently doing to minister to divorced and single parents?" The reply came back, "Oh, they aren't welcome here!" You can imagine my shock. I'm pleased to say that within a few months we discovered there were people who wanted to become a part of developing a ministry of support for single

103

BALANCING YOUR SINGLE ADULT MINISTRY

	PURPOSE Biblical Basis for Ministry	PLAN Involvement Required	PROGRAM Accomplishing the Purpose
CONTACT	**LEAD AND EQUIP OTHERS** Ephesians 4:11-15 Development of Mature Christians 1 Peter 4:10 "God has given each of us special abilities; use them to help each other."	**COME AND LEAD** Be an equipper of others to develop multiplying disciples — those who will disciple others. Expose people to opportunities to serve others by leading Bible studies, mission trips, discipling others. Use your spiritual gifts to serve others.	**MEETING NEEDS FOR GROWTH** Leadership training, small discipleship groups, class teaching, leading outreach activities, and mission trips.
CONTENT	**DEVELOP SPIRITUALLY** Hebrews 10:24-25 Stimulate one another toward love and good deeds; meet together, encourage one another. Matthew 28:19-20 Go and make disciples.	**COME AND GROW** Learn and apply basic biblical principles for spiritual growth. Build one another up through commitment to Christ and to each other. Learn to become accountable to others by being a regular attender of the ministry.	**MEETING SPIRITUAL NEEDS** Church services, home Bible studies, retreats, afterglows, Sunday A.M. and special seminars.

	PURPOSE Biblical Basis for Ministry	**PLAN** Involvement Required	**PROGRAM** Accomplishing the Purpose
COMMITMENT	OUTREACH Acts 1:8 You will be My witnesses. Luke 19:10 Christ came to seek those who were lost.	COME AND INVESTIGATE Come to activities and be exposed to the Gospel. Become a part of activities which appeal to Christians and non-Christians. Be given the opportunity to respond to the claims of Christ.	MEETING FELT NEEDS Recreation, sports, special outings, workshops (self-esteem, divorce recovery, single parents, children of divorce, codependency), and evangelistic Bible studies.

© G. Jerry Martin

parents, and for those who were divorced.

● Commitment. The move upward to the commitment level thins out the number of those who are willing and able to give themselves to leadership and discipleship. As we challenge our people to consider opportunities to ministry and be in leadership, they will understand better the spiritual gifts they have to contribute to the body of believers. They will be able to discover the requirements and responsibilities of leadership, teaching, missions, caring for others, and administration.

When given the opportunity and challenged to serve, single adults will rise to the occasion with depth of dedication. Serving and impacting another person's life can be the most challenging and rewarding experience on the path of growing to spiritual maturity.

Effective prayer, planning, preparation, and communication coupled with the guidelines given on the chart and a lot of hard work begins the development of a balanced ministry for single adults.

The progression of ministry involvement is not an evaluation of spirituality. The progression is a degree of commitment one has made of the time and energy they are able to give to the ministry. The plan chart, Balancing Your Single Adult Ministry, helps to evaluate present ministry; it is also a planning device and a challenge to your group members to evaluate their own commitment to ministry. Use the ministry plan sheet to see the progression of commitment of ministry and the various levels in which a person can enter into a single adult ministry.

Relaunching a Single Adult Ministry
We are attracted to a sign which reads, "Under New Management." Those who liked what was going on can't believe it will be better, and those who were dissatisfied can't believe it will be any worse. You are in a win, win position.

The key to relaunching a vital ministry to single adults is to: 1. Communicate, 2. Communicate, 3. Communicate.

● Communicate through leadership. At this time your Task Force will conclude their responsibility. After they have evaluated the ministries and designed a balanced ministry, they will have fulfilled their reason for existence. The continued development of the ministry will be done by the present established leadership team, an entirely new team or new people added to the present leadership team.

Depending on the size of your group, you will need several people to give oversight of each ministry. Be careful not to build ministry around one person, but let several people share leadership responsibility. Also be careful you don't fall into the trap of running a Single Adult Ministry like a Youth Group. These are adults and they need to "own" this ministry.

The Leadership Team will need to carry the message of this ministry to others. Each of them has a network of friends at church, where they work, and where they live.

• Communicate a major emphasis. To relaunch your ministry, focus on a key time when you can make an impact on the most number of people. Determine to make this a quality experience for those attending the event. For some churches this major emphasis will be on Sunday morning, and for others a week night will be best.

In one church I served, the Sunday morning design of the worship services and the other departments of the church made this the best time for inviting new people; consequently, this was our major focus time for people to sign up for seminars, support groups, trips, recreation, and hear a message designed to meet a felt need from a biblical perspective.

At another church, we found it advantageous to use Thursday night as our inviter time. The evening was designed with a variety of ice-breakers, recreation, skits, and a need-related talk/discussion and refreshments. The variety and the informality appealed to this group.

Determine a date for your major emphasis and design a plan to communicate it. Choose a date at least four to six weeks away. Your focus may be to start a new topics series, bring in a guest speaker, or put a new twist such as recreation or a barbecue.

To publicize the event, design a flyer, write a news release for the church newspaper and the local community paper.

• Communicate churchwide. Since your Single Adult Ministry is an essential focus at your church, you and your leadership team need to let it be known that you are committed to it. As the ministry gains visibility, you will see this enthusiasm become more contagious. People want to be a part of something positive.

The purpose of the big announcement is not to draw attention to you or create some unusual hype for the group, but to communicate that this is an important area of focus in your church. It is essential that the senior pastor declare his support for this ministry. Make effective use of the regular publications of the church such as the church bulletin, church newspaper, and bulletin boards.

You may also gather prospects for your Single Adult Ministry by including a single adult contact card in the church bulletin. The card will ask for people to include single adults with phone numbers and addresses for your contact list. Many of your prospects will come from their family and friends. Contact prospects as soon as possible to let them know of your major emphasis.

Keep It Going

Whether you are the single adult minister, associate pastor, senior pastor, or a volunteer lay person assigned to this ministry, the following steps can help you have a more effective Single Adult Ministry.

• Tend your own spiritual passion. Whether we are in ministry vocationally or a volunteer, most of us readily acknowledge the necessity of maintaining a strong, consistent, and stable spiritual life. However, with the pressure of schedules, problems, programs, and activities, we struggle with our relationship with God. Thus, we neglect that which is most important, our own spiritual maturity. Jesus told His disciples, "I am the true vine, and My Father is the gardener. He cuts off every branch in Me that bears no fruit, while every branch that does bear fruit He prunes so that it will be even more fruitful. Remain in Me, and I will remain in you. No branch can bear fruit by itself; it must remain in the vine. Neither can you bear fruit unless you remain in Me" (John 15:1-2, 4).

• Establish your own personal/family time. You will not be effective in ministry if you are not spiritually, emotionally, and physically refreshed. You need to schedule your time so your family is first priority after God. This applies to leaders who are married and those who are not married. You need a "family" where you can be mutually committed and accountable to one another. Your family should complement your ministry, rather than be a hindrance to it. Do not neglect your family when ministering to others.

• Create a relational ministry. Begin by modeling to your leadership team a ministry that desires to meet the needs of individuals. From that base of caring will come communication of a relationship with God and others being the basis of the ministry. In scheduled meetings plan for relationship building.

A busy executive ran through the double doors into the train station, leaving behind him the pressures of his job. His only thought was his beautiful, warm family. He dreamed of playing with his children and could almost taste his wife's good cooking. He had to hurry to catch the train out of the city to the suburbs, so he ran down the station's long, crowded corridors. As he turned the corner onto the final stretch to his homebound train, he did not see a little boy who was squatting down, playing with some marbles. The running executive ran into the boy and the marbles flew everywhere. But the man kept running, thinking, "If I stop, I'll miss my train, my time with my family, my dinner!" A few steps later, however, he stopped. He walked back to the boy and helped him gather the marbles. Amazed, the little boy looked into the man's face and asked, "Mister, are you Jesus?"[4]

May we minister in such a way that those we serve will see Jesus.
• Select leaders. Certainly we don't know what the Lord will do with gems in the rough if they are willing to be servants to others (Mark 10:42-45). It is exciting to see how the Holy Spirit works as people commit their lives to Him in ministry.
A leader must be teachable, willing to follow another person's leadership, and desirous of learning to be an effective leader. A good leader should be flexible and should also be able to prioritize responsibilities so as to have enough time to serve on the leadership team.
• Build the ministry team. The care and equipping of the leadership is an ongoing process. Our leadership team development must be based on a biblical foundation (Eph. 4:11-18).

The importance of teamwork is found in a parable for staff members. Once upon a time a church called three members to serve on the leadership staff. The first said, "Here am I; now your troubles are over. I will do everything that needs to be done." But his job was given to another.
The second said, "Here I am. You do the work while I give orders." But his job went to another.
The third said, "Let us pray and plan, and work together, that we may serve Him who has chosen us and appointed us that we should go and bear fruit and that our fruit should abide." And the seeds which they sowed fell in good soil and brought forth abundantly.[5]

If the ministry is going to work, there must be a systematic plan for developing leaders. It was Jesus' "job" to develop His disciples. "Believers are to be cared for and serviced. If leadership is not being developed to provide service, growth stops."[6]
The leadership team will need to meet regularly to maintain a quality relationship with each other and to care for the various ministries. At

each leadership team meeting, in addition to a time of ministry to one another and report from ministry areas, we need to include the following steps to keep the ministry fresh:

1. Evaluate and brainstorm. Ask questions, tough questions. Then consider how you may improve what you are already doing. Also consider what other possible ministries you can include to meet the needs of single adults.

2. Decide. Consider what could be implemented from the brainstorming session. Maybe you will only decide on one thing to implement. Don't try to do everything at once, but make a decision. Trust God for the results. Be sure the ministry is compatible with your Ministry Statement's objectives and goals.

3. Plan. Put someone in charge. Consider who will be the point person for the ministry, what recruiting will be necessary, what training will be needed, and the financial responsibility for the program.

4. Begin. Determine a launching date. Communicate when this renewed ministry will begin, then make it a quality ministry.

5. Evaluate again — and again. A ministry worth doing now may not be needed in six months. At your regular leadership team meetings have a mini-evaluation through reports. At least twice a year have a leadership retreat to consider the whole ministry.

Conclusion

It is important to design a ministry model around a "community of family" environment that is nurturing people to spiritual, mental, and emotional health. Ministry is much more than programs.

Single Adult Ministry must be meeting needs within a balanced program of evangelism and discipleship. A program will die quickly if it only exists for itself.

Serving others is imperative. In service we take the focus off ourselves and place it on the Lord and the needs of others. Many people who are "too busy" or who are in crisis feel they don't have anything to give. But even in times when we don't believe we have anything to give, we grow by giving of ourselves. People need a sense of mission in which they can make a contribution.

Building ministry by equipping leaders will add stability to individual lives as well as to the group. Through equipping, a leader finds affirmation and healing. As we focus our attention outward, our ministry will be defined by the needs of the community. This will sharpen our focus on continued and future ministry.

G. Jerry Martin
Associate Pastor, Education
First Baptist Church
936 West 5th St.
Oxnard, California 93030

Notes

1. Terry Hershey, *Young Adult Ministry Group Books* (Loveland, Colorado, 1986), 29.
2. Andrew Greeley, *Sexual Intimacy* (London: Thomas Moore, 1973), 161.
3. Hershey, 29.
4. Hule Goddard and Jorge Acevedo, *The Heart of Youth Ministry* (Lexington, Kentucky: Bristol Books, 1989), 152.
5. Dobbins Gaines, *A Ministering Church* (Nashville: Broadman Press, 1960), 91.
6. Ron Jensen, *Dynamics of Church Growth* (Grand Rapids: Baker Books, 1981), 112.

9. A NEW PARADIGM: WEEKDAY MINISTRY

"Effective weekday ministry opens wide the portals of entry for unchurched single adults to step into the flow of your ministry, the life of your church, and the arms of the Savior."

Mark Thrash

One year ago a group of distinguished ministers to single adults were sitting at a retreat center in Roundtop, Texas dialoguing about the future of single adult ministry, the new trends that are emerging, programs and activities that are successful and those that are not. The ministers present are distinguished not because of social or economic standing, nor academic degrees, but because they oversee the largest single adult ministries in our country. In the midst of this casual dialogue, the most innovative, respected, and talented pastor suddenly blurted out, "I believe we have entered a 'black hole' of single adult ministry. For the first time in my career, I am not sure what will work anymore . . . or how I am going to continue to reach single adults. I am at a loss."

His statement caused me to return to my home church and ministry pondering the question, "What will it take to reach single adults in the 1990s and beyond?" Have we indeed entered a "black hole" in ministry to single adults where everything is in flux? What are we to expect in the years before a new millennium? How are we to plan, program, and strategize to effectively impact a growing population of single adults in this country?

The New Paradigm

In politics, medicine, theology, or academics, the catchword of our day is *paradigm*. A paradigm is defined as "a grid of values and rules through which we interpret and understand life." Paradigms provide the framework and structure by which we approach circumstances, situations, and

113

difficulties looking for solutions. Paradigms involve strategies by which we accomplish our goals. Paradigms are the "why" we do things and the "how" we believe those things should be done. Paradigms are the lenses through which we see and interpret our world . . . and our ministry. In one statement, paradigms are the way we've always done things, thought about things, and follow through with things.[1]

Time magazine (January 14, 1991) ran an essay on paradigms in which the author observed:

> The world was a surreal, decisive crispness, has been sorting itself into categories of Old Paradigms and New Paradigms. The 1990s have become a transforming boundary between one age and another, between a scheme of things that has become disintegrated and another that has taken shape. A millennium is coming, a cosmic divide. The 20th century is almost an extinct volcano; the 21st is an embryo.[2]

Ministry to single adults is also struggling between old and new paradigms, between old tried-and-true methods that have always worked and the present-day reality that many of those paradigms are outdated, antiquated, and ineffective. The struggle single adult ministry faces is pivotal because the outcome determines whether the ministries of this next century will influence and impact our world and to what degree. The magnificent and glorious cathedrals of Europe, once vibrant and full of life, now stand as silent sentinels. They are present-day reminders of the minimal influence of Christianity on the lives of the masses. We find ourselves at a critical crossroad in ministering to single adults. Should we hold onto old paradigms as the world around us changes?

You know you need a new paradigm for your church or single adult ministry when the paradigm you presently employ is no longer solving the problem or accomplishing the mission as it once did. New paradigms must be hammered out on the anvil of a changing world to provide new, fresh, innovative, creative, and effective methods of achieving your goals.

If indeed we need new paradigms for ministering to single adults, what are they? How can we move from this "black hole" to forge a new framework and structure around which we build a solid and stable single adult ministry? Where do we begin?

I believe we begin with the realization that new paradigms are within our grasp, at our fingertips. The crossroad we face, however critical, is strategic, one with great potential to reach a new segment of the popula-

114

tion that has never been touched by the Good News of Jesus Christ. We face an enormous opportunity pregnant with potential and promise, rather than an overpowering obstacle.

A New Paradigm of Time

The 1980s can be characterized as an era of monetary excess. Individuals like Ivan Boesky and Michael Milliken typify the monetary mismanagement that occurred during the Reagan administration. An entire nation was caught up in the financial boom trying to make as much money in the shortest time possible with the least investment. Money was the most valuable commodity of the 1980s.

Recent studies indicate that what *money* was to the 1980s, *time* will be in the 1990s. Time will be the most valued commodity among the single adult population, since they will be driven more by time value than by money value. They will tend to be more selective and frugal as to who occupies their free time and in what capacity. Already the church must vie with hosts of other activities, amusements, and hobbies that lobby for attention.

For the vast majority of the American population, Sunday is not sacred or set aside for the worship of God. Blue Laws prohibiting Sunday commerce are a relic of the past in most communities. Single adults have a variety of activities and opportunities available to them every Sunday, and they will look critically at all the options, choosing for themselves those options that will most meet the immediate needs of their lives.

Single adults are less likely than before to come to the church for the activity your ministry has scheduled, no matter how big and important it might be. They are more likely to give you "blocks of time" during any given week and no more. An example of this is your Sunday morning schedule of activities. Most churches typically offer a Bible study hour followed by a worship service. The time commitment to participate in those two activities is close to three hours, or one block of time. Another block of time might be a regularly scheduled social or athletic event taking place later in the week or on the weekend. Your single adults might commit themselves to give you that second block of time, but that will be all. Any other event you plan or promote, regardless of how exciting or grandiose (or free), will not be attended. Why? It would overdraft their time account.

Many of the single adults in my church will give eight to ten hours a week to the church. If I schedule more ministry events and opportunities than the allotted hours, I force them to choose to attend some and disregard others. Why? Their time is of utmost value and is tenaciously protected. As a minister to single adults, I should not expect leaders to participate and involve themselves in this ministry if I do not give them strong "time value." Society and the world will see to it that their attentions and affections are focused elsewhere.

The Sunday morning schedule of activities is the hub around which most churches and singles ministries revolve. It is vital for the growth, affirmation, and communication of the corporate church body. For many ministries — mine included — it is the focal point of the week. Hundreds of single adults gather each week for strong biblical preaching and teaching, worship, praise, and relationship building. Numerous single adult ministries offer a strong Sunday morning schedule and continue to experience growth in that block of time.

In addition to the Sunday morning experience, there is a trend emerging toward strong weekday programming. Collectively, single adults are searching for quality programming the "other" six days of the week. Thus, it would behoove anyone involved in ministry to single adults to take a hard, critical, and objective look at weekday ministry opportunities and programming.

A New Paradigm: Weekday Ministry

Let me begin by stating that weekday ministry is not a new idea. Numerous churches have been involved in weekday ministry for decades and are doing a bang-up job of meeting single adult needs throughout the week. However, for the vast majority of churches claiming to have ministries to singles, weekday ministry is a new and important paradigm. Many congregations view singles ministry as solely providing a "Sunday morning event," with one or more Sunday School classes for singles. Typically, these classes are characterized by broad age spans or by one class for the "college and career" single and another for "single again" folks. And if you were to happen upon these churches and inquire about opportunities available for the rest of the week, the calendar would be void of programming. Weekday ministry is the new paradigm. The future and life of such ministries rests on the ability of its leadership to successfully integrate weekday ministry into the existing structures.

Why is weekday ministry emerging as the newest paradigm? Why will our response or lack thereof dictate our effectiveness in the future? With the nation's economy in recession, companies laying off blue and white collar workers, increased unemployment, the rise of single-parent homes, and increased flexible hours for shift employees, work schedules have become hectic. The 8 A.M. to 5 P.M. workday is long gone for many. Part-time employment has replaced full-time work as individuals are laid off and as the job market is flooded with applicants. One paycheck is no longer sufficient to make financial ends meet, thus causing many to seek multiple employment. Single parents must juggle jobs as well as raise children, and they see no relief in sight.

Many employees are now required to work four ten-hour days with three days off per week. Hospitals offer employees the option of working a forty-hour week in the span of one weekend. Saturday and Sunday work schedules have become a necessity. For many, the fourth commandment has become a virtual impossibility. Others use their weekends to catch up on the responsibilities and domestic chores they have ignored throughout the week. Many use Sunday mornings to sleep in or to participate in their favorite sports, hobbies, or leisure activities. The old paradigm of Sunday morning Bible study and worship must be expanded to include a new paradigm of weekday ministry.

Formulating a strategy to meet this burgeoning paradigm begins by examining the weekday calendar in light of the needs and schedules of your single adult population. Below are listed some questions you should ask yourself as you prepare your monthly calendar.

- What are the real needs versus the perceived needs of single adults?
- When was the last time I surveyed the needs of my people?
- What time commitments are single adults willing to give?
- How can I best utilize their abilities and gifts while giving them maximum time value?
- Are the activities and opportunities scheduled adequate to meet their needs and impact their lives for the kingdom of God?
- Is there a healthy balance between the social, intellectual, educational, physical, and spiritual needs that my people have?
- Is the weekday schedule achieving all the intended goals we set forth in this ministry?
- Does my present paradigm adequately address the obstacles/problems that I encounter in the process of pursuing my mission and vision?
- If I had the opportunity to begin from scratch to plan and program my ministry, would I be doing what I am doing now, using the same methodology?
- Would people who are not "church professionals" go about accomplishing the vision and mission of this ministry in the way I am presently operating?

- Am I meeting in one specific time and place, or do I have numerous meeting times and places?
- Am I employing an age-graded or lifestyle-graded methodology? Is it working?
- Is my ministry focused solely on Christians, or is there opportunity for Christians and non-Christians to interact?
- Am I presentation- or participation-oriented?
- Could I achieve in a weekend, what often requires ten weeks of scheduled meetings?

Weekday programming arises from needs, not presumptions. The needs of your people are paramount to your programming. Do not presume that you are the "guru" knowing exactly what your people need. The large percentage of single adult ministers in America are married and find themselves rather distant from the single adult who is playing the field. Take time to talk with the single adults in your ministry. What itches do they have that need to be scratched? Give them opportunity to voice their opinions and then act upon their opinions with need-oriented programming. Mundane programs and activities attract very few people.

Our single adult ministry has a few short, powerful phrases which summarize our vision and philosophy. "Find a need and meet it." "Find a hurt and heal it." "Maximize your singleness." As we have focused on these statements, we have discovered that as real needs are met, other real needs emerge. Years ago we began a weekday Divorce Recovery Ministry, the first of its kind in our area. Hundreds of singles we had never seen before came to attend a seven-week seminar. And as we began to program for singles who had experienced divorce, we were forced to program for their children. Thus began our Pastor's Pals Ministry, a program sponsored and run by many of our single men for children from single-parent homes. That ministry grew so rapidly that we soon had to employ part-time staff to work with the children. As our Divorce Recovery Program was completing its first year, many graduates inquired about an advanced course of study, and we began to study the feasibility of offering such a program. Alongside our Divorce Recovery Ministry grew our Single Parent Fellowship, comprised of single parents coming together for support, education, social activities, and Bible study.

A further development of these programs was the institution of an Overeaters Anonymous and various twelve-step programs. White-collar singles approached me to begin a Professional Singles Group, and soon we had all these single adult groups meeting on a Thursday evening in our church building. Talk about Time Value! What began as a narrow window of ministry became a door of opportunity.

Another interesting phenomenon began to occur in this same time frame. Week by week, looking over the sea of faces in our congregation on Sunday morning, I began to see many familiar faces, sporadic at first, but fairly regular in attendance. In any given year, hundreds of singles find entry into our church via our single adult weekday ministry. The open-ended funnel of weekday ministry to single adults introduced them into the life and body of the church.

A New Paradigm: Learning to Count

The paradigm of weekday ministry mandates that we begin to count our singles in a different manner. No longer do we count them only on Sunday morning like sheep . . . one, two, three. It is still important to keep weekly Sunday morning Bible study statistics, in order to compare this year against previous years. But the new paradigm requires that ministry be viewed as a seven-day event, the number of "touches" we make on individual lives. The rise of our weekday ministry necessitates that I look specifically at two numbers each week. First, I look at the attendance figure for the Sunday morning Bible study hour, per department, per class. A second number I must consider is the figure representing those single adults we have touched and ministered to through our weekday programs. The second number is a much bigger and broader statistic as our weekday programs increase.

Ron Lewis, the founder and president of Church Growth Designs, a firm that consults with individual churches on church growth and societal trends, shared with me, "Mark, we have not only got to make the Sunday morning experience exciting and alive, but we must begin to broaden our scope to include nontraditional methods and days to reach more singles."[3]

How many new individuals did we touch in a month's time? How many singles attended Bible study this last month? How many new people attended the Sunday morning specialized classes on Stress Management or Managing Your Money? How many singles were at the apartment clubhouse for the informal Bible study at 10:00 last Sunday morning? How many were at the country club? What percentage of regular attenders participated in the citywide Monday night home Bible study groups? How many prospects attended the Single Life Series held at a local hotel during the month of January? Of the sixty Shandon Baptist singles who fan out all over the city on Tuesday Night Outreach, how many visits and contacts were made? How many postcards were mailed out? Were there any first-time singles in the interchurch coed softball, basketball, or vol-

119

leyball league? Out of the hundreds of singles who sign up to attend our annual oyster roast, barn party, fish fry, rafting trip, Ladies' Night, For Men Only, weekend survival outing, who will be touched for the first time? The second time? The third time? Are our single adults inviting their work colleagues to attend the business luncheon this next week? How many single adults will we send on a two-week mission trip to Brazil this year? What funds do we need to raise through the Bachelor/Bachelorette Auction two months from now in order to support a short-term mission trip to New Orleans? How can we effectively target single adults who have lost a spouse by death for the upcoming Grief Workshop? Who will take the responsibility to invite and bring an un-churched friend to the upcoming July 4th picnic and fireworks? To the water-ski party? To this weekend's barbecue? How many are planning to attend the church-sponsored Christian Comedy Club, and how many guests do we anticipate to be in attendance?

Effective weekday ministry opens wide the portals of entry for un-churched single adults to step into the flow of your ministry, the life of your church, and the arms of the Savior.

Mark Thrash
Minister to Single Adults/ Evangelism
Shandon Baptist Church
819 Woodrow Street
Columbia, South Carolina 29205

Notes
1. "The Win Arn Growth Report," *Church Growth Newsletter*, 32, California, 1991.
2. Lance Morrow, "Old Paradigm and New Paradigm," *Time*, 14 January 1990, 65.
3. Ron Lewis, Church Growth Designs, Conversation in March 1992.

10. DEVELOPING AN OUTREACH MINISTRY

"Our culture claims to have a supernatural out-look; yet when Christians try to share a message of faith which is supernatural at its very core, it is often rejected in the marketplace of ideas because it doesn't conform to the self-absorbed spirituality in vogue today."

Gary Gonzales

For the church to survive at the end of the twentieth century, it must be willing to die and be reborn as a mission." When I first read those words fifteen years ago, I was struck by their frankness. As the years have passed, I have been impressed by their accuracy. Reaching modern Americans and especially singles, demands that we adopt a "go and tell" rather than a "come and see" strategy.

As we enter the final decade of the twentieth century, it's obvious that the traditional church in America is lying flat on the mat—and the ten count is well underway. Recent statistics on church vitality show that a solid 85 percent of churches are plateaued or declining. But why?

Cultural and Social Shifts
The last fifty years have been an era of unprecedented social upheaval and change. Most experts agree that these shifts are radical and all-pervasive. One social observer notes that as we move into the next millennium, change will be so rapid that future historians will look back with nostalgia on the last decade and refer to it as "the stable '80s."

As is too often the case, most churches are twenty years behind the times, oblivious to the implications current trends have for their ministries, and are continuing to do "business as usual." But these shifts are of monumental significance. Let's take a moment to review some of the major ones:

• From rural to urban. In 1900, 90 percent of Americans lived or worked on the farm. Today only 2 to 3 percent make their living on the farm. A recent survey revealed that 61 percent of Americans live in the thirty-nine largest U.S. cities. We have become an urban world.

It has further been suggested that within a couple of decades most of us will live in one of three "megalopoli." Their names: "San-San" (San Diego to San Francisco), "Bos-Wash" (Boston to Washington) and "Chi-Pitts" (Chicago to Pittsburgh)!

This urbanization has altered the personality and psyche of the people we're trying to reach. *The Four Spiritual Laws,* for example, although still effective with middle-class Anglo-Americans who share a common set of values, is often ineffective in evangelizing modern urban people who share a whole different set of values, beliefs, definitions, understandings, and needs.

• From homogeneous to multicultural. Not long ago a friend of mine who is an internationally known urban expert spoke in my inner-city church. He made a striking observation, "The West Coast is no longer the backbone of America, now it's the front door of Asia." Then he added, "The United States is currently the third largest Spanish-speaking nation in the world, following Mexico and Spain." The Los Angeles public schools claim to have eighty-six language groups represented in their classrooms.

Whether you view these changes as an affront or an opportunity, the fact remains that they strongly impact the way we need to do evangelism today. Failure to recognize this rich diversity can lead to personal frustration.

While I was pastoring a church in the Los Angeles area, a well-versed man in my church asked me if I could help him understand why his evangelistic attempts were unfruitful. He had been trying to reach a number of his neighbors through lifestyle evangelistic methods for some months. He had done all the right things, but his efforts had proven unproductive.

I said, "Describe for me the kinds of people you're trying to reach." Without seeing the implications he said, "Let's see, the couple across the street just moved here from China. And then there's the Mexican family next door. And just down the block is a black single mother my wife has been witnessing to."

I stopped him and said, "Wait a minute. Listen to what you're telling me. What you're describing is a foreign mission field!" The era of the homogeneous church is over and a new day has dawned.

• From Judeo-Christian to rampant secularism. In about three-quarters of a century, we have gone from a Christian consensus to a caricature of pluralism. Virtually every kind of freedom of expression is available in America today, except one that embraces a belief in God.

The irony is that pollsters George Gallup, Jr. and George Barna keep cranking out research that indicates the vast majority of people claim to have a personal belief in God. Of these, 25 percent admit to having had some kind of Christian conversion experience. In response to such testimony, William Iverson writes with thinly veiled doubt, "A pound of meat would surely be affected by a quarter pound of salt. If this is real Christianity, the 'salt of the earth,' where is the effect of which Jesus spoke?"

• From marriage-oriented to single-oriented. Another factor often overlooked or downplayed in Bible-believing churches is the national trend toward broken marriages, or postponing the marriage decision, coupled with an increased willingness to choose a single lifestyle. A recent special report in the *Single Adult Ministries Journal* (January 1992) stated that while Protestant churches are very sensitive to the needs of families and the elderly, they are all but oblivious to the concerns and needs of single adults generally, and single parents specifically.

This attitude is radically out of step with the times. While we should never value one segment of society over another, we need to know the demographics of our constituency. How else can we hope to reach them or meet their unique needs?

When I was living in Southern California, four large Presbyterian churches surveyed their congregations during a Sunday morning worship service to see how many of them were single adults. Each church was shocked to discover that over 50 percent of their regular attenders were single.

Overcoming a Hardening of the Categories

An ancient bit of doggerel can serve us well as we attempt to reach single adults for Christ in this time of change.

Methods are many,
principles are few.
Methods always change,
principles never do.

As Americans we have a built-in penchant for packaging. After all, we're a world-class consumer society. Give us a product — any product —

and we know how to wrap it, advertise it, price it, position it, and market it. Even Christian ministry. Too often the focus of our attention is on method rather than principle. And while principles are timeless, methods are time-specific. Rapidly changing societies demand rapidly changing methodologies.

The key, as regards the Gospel, is to translate its message into understandable terms for a new generation of hearers without transforming it. This is a delicate art, so, let me try to offer some handles.

• Start with felt needs rather than real needs. Right off the bat, I've attacked—and I hope, mortally wounded—a sacred cow. Felt needs are front burner, real needs generally back burner.

Most of our attempts to reach unchurched people—single and married—are too direct for our suspicious-of-institutional-religion day. For example, we invite people to come to our Bible study, on our turf, and when it's convenient for us. That usually translates into something like, "We'd like you to come to our church (or home) to study the Book of Leviticus at 7:30 on Tuesday night."

That kind of approach is doomed to failure from the start. It asks too much of the seeker, although it may be just fine for believers. It expects them to enter unfamiliar surroundings (the current number-one fear of Americans), to study a book of the Bible they couldn't spell even if their life depended on it, and at a time of day that might be inconvenient or inappropriate (how many women want to stroll urban—or suburban—streets at night in these days of random violence?).

A friend of mine faced these important issues by developing an outreach to his target audience of professionals in high finance that took place on Thursday at lunch time (one-hour time limit), in a popular watering hole located in a large hotel that caters to business people. Following a brief lunch and informal time of conversation around the tables, he led an in-depth Bible study on Leviticus (though they never knew it) in the seminar-style to which they are accustomed. Rather than entitle his talk to these real estate and financial moguls, "A Layman Looks at Leviticus," he called it, "How to Stay Afloat in a World That's Circling the Drain."

Formerly a successful business entrepreneur, he spoke their language from the outset by talking about the fast track, get-rich-quick scams that stimulated the economy of the 1980s but proved to be bankrupt in the 1990s. After several minutes of this, he introduced the biblical teaching on the Year of Jubilee into the discussion. Using sound financial principles that would cause even Alan Greenspan to smile approvingly, he showed how God had a better way to avoid reversals of financial fortune by implementing a plan of economic fairness for all.

My wife and I sat and marveled at the skill with which he held his audience in the palm of his hand without "missing a biblical beat." He began with their felt needs in mind and then gently moved toward addressing their real needs—God's provision for the safety and security of mankind. The felt needs of single adults are multitudinous. There are many places to begin.

• Contextualize the message. It's more than cliché to say that we are called to be interpreters of both "the Word" and "the world." In his excellent book, *Dying for Change,* Leith Anderson points out that "... evangelical Christianity has done well on revelation (the Bible), but poorly on relevance (the culture)." To contextualize the message means, essentially, to put it in user-friendly terms for a particular class of people.

Think about it for a minute. The basic makeup of humankind hasn't changed much since Jesus' day. Was the centurion with a deathly sick slave really that much different than the father who finds out that his twenty-seven-year-old son is dying of AIDS? Or, was the unwed woman at the well in John 4 faced with any more pain or pariah-status than the contemporary single-again mom who's been touched by divorce for the second or third time?

The would-be evangelist in every era must ask similar, hard questions. "What is the cultural key I can use in unlocking this person's heart in order to help him hear the Gospel of Christ in terms he understands?"

My wife, who served as a missionary in western Europe for almost a decade, found that although people held widely different political, economic, and philosophical views, they had the same desires for love, hope, health, and happiness. She and her fellow missionaries further discovered that their once-narrow view of the people they were trying to reach as "heathens" was transformed over time to an important appreciation that "these people are more like us than they are different."

Spanish philosopher Miguel Unamuno said, "If we ever got honest enough to go out into the streets and uncover our common grief, we would discover that we are all grieving the selfsame things."

• Give them time to change and grow. In recent decades evangelism was committed to seeing instantaneous life change. Converts were expected to walk the aisle or pray the prayer and change once and for all. The more contemporary—and currently effective—approach is to recognize that people who have lived thirty or forty years in unbelief may need more time to be transformed. While this doesn't make salvation any less an "act of God," it does suggest the need to build relationships with people who may come to Christ over a period of months rather than minutes. Friendship Evangelism operates on the premise, "If you want a healthy birth, you've got to have a healthy pregnancy."

This approach is realistic and workable. But it is also difficult, time-consuming, and often discouraging.

It is *difficult* because there is no longer such a thing as one-size-fits-all evangelism. In today's complex world, the "just add water and mix" approach has fallen by the wayside. Prepackaged evangelistic tools and strategies will continue to have their place, and may even work well on occasion, but they are far too simplistic in a pluralistic society. The other problem with relying too heavily on them is suggested in this saying, "If the only tool in your toolbox is a hammer, you tend to see every problem as a nail."

Reaching people with the Gospel is *time-consuming*—and time is increasingly viewed by moderns as their most precious resource. VCRs, microwave ovens, and voice mail all attest to that. The myth that singles have extra free time is just that—a myth.

Christian writer Joe Aldrich has noted, "Excessive relational demands have hindered our relational capacities." In other words, most of us are reluctant to invest our limited time and energy in developing new friendships because they demand too much output from already overloaded people. Yet, reaching today's single requires just such an investment because, more than ever, the Gospel has to be seen as need-meeting in a practical, day-to-day sense.

Contemporary evangelism can be a *discouraging* enterprise because many people we're trying to reach have other, deep-seated problems. Broken and blended families, addictions, and codependent relationships are more than mere buzz words. They are realities. The odds are high that single adults coming out of a painful past will need to be dealt with and ministered to on more than a superficial or even single-issue level.

Bill Hybels, popular author and pastor of Willow Creek Community Church near Chicago, recently stated in an interview for *Preaching* magazine that their church is discovering that before they can disciple new converts in earnest they must first reparent them. That's an incredible undertaking and one for which few churches are equipped.

Don't Give Up the Ship!
The reason evangelism seems so hard today, especially among singles, is that we're living in a new world. Before we can even hope to compete on

a level playing field with cultic groups, Islam, Neo-paganism, and New Age religions, we've got to find the stadium where the game is being played.

However, the good news for us would-be evangelists is twofold. First, biblical Christianity has always flourished in hostile environments. It's no accident that the blood of the martyrs was the seed of the church. Today's world is tailor-made for the Gospel message. Paul, the greatest evangelist of all time, wasn't kidding when he wrote, "I am not ashamed of the Gospel, because it is the power of God for the salvation of everyone who believes: first for the Jew, then for the Gentile" (Rom. 1:16).

Second, we have been given the unlimited power of the Holy Spirit. Jesus promised we wouldn't have to "go it alone" (Matt. 28:20). He would leave Planet Earth, but only so the Comforter might be sent. The Greek word for Comforter is *paraclete* which literally means "advocate," or "to come alongside of." So, we're not abandoned by God in the task.

Words — and Music Too

Our culture claims to have a supernatural outlook, yet, most people live with an antisupernatural bias. When Christians try to share a message of faith which is supernatural at its very core, it is often rejected in the marketplace of ideas because it doesn't conform to the self-absorbed spirituality in vogue today.

Christians too often try to evangelize lost people without taking time to listen to what they are really saying and thinking. Still more dangerous, we assume we have to be able to answer every question asked of us — and on a moment's notice. Let me remind you, "A fool can ask more questions than a wise person can answer."

A better approach in today's combative climate is to turn the tables by asking questions. Ask single adults you're trying to reach not only *what* they believe but *why* they believe it. Perhaps then they will see the contradictions in their thought process. Jesus confounded the religious authorities of His day with questions. Socrates and other master teachers did the same thing. Maybe it's time for Christians to start playing offense rather than defense.

Many of today's singles see mainstream Christianity as stifling and restrictive. They may have grown up in environments that emphasized "do's and don'ts." As a result, they're often angry and antagonistic toward "oldtime religion." To try to confront or "preach" to a person with that mind-set is to invite argument and animosity. Raising pertinent questions is a far less confrontational approach and one that encourages honest dialogue.

In the final analysis, evangelism to single adults must remain a fluid process. While it ought to be done intentionally, as the old saying goes, "There's more than one way to skin a cat."

I've mentioned the role of words in evangelism, yet words often get in the way. Some years ago when I was in seminary, an astute professor reminded us that we ought to play the "music" of the Gospel before we play the "words." Most of us are more tuned in to another's attitudes and actions than we are to his or her answers. I've never forgotten the wisdom of that remark.

Recently I was talking to a single man who was caught up in the drug culture and related vices of the '70s and has since returned to the Lord. Having felt the call of God on his life for some time, a few weeks ago he began attending a nearby Christian college while holding down a full-time job. He reminded me of the following story.

Some centuries ago a young priest was invited by an older priest to go to a nearby town in order to evangelize it. When they got there, all the older man did was to mingle in the town square and talk to people. After several hours the young priest grew weary and impatient with his mentor. He asked, "When are we going to evangelize the people?" The wise old man said, "We just did."

While the debate will continue to rage about when evangelism is actually taking place, we must never forget that spreading the faith requires relationship. This is especially true in the single adult community where empty words and promises fall on deaf ears. The Scots have a saying, "The Gospel is more felt than telt."

So, back to discovering the felt needs of single adults. Then address them with a love that is genuine and with contemporary understanding.

Contextualize the Gospel message to make it clear. It *is* a relevant message. Then, give God time to draw single adults to Himself and bring maturity to those who respond.

Single adult ministry can provide the context and acceptance for effective evangelism. We have the infallible message. We must train and encourage singles to build relationships where God's message of salvation can be heard and received. If we don't, no one else will.

Gary Gonzales
Pastor
Elim Baptist Church
2731 McKinley Street NE
Minneapolis, Minnesota 55418

11. DEVELOPING A MISSIONS MINISTRY

"The greatest destiny any of us can have is to move in the direction that our infinite, sovereign God has chosen to go. In the Bible God has clearly revealed that He is moving in the direction of world missions."

Gilbert E. Crowell

A prevalent myth among single adults today is that missions is a unique specialty that should be pursued or investigated only by those with a professional interest in the subject. I want to dispel this myth from the outset!

As a young, unmarried Christian single adult, I was pursuing career and women, not necessarily in that order. For me, a "mission" was a bombing run by a jet pilot or a task to be completed by the supply department of a naval vessel, or a Friday night search for Miss Right at the junior officer's club!

I had no idea what missions was all about from God's perspective until one unsuspecting day when I was challenged by the single adult pastor at my church to sign up for a two-week mission trip to Guatemala. I had the time and the money and I liked the other people who had signed up, so why not? One of my favorite pastimes was travel; after all, isn't that one of the reasons why I had joined the Navy? Boy, was I naive to the purposes of God for my life!

Purpose

Single Adults and Missions is an issue that should be considered by every pastor, associate pastor, or single adult leader in beginning, developing, or enhancing any ministry with single adults. God desires that we line up our lives with His sovereignly revealed will. But this poses the question, "What is God's overall governing purpose for missions that

129

includes all of us, not just a select few?"

The answer is found in the Bible, beginning with God's promise to Abraham in Genesis 12:3, when He said, "All peoples on earth will be blessed through you." God swore that, beginning with Abraham, He would move through time/space history using those people who understood and believed His promise to pass on the good news of how one can have a personal relationship with God forever! This promise can be traced through the Bible from Abraham to Christ to every believer living on the earth today. Jesus Christ was the full and complete disclosure of God in the flesh. Some of the last words of our Lord on this earth were, "All authority in heaven and on earth has been given to Me. Therefore go and make disciples of all nations, baptizing them in the name of the Father and of the Son and of the Holy Spirit and teaching them to obey everything I have commanded you. And surely I am with you always, to the very end of the age" (Matt. 28:18-20).

Peter declared to the Jews that this ancient promise of God was for them (Acts 3:25-26). Paul announced to the Gentiles that they were recipients of God's promise to Abraham because of their faith (Gal. 3:6-9). John's Revelation shows that God's ancient promise will be fulfilled with peoples from every tongue, tribe, and nation worshiping God around His throne (5:9-10 and 7:9-10).

Surely, the greatest purpose that any single adult could have is to be involved in the cause of God that is destined to succeed—the extending of spiritual blessing to yet unreached peoples of the world!

Facts and Objectives
A short-term missions project for a group of single adults can be as brief as one day or as long as three years, depending upon the purpose and the location. The four most common types are education, evangelism, service, or a combination of the three.

Depending on your location, you may want to begin with a one-day or weekend trip. For example, if you are near Los Angeles, you may want to consider a one-day educational field trip to the headquarters of Wycliffe Bible Translators in Huntington Beach. Or, if you are near Washington, D.C., you might want to arrange with Pioneers in Sterling, Virginia to volunteer a group of ten single adults to handle all aspects of their next major mailing. Regardless of your location, you are probably not far from the U.S. office of an overseas mission that needs your help. *The Mission Handbook to USA/Canada Protestant Ministries Overseas,* co-published by MARC and Zondervan, will give you the name, address, and telephone number of a mission agency near you.

If all of this missions emphasis is new to you or your singles group, you might want to do some research, get some input from others who have done various projects, and learn from them. If your group is considering an overseas trip, it is definitely to your advantage to go with an agency that has several years of experience in hosting groups. For example, Greater Europe Mission has a summer Eurocorps project that is excellent for first-time exposure to overseas missions. Operation Mobilization has years of experience in leading groups to missions involvement in places like Mexico or Europe.

Another good suggestion is to talk with Bridgebuilders, an agency designed for the express purpose of helping single adult groups plan, organize, execute, and evaluate short-term mission trips. The founder of Bridgebuilders, Chris Eaton, has coauthored a book with Kim Hurst entitled *Vacations with a Purpose: A Planning Handbook for Your Short-term Missions Team* (NAV Press) that is an excellent planning resource for your team. The book comes with a leader's guide as well as a manual for each team member. Do not make the mistake of thinking you have to "go it alone" or "reinvent the wheel" when it comes to planning a missions project. There are many people who are standing by ready to help you each step of the way.

Once you and your leadership team have decided on the purpose of your short-term missions project, you are ready to set some objectives, such as agency, time commitment, skills required, and financial factors.

For example, one year the singles group from my church chose to do a missions service project. They investigated agencies and decided to help Habitat for Humanity build a home in inner-city Atlanta for a needy single parent. Working with a project coordinator from the agency, they established a construction schedule, raised $20,000, and constructed the home from start to finish, working together on Saturdays over the course of a summer. The home was completed on schedule with over $7,000 left over! Almost 200 single adults were involved in the various phases of the project, and they still talk about the spiritual impact this had on their lives.

Another year, the singles decided to do a combined evangelistic/ service-oriented missions project. Knowing their purpose, they chose to work with the Evangelical Association for the Promotion of Education, E.A.P.E., an agency founded by Tony Campolo. Six single adults went to Haiti for two weeks that summer, and assisted in the construction of a small church building during the day, with numerous opportunities to

131

share their faith in the late afternoon and evening. Talk about vacation with a purpose! As a result, a bond of continuing love and partnership was formed between the two churches.

The purpose of the project will lead you to the appropriate agency to assist your team in formulating your objectives. At the end of the project you will want to assess whether those objectives were achieved.

Recruiting the Right People

The first person to recruit is the pastor of your church. If *you* are the pastor of a local church and have never been on a short-term missions trip overseas, you owe it to yourself and your single adults to go with them at least once. Our pastor accompanied us on a trip to Guatemala fifteen years ago. After the first night sleeping on the dirt floor of a hut in a mountain village, he returned to Guatemala City and checked into a hotel for the remainder of our time in the country. However, rather than that being a negative aspect, it was such a positive that he was with us in the country on the trip, supporting and encouraging us from the beginning, and providing high visibility of leadership for the project to our home church, that it hardly mattered in the least that he was not with us every day of the trip. Even the ribbing that we gave him about checking into the hotel was well received, and endeared him to our hearts.

The next objective should be to solicit the support and encouragement of the entire church through the leadership of the pastor, the elders, the deacons, and the missions committee. Failure to request the approval and involvement of the church's spiritual leadership can severely restrict the spiritual impact of the project upon the life and ministry of the congregation.

Don't neglect the children and youth as you publicize your mission trip. Go to the early childhood classes and let them know about the project. Consider providing stickers to all the children so they can know, pray, and tell their families about what the single adults are doing to tell others about Jesus. The kids will talk about the stickers with their dads and moms, brothers and sisters when they go home from church, especially if the teachers and singles have made it fun for them and stressed the importance of their involvement. In this simple way, you can easily have the entire church talking about the missions project in their homes! It will be a blessing to everyone in the church and the Single Adult Ministry in the long run.

Involve the youth and the adult classes in creative ways also. Car washes, dramatic skits, or sports can all be used to advance the cause.

One church that I know of has an annual Run for Missions where they have a Saturday Olympics type competition among the different departments, capped off by a family fun run that includes everyone!

If the single adult leadership is committed to a unified, church-wide approach rather than "doing our own thing," it will be recognized by the spiritual leadership, affirmed by the church body, and blessed by God to the building up of the entire church!

Be careful to encourage the involvement of all the single adults from the outset, even though only a select number may take part in the mission ministry. All the single adults can be involved in praying, planning, organizing, and evaluation and reporting phases. Of course, it is necessary to know the strengths, talents, and spiritual gifts of each single adult who desires to be involved so that the best possible match can be made of abilities and function. A simple survey that asks single adults their skills and interests, along with the level of spiritual commitment (beginner, intermediate, or advanced) is the place to start.

Cost Factors
Sometimes, the leadership of churches that have not been involved in missions look at the expense factor and fall victim to the fear that encouraging people to give to missions will somehow drain the already stretched church budget. Nothing is further from the truth. The more involved we become in what God is doing, the greater the blessing that will be extended to others, spiritually, physically, and financially. In the time I have gone from being a nearsighted Christian to more of a World Christian, my giving to the work of the local church has increased significantly, and my support of missions has grown steadily over the past fifteen years. Once churches realize that they exist for a far greater reason than just to pay their own bills, they become empowered by the Spirit of God to fulfill the purposes of God. Jesus Himself said, "Seek first His kingdom and His righteousness, and all these things will be given to you as well" (Matt. 6:33). This spiritual principle is applicable to churches as well as individuals.

One church in Barbados was meeting in a leaky tent and desperately needed a new building. Yet, they sensed that God was leading them to invest their building fund in a missions project. They did so, and a few months later God provided all the money they needed for their church building! God blesses us in order that we might be a blessing to others who have not yet heard of Christ.

Money should not be the number one issue. The money will be there.

Single adult leaders need to inspire and motivate single adults to give their lives to a cause greater than themselves, the advancement of God's kingdom on earth!

The best way to inspire singles to adopt God's cause is to lead by example. The heart of a leader will always challenge and motivate others to follow.

Even though financial support is not the primary issue, it deserves adequate forethought. It is good when the church makes a commitment to provide a certain percentage of the support for the mission team, and the single adults agree to provide, raise, or develop the funding for the remaining amount. Each church will determine the percentages that work best. The numerous ways funding can be developed are really limited only by the creative thinking of the leadership or the policies established by the church. If faith promise, pledging, or even selling raffle tickets is contrary to your church's fund-raising policies, you might consider ideas like a complimentary spaghetti dinner or a pancake breakfast where the team can share the vision for the project and ask attenders to prayerfully consider supporting the project.

The single adults in my church had a Bowling for Bibles night. They took pledges based on their bowling averages, went bowling one Friday night and received almost $400, which they used to purchase Bibles for Romania! It was an event that everyone could be involved in, even the non-churched seekers! Unleash those creative mental juices to discover how God will provide the funds for your group's missions project.

Team Dynamics
The success of any team, whether it be the Minnesota Twins in the World Series or the Single Adult Missions Team in your church, is dependent upon five key elements: common goal and purpose, accepted leadership, solid relationships, good communication, and division of labor/specialization. We have previously mentioned common goal and accepted leadership; now, let's consider for a moment the other three.

● Solid relationships and good communication are the result of spending committed, quality time together. Too often, mission projects are undertaken with the naive idea that the project will come off "on its own." Nothing could be further from the truth! Six to nine months of planning and meeting together regularly is essential to a good, short-term summer project. This time enables the group to pray for one another, to grow in their understanding and caring for one another, and to cultivate their faith for the unexpected.

134

The group needs to be prepared for the spiritual obstacles that they will encounter, as well as the spiritual threats to their own unity and oneness that are certain to come. After all, missions is a spiritual venture into enemy-occupied territory! Be prepared for the enemy to fight back; yet, resist him, firm in your faith and unity as a team, trusting the Lord Jesus Christ for spiritual victory. Learn to work together and to play together as a team.

● Division of labor/specialization is simply the use of each team member's unique gift, talents, and abilities in functional roles that enhance the team's productivity. You would not want a defensive end playing wide receiver on a football team. The same principle holds true for a missions team. Make sure each person's talents and abilities are being used; affirm and encourage their use; and create opportunities for their use if they do not presently exist.

Except for prayer, there is probably nothing that will reduce interpersonal conflict more than giving people the opportunity to use their God-given talents and abilities in ways that fill them up rather than wear them out. Survey the team at the outset to find out their unique talents, background, experience, or training, and be a good steward of the human resources the Lord provides. Each team member should have a unique role and possess a clear understanding of what is expected. It is amazing the increase in impact that can be achieved when team members work in harmony, using their gifts and abilities to their full extent.

When the day of departure arrives, it should be a time of celebration, involving everyone in the church if possible. Such a send-off can be compared to the one a high school or college athletic team receives prior to departing for an out-of-town championship game. Win or lose, it is the memory of their supporters' love and devotion that remains in the hearts and minds of the participants. The church should do no less for its missions teams!

To this day, I can still recall the day of departure at the airport for each one of the mission trips I have taken. I can still see the friends, family, and other church members who made the special effort to turn out. Take advantage of the time of departure to build memories for the church family and your single adults. Later you will cherish these memories.

Reporting and Evaluating

Part of the long-term planning is the *reporting* phase. Like the project itself, this may be as short as one evening or as long as several months, but should be recognized as a vital phase of the overall project.

Short testimonies in worship services or classes, potluck dinners in homes including a lively discussion and sharing time, or a full-length creative sharing service, are just a few options your team will want to consider.

Don't forget to greet the team upon their arrival back home, but be sensitive to the fact that they may be physically fatigued from the rigors of the project and the travel time back home. Give them a chance to recuperate and prepare before asking them to share extensively about their experiences.

Times of reporting should be uplifting, yet realistic and honest. The team should be prepared to share not only the glory and the successes, but the hardships and difficulties encountered as well. Communicate accurately about the host country's cultures and lifestyles. Remember, a few short weeks in a host country does not make one an expert on all the spiritual and social dilemmas a country or people group may be facing. Be sure to include opportunities for continuing and ongoing involvement.

Probably the most crucial yet most often neglected phase of most short-term missions projects is *evaluation*. The leadership team needs to be disciplined in its determination to evaluate all aspects of the project in order that the insights and experience gained will not be lost. A written report to the church leadership will enhance future mission projects, regardless of the success of the immediate project.

Did the missions project accomplish its stated purpose and goal? Was the investment of time and money a good one in terms of the return on investment? Keep in mind that the return on investment can be subjective as well as objective. The spiritual lives of most short-term missions participants are dramatically changed for the better; believe it or not, they usually benefit even more than the target group they set out to assist or serve! In light of all that was learned and experienced, what recommendations should be made to the leadership group for the next missions project? These are the types of questions that need to be asked and answered in writing before the project is considered complete.

Conclusion

If we truly believe that God is in the process of bringing to Himself representatives from every tribe, tongue, people, and nation to worship Him before His throne, as the Bible so vividly describes in Revelation 5:9-10 and 7:9-10, then what remains for us to do?

The greatest destiny any of us can have is to move in the direction that our infinite, sovereign God has chosen to go. In the Bible God has clearly revealed that He is moving in the direction of world missions.

Some fourteen years ago, I went on a short-term missions trip to Portugal for two weeks. During that time, I was involved with about ten American single adults and ten Portuguese singles in an evangelistic campaign. During the day we would distribute flyers at the public markets and train stations, inviting people to come to evangelistic meetings that night. I vividly remember my anticipation in waiting for all the people to show up for our meetings, after passing out over 5,000 invitations! The first night one elderly woman came. With the other twenty team members present, at least she did not know she was the only one who came! Our meetings continued, and at the end of the two weeks, three new believers in the Lord Jesus Christ were baptized in the Atlantic Ocean. What a joy it was to experience with them their excitement over their new life in Christ!

One of the team members, who went on to become a career missionary in Portugal, is now dying. He hardly has enough strength to get up from his bed. Unless the Lord heals him, he will leave behind a wife and two young children. Yet, I am sure he would say today that it has been worth it all to give his life away in a cause that was truly worth living for!

There are many, many single adults who are living and dying without a cause. As single adult leaders, we have the opportunity to challenge them to become involved with the Lord Jesus Christ in advancing God's kingdom on earth. Let's make the most of the time and opportunity we have been given. Let's get started today!

Gilbert E. Crowell,
Associate Pastor (Singles & Missions)
Eastside Baptist Church
1821 Chondra Drive
Marietta, Georgia 30062

For Further Reading

Missions Handbook: USA/Canada Protestant Ministries Overseas, Editors: W. Dayton Roberts and John A. Siewert. Co-published by MARC and Zondervan, 14th edition, 1989.

Lifetime Memories: Summer Missions Handbook 1991. Compiled by Lara Jean Kauwling. Published by the Student Missionary Union of Biola University, 13800 Biola Avenue, La Mirada, CA 90639, (213) 903-4881.

Vacations with a Purpose: A Planning Handbook for Your Short-Term Missions Team by Chris Eaton and Kim Hurst. Published by NAVPRESS, Single Ministry Resources, 1991.

Perspectives on the World Christian Movement: A Reader. Edited by Ralph D. Winter and Steven C. Hawthorne. Published by William Carey Library, P.O. Box 40129, Pasadena, CA 91104.

Operation World: A Day to Day Guide to Praying for the World. Edited by Patrick Johnstone, fourth edition. Co-published by STL and WEC International, 1986.

From Jerusalem to Irian Jaya: A Biographical History of Christian Missions by Ruth A. Tucker. Published by The Zondervan Corporation, 1983.

In the Gap: What It Means to Be a World Christian by David Bryant. Published by Inter-Varsity Missions, 233 Langdon Street, Madison, Wisconsin 53703, 1979.

12. DISCIPLING SINGLE ADULTS

"When we enter the freedom that comes with a relationship with Jesus, we carry a responsibility for sharing this with others."

Norm Yukers

One Saturday in February 1991 I was leading a workshop at an NSL (Network of Single Adult Leaders) Conference. My topic was "Discipling Single Adults." I had planned for twenty participants and was surprised to see more than fifty people in the room. I realized then what I had been suspecting for a while—singles and their leaders are starved for discipleship and need the tools to develop this vital area of ministry.

Discipleship actually started for me in 1981. I was not attending church anymore and didn't give two hoots about God—or so I thought. But that year, someone took the time to tell me about Jesus Christ and how I needed a personal relationship with Him. The next week I was in a church and two weeks later was being discipled by the pastor. Of course, I didn't know I was being discipled; I just knew I was hungry and someone was taking time to feed me.

Because of that nurturing, I was able to grow quickly. Fourteen months after my realization of a need for a personal Savior, I was leading a group of single adults on that same journey. It was at this time I felt called by God to full-time ministry as a singles pastor.

Several years later, I found myself in seminary and being discipled by a professor who challenged me to begin a discipleship emphasis to my ministry.

A friend in my singles ministry and I set out to create a discipleship emphasis where Christians would grow up straight and tall and connected together in a common root system—Jesus Christ. We called our course "The Redwood Program." Some of our ideas and principles will be shared in the following pages.

Discipling Single Adults

Dietrich Bonhoeffer describes discipleship as "adherence to Christ, and because Christ is the object of adherence, it must take the form of discipleship." He goes on to say, "Christianity without discipleship is Christianity without Christ."

In this day of *cheap grace* with its emphasis on freedom and equality, and with so many people unchurched, it is not popular to teach total obedience. But the Bible does not present any other message. Discipleship is obedience, and we should not try to make light of it.

But why should we have a group that ministers just to singles? In other words, what is the purpose of our singles group? It should be no different than the scriptural purpose of the church. Ephesians 3:14-21 gives us a picture of this purpose with a bottom line of *bringing glory to God.*

> For this reason I kneel before the Father, from whom His whole family in heaven and on earth derives its name. I pray that out of His glorious riches He may strengthen you with power through His Spirit in your inner being, so that Christ may dwell in your hearts through faith. And I pray that you, being rooted and established in love, may have power, together with all the saints, to grasp how wide and long and high and deep is the love of Christ, and to know this love that surpasses knowledge—that you may be filled to the measure of all the fullness of God.
>
> Now to Him who is able to do immeasurably more than all we ask or imagine, according to His power that is at work within us, to Him be glory in the church and in Christ Jesus throughout all generations, for ever and ever! Amen.

You may be saying to yourself, "What a profound mystery. Our singles group is to bring glory to God! But how do we know if we are succeeding?" The answer is actually quite simple. Our goals must be based on the purpose. Fortunately, the Bible gives us those goals.

Ephesians 4:11-14 clearly tells leaders that our charge is to help people mature in the unity of the faith and grow in the knowledge of the Son of God. Matthew 28:18-20 challenges us to go and make disciples, teaching them to obey all that Jesus had commanded.

Nothing glorifies God more than a Christlike person who is living out a Galatians 5:22-24 lifestyle: "But the fruit of the Spirit is love, joy, peace, patience, kindness, goodness, faithfulness, gentleness, and self-control.

140

Against such things there is no law. Those who belong to Christ Jesus have crucified the sinful nature with its passions and desires."

You might be asking, "How do I begin?" Well, as the writer of Ecclesiastes said, "There is nothing new under the sun" (1:9). Therefore, the tools we need are already in existence. Let us now identify them and see how to use them.

You Begin with People

The first tool is people. Without people, there is no discipleship program. I believe in horizontal or continuum discipleship as opposed to vertical. Jesus is the discipler, and all believers are somewhere on the continuum as disciplees. One may be further along the line than another, but the learning goes both ways.

In the vertical discipleship model, there is Jesus and the disciplee, but the discipler is plugged in the middle, a contact point between Jesus and the disciplee. I cannot find reference to that model in Scripture.

People, the ones chosen for discipleship, should exhibit certain qualities. These qualities or characteristics all begin with the letter *C*.

• A person must be *converted* in order to be considered for discipleship. Until one's eyes are opened to spiritual things, obedience at all cost is not an option.

• The second characteristic is *churched.* I am not saying that parachurch organizations cannot do discipleship. Rather, I am pointing out that just as Christ ordained the local church to carry out His plan, so we also should look for those individuals who are active in the local church. More will be said about this later.

• A third characteristic is *compassion* for the lost. This could manifest itself in at least three ways: the first and most basic is personally praying for those apart from Christ; the second is bringing an unsaved/unchurched person to a place, activity, or meeting where they would hear the claims of Christ; the third is giving personal testimony and actually sharing with someone about Christ.

• The fourth observed characteristic is a *craving* for the Bible (1 Peter 2:1-2). The learner should desire, above all else, to know Christ in an intimate way; through a greater understanding of the Bible, he or she can begin the journey to this intimacy. Just as a hungry person is first in line at a picnic with his plate and plastic silverware, so should a discipler be ready with Bible, pen, and paper to be fed spiritually.

• The final characteristic should be a willingness to lead a Romans 12:1-2 *consecrated* life.

Therefore, I urge you, brothers, in view of God's mercy, to offer your bodies as living sacrifices, holy and pleasing to God—this is your spiritual act of worship. Do not conform any longer to the pattern of this world, but be transformed by the renewing of your mind. Then you will be able to test and approve what God's will is—His good, pleasing and perfect will.

Willingness is the operative word. A person will grow to be a Romans 12:1-2 Christian as he is exposed to the commands and teachings of Christ and has the willingness to obey them.

The Well-Balanced Christian Life

Hub—Christ (2 Cor. 5:17; Gal. 2:20)
Rim—Obedient Christian life (Rom. 12:1-2; John 14:21)
Spokes—The Bible (2 Tim. 3:16; Josh. 1:8)
    —Prayer (John 15:7; Phil. 4:6-7)
    —Fellowship (Matt. 18:20; Heb. 10:24-25)
    —Witnessing (Matt. 4:19; Rom. 1:16)

● The Bible . . . God's Word. As we look at the spoke called "The Bible," we see at least five ways to get God's Word into our lives. These five ways are often illustrated as a hand.

The thumb is *hearing* (Rom. 10:17), and is characterized by listening to

142

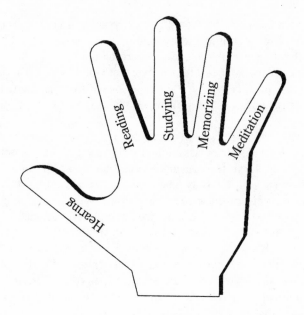

audio cassettes, attending preaching services, and taking notes during sermons.

The index finger represents *reading* (Rev. 1:3) the Word. There are many one-year Bibles on the market that will allow you to read the complete Bible with planned variety. It is my opinion that every Christian should read through the Bible yearly.

Studying the Word (Acts 17:11) is the middle finger of the hand. Many good Bible study systems are available at Christian bookstores.

Just as the ring worn on a ring finger is often something very special, so is *memorizing* (Ps. 119:9-11) a special part of our life. Again, many good systems are available, including the Navigators' "Topical Memory System."

The pinkie finger represents *meditation*. Lately, some Christians have been frightened away from meditation, thinking it to be part of Eastern mysticism. Psalm 1:2-3 clearly tells us that meditating day and night is a good thing.

Now that we have the hand completed, let's consider our need for all these approaches to the Bible. Try to hold a book by the thumb only.

Even if you could balance it, it would be very easy to snatch it from you. If you hold it with your thumb and index finger, the book is a little more stable, but still not secure. As you add each remaining finger, the stability and security increases. So it is with the Word of God. As you put yourself under the hearing of it, regularly read it, seriously study it, memorize it, and meditate on it, you will find it bringing stability and security to your life.

● Prayer. The spoke of the wheel entitled *prayer* is the next element of discipleship. The disciples asked Jesus to teach them to pray. He responded by giving them the prayer recorded for us in Matthew 6:9-15. Here Jesus was teaching not only *how* to pray, but *what* to pray. We are able to follow this pattern because we are disciples of Jesus, who mediates for us to God the Father. Because we have placed our faith in Jesus, we can pray to *our* Father. For an excellent treatment on prayer and discipleship, see *The Cost of Discipleship* by Dietrich Bonhoeffer.

● Fellowship. The next spoke that keeps the wheel of the discipled life balanced is *fellowship*. As we see in Acts 2:42-47, among all the things the disciples were devoted to, fellowship was right in the middle. This is the context for disciple-making.

> They devoted themselves to the apostles' teaching and to the fellowship, to the breaking of bread and to prayer. Everyone was filled with awe, and many wonders and miraculous signs were done by the apostles. All the believers were together and had everything in common. Selling their possessions and goods, they gave to anyone as he had need. Every day they continued to meet together in the temple courts. They broke bread in their homes and ate together with glad and sincere hearts, praising God and enjoying the favor of all the people. And the Lord added to their number daily those who were being saved.

In fact, the desire for community is a mark of a true disciple. Community may be two or three nurturing each other, holding one another accountable. Or, a small group of six to twelve may covenant together for spiritual growth and accountability. Regardless of the number, the communal commitment is imperative.

True disciples are a glad and joyful people, and thus enjoy being with each other. A healthy and dynamic discipleship ministry for single adults will include both one-on-one and small group fellowship. This intimacy through community development is a discipleship imperative.

144

• Reproduction. The final spoke of the discipleship wheel is *reproduction*. When we enter the freedom that comes with a relationship with Jesus, we carry a responsibility for sharing this with others. Some people freeze up at the thought of this area of discipleship. They think, "Oh no! Here it comes! I knew it! They want me to go in the street and pass out those Gospel tracts! I'm not an evangelist!"

Instead of viewing the reproducing of our Christian lives as an action, let's view it as a lifestyle. Jesus told us that the field is ready for harvest. "Do you not say, 'Four months more and then the harvest'? I tell you, open your eyes and look at the fields! They are ripe for harvest' " (John 4:35). We need to view the world and the people in it as Jesus does.

Paul told us to prepare ourselves as soldiers preparing for battle! This requires a team approach. Reproducing together through ministry teams is a powerful arena for individual growth. "Endure hardship with us like a good soldier of Christ Jesus. No one serving as a soldier gets involved in civilian affairs—he wants to please his commanding officer" (2 Tim. 2:3-4).

In *Disciples in Action* Leroy Eims wrote, "Every heart without Christ is a mission field. Every heart with Christ is a missionary." We are Jesus' plan to carry the message to those in need. A good disciple knows that and does his/her part.

For the single adult the Christian life is not easy, but if we prepare them for it in Christ, they will not be overwhelmed, but can be overcomers.

Once single adults have learned and put into practice the principles shown in the wheel and hand illustrations, they are well on their way to becoming Romans 12:2 believers and true disciples of Jesus Christ.

Norm Yukers
Associate Pastor with Single Adults
Los Gatos Christian Church
16845 Hicks Road
Los Gatos, California 95032

For Further Reading
Bonhoeffer, Dietrich. *The Cost of Discipleship*. New York: The Macmillan Company, 1949, 1960.

Campus Crusade for Christ. *How to Make Your Mark* (A Manual for Evangelism and Discipleship). Here's Life Publishers, Inc., 1983.

Eims, Leroy. *Disciples in Action* (Witnessing, Making Disciples, Equipping Laborers, Training Leaders). Colorado Springs: NavPress, 1981.

Pratney, Winkie. *A Handbook for Followers of Jesus.* Minneapolis: Bethany Fellowship, Inc., 1977.

Ridenour, Fritz. *Lord, What's Really Important?* (Discovering a Biblical Lifestyle). Regal Books, 1978.

Riggs, Charles. *Thirty Devotional Exercises* (A Discipleship Tool). Minneapolis: Billy Graham Evangelistic Association, 1980.

13. TEACHING SINGLE ADULTS

"Single adults are hungry for meaning and are not satisfied with shallow answers. They need truth, not probability, substance, not techniques. They need community, not commiseration. They need to prevail, not merely to cope."

L. Daryle Worley, Jr.

Specialized ministries exist to enhance the ability of the local church to address effectively the varied and unique needs of its people. Singles ministry is a specialized ministry. Therefore, its primary objective must be to accomplish the purpose of the church in the lives of the group it was created to reach.

What, then, is the purpose of the church? This subject has received no small amount of attention in recent years. Questions concerning the methodologies of the church, and even its relevance in contemporary society, have challenged everyone from the theologian to the very infrequent church attender. And the result has been widely divergent philosophies and strategies of ministry, each seeking to ensure that the church keeps up with the pace of North American cultural change.

But these are only the philosophies and strategies; the actual *purpose* of the church cannot be so hotly contested. The Apostle Paul instructed the church at Ephesus that God had especially gifted, among others, teachers "to prepare God's people for works of service, so that the body of Christ may be built up until we all reach unity in the faith and in the knowledge of the Son of God and become mature, attaining to the whole measure of the fullness of Christ" (Eph. 4:12-13). This is a clear statement of purpose; the church exists to bring people to spiritual maturity — which is the state of experiencing all that God has to offer. And we know from other passages, that pursuit of spiritual maturity involves, first and foremost, consistent obedience to the commands of Christ.

Following this inquiry, we need to ask what the commands of Christ are. Doubtless there are many, but some essential ones stand out above the rest. Christ Himself said, " 'Love the Lord your God with all your heart and with all your soul and with all your mind.' This is the first and greatest commandment. And the second is like it: 'Love your neighbor as yourself' " (Matt. 22:37-39).

Jesus also gave a related command just before returning to His Father, what we know as the Great Commission. This one is related to the previous two because it is essentially entailed by them. The most loving thing we can do for God is to be so fulfilled by our relationship with Him that we share it with others. And the most loving thing we can do for people is to recognize and respond to their greatest need. Clearly, the greatest need people have, regardless of the relative pain and pleasure of their lives, is to know that they will spend eternity with their Creator.

Thus, the most basic commands of Christ include a lifestyle so characterized by love for God and people that it leads naturally to introducing our two loves to one another.

What we have established so far is that a singles ministry exists to enhance the ability of the local church to address the varied and unique needs of single adults. Therefore, it must focus primarily on moving those single adults toward maturity in their individual relationships with Christ, and the core of such maturity is a genuine love for God and people.

In the Scriptures teaching is vital to the achievement of this process. Jesus included teaching as integral to the Great Commission. Paul recognized it as one of the five gifts given specifically to accomplish the purpose of the church. Our Lord took teaching so seriously that He even warned us through James that teachers would be judged more severely, thus underscoring the profound weight of their responsibility. With this sort of importance placed upon teaching by God Himself, it is arguably unwise to begin our teaching with anything other than His own Word as the primary curriculum.

Why Should We Teach the Bible?

Some questions may be running through your mind. For example, "Is the Bible truly relevant to the needs of contemporary single adults?" or "Are single adults really interested in what the Bible has to say?" or "This is all fine, but I am not a gifted teacher; how do I teach from the Bible without an established curriculum?" Let's look at these questions.

• First, the Bible is, without question, relevant to the needs of single adults. And if this statement appears untrue in any given ministry, it is more an indictment of the teacher than the text! Single adults, like the rest of society, are hungry for meaning in the confusion of day-to-day life. They are not satisfied with shallow answers. Single adults need truth, not probability. They need substance, not techniques. They need community, not commiseration. They need to prevail, not merely to cope. The Bible meets these needs above and beyond the insights of the wisest people-helpers in human history; because of its origin it has an authority which all other thinkers and systems cannot rival. If the Bible seems irrelevant to single adults in the church, it has not been understood. And if they have not understood it, it has not been clearly taught.

 • Second, if the relevance of the Bible is perceived and communicated by the teacher, single adults will be interested in what it has to say. People are not always able to recognize the best source for answers to core issues. Therefore, it is a teacher's calling to locate that source and communicate the answers with competence. There is no shortage of spurious fountains of wisdom these days, nor of teachers to herald them. And there are whole assemblies of people who are quite ready to receive each of these teachings as authoritative, with little or no objective verification. The Bible, however, surpasses them all in objective verifiability. It has peerlessly demonstrated its truth and power to change lives. It has passed the tests of time, skepticism, and scrutiny. When single adults are looking for a solid foundation, and authoritative answers for their lives in a generation of ethical and moral anarchy, they will receive the truth of the Bible when it is communicated with insight.

 • Third, several Christian publishing houses provide Bible curriculum. One, for instance, offers a system which takes you through the Bible in ten years, offering teachers bona fide job security! However, approaches like this one can actually contribute to a perception that the Bible is irrelevant. It is not that the material is poorly researched or organized; rather, some of it lacks the audience-specific application which makes the Bible truly live. An obvious next step would be to locate a Bible curriculum written specifically for single adults. Unfortunately, there is precious little available. (Write NSL, P.O. Box 1600, Grand Rapids, MI 49501 for ideas.) What remains, then, is to consider preparing your own material. I know this sounds like a big job, but I want to suggest a system which, for me, has actually made teaching preparation a delightful experience!

How Do We Teach the Bible?
 • Know our single adults. Relevant teaching answers the questions its hearers are asking. When Jesus spoke with the woman at the well in

Samaria, He did not explain end-time events. Rather He got right to the heart of the matter for her personally. We do not possess Jesus' insight into people; but when we presume to instruct a group, we must strive to know them, their needs, their life situations, their strengths and weaknesses corporately and individually, etc. Gaining such knowledge can take time, and all the while the group is changing. But we need to stay with it. Without knowing our audience and tailoring especially applications with them in mind, our teaching material will ultimately prove unsatisfying to all involved.

• Choose a Bible passage. The Bible is a large book; where do you begin? Assuming you are already defining the needs of your audience, let's look at three criteria which can help you determine a starting point.

First, be aware of what portions of the Bible broadly address the unique needs of your group. A new Christian desiring to be instructed in the basics of his relationship with Jesus Christ, for example, will not gain a great deal from an examination of the Law in Leviticus. Similarly, someone seeking to clarify her thoughts on biblical creationism will not be best served by studying the Pauline Epistles. Although all Scripture is profitable for instruction in righteousness, a specific issue is best addressed by a passage which focuses on that issue.

• Having identified a relevant section of the Bible, progress through it systematically. Some teachers today tend to ignore the "whole council of God." A natural inclination is to teach favorite passages over and over. Romans 12, for instance, is a rich text full of instruction on how to live the Christian life to its fullest. But if you always teach Romans 12 without progressing systematically through a book or section, you may never land on chapters like Romans 9–11. However difficult the thorny issues of God's promise to Israel and purpose in election and predestination may be, you cannot simply ignore these chapters of His Word. You may think only a fool would rush into such topics in a large group study, but even Romans 12 cannot be properly appreciated when isolated from the context of Paul's entire argument in that letter.

• Recognize that not every opportunity to teach the Bible is long term. What do you teach when you only have one opportunity with a group? Obviously, the need to understand the audience still exists, as does the need to know what portions of Scripture best apply. Then, from among those portions, prayerfully choose one which you feel appropriately addresses their circumstances. But even in these situations, understanding the context of a passage—so that you could teach it on the spot if opportunity were given—is essential for richness and relevance. It is

150

also the only way you can be certain that you are handling the Scriptures responsibly.

How Do We Interpret the Bible?

Vital to teaching the Bible effectively is knowing how to interpret it properly. Because of the uniqueness of the Bible, some might object to the suggestion that there are proper and therefore *im*proper methods of interpretation. After all, Christianity is first and foremost a relationship and the Bible is God's means of communicating with His people. Why, then, should someone else presume to inform me of the true meaning of God's communication to me? Good question! But let's remember that the Bible is also an ancient literary document, and as such must be approached carefully according to a consistent set of interpretive principles in order not to be abused. Universities are populated with professors who dedicate a lifetime to handling accurately the writings of a Plato or a Kant. Hermeneutics, the science of literary interpretation, is essential to virtually every academic field: philosophy, history, literature. Yet when it comes to the Bible, there seems to be an unwritten but often accepted maxim that everyone has a right to his own opinion concerning its true and intended meaning. As all literary scholars recognize, that is false. It is impossible to present a thorough system of biblical interpretation in this chapter. But let's look at three basic principles which can certainly get us started in the right direction.

• First, the clear, obvious meaning of the words in a passage is preferred over a more complex or obscure meaning. When we hear great Bible teachers, we are often astounded at their keen insights. They see things we never saw. Unfortunately, our lack of understanding of the process by which they arrive at their insights *could* lead us to misuse the Bible. One way to avoid such error is to make sure that our insights are actually birthed by the text, as opposed to going to Scripture simply attempting to find support for our own preconceived ideas. In technical terms, favor *exegesis* over *eisegesis;* read your insights *out* of the text; don't read your insights *into* the text.

• Second, know the context of the passage. I made this point earlier but I repeat it for emphasis; most interpretative errors can be avoided simply by knowing context. This is also the case with verbal discussions and disagreements in daily conversation! In fact, it is difficult to overestimate the importance of context in rightly understanding any form of communication.

In biblical interpretation, however, context does not consist exclusively of knowing the content of surrounding chapters. It also includes knowing something of the historical, social, and cultural climate at the time of writing. It includes knowing the purpose for the writing. All four Gospels, for instance, intended to give an account of the life of Jesus, but each had a different purpose and/or target audience. Matthew was written to the Jews, John to seekers. Paul's letters to the churches commonly dealt with specific difficulties the new Christians were experiencing. Context includes knowing something of the distinctiveness of the writer's style and his/her cultural and geographical background. I realize this sounds vast, but it is really no more than is offered in any standard commentary, and even in some study Bibles, as introduction to each biblical book. Don't skip over the introductions!

• Third, understand the nature of application. The most effective method of specific biblical application is to give relevant examples, not nonnegotiable directives. Remember that the Bible essentially establishes a set of attitudinal and behavioral principles—an ethical code, as it were—as opposed to a list of absolute do's and don'ts. That is to say, the behavior of two people, both of whom are seeking to live according to the very same word of instruction, can end up looking quite different. This is what allows the Bible to transcend time and culture while remaining specific and pertinent. Therefore, an essential aspect of handling Scripture well is to convey its relevance to your hearers' life situations, without unduly limiting the scope of their individual expressions of obedience to it. People need to learn how to apply the truths of the Bible themselves. Just as a counselor seeks to build the counselee's independence rather than dependence, so teachers must seek the same for their students. Application, therefore, is best when it consists of relevant *illustrations* which bring contemporary clarity to the text, rather than rigid *instructions* which define how this teaching ought to look in the hearer's daily life.

Without a doubt there are many more hermeneutical principles which we could discuss. But I believe these very basic ones are sufficient to underscore the indispensable role of interpretive science and to whet the appetite for further study.

How Do We Organize Our Thoughts?

Interpreting the Bible properly is not the sole preparation for teaching it well. Like a symphony, a lesson must have good form in order to be worth hearing. There is no shortage of instruction on how to organize our thoughts for public presentation, and it is really up to each individual to find one which fits his personal style. I would like to summarize my favorite as an example, because it has so streamlined my outlining of Scripture that now I find preparation as personally rewarding as teaching. The system I use was developed by Lloyd Perry and is presented in his book, *Biblical Preaching for Today's World* (Moody Press, 1973). Now don't be scared off by the word *preaching*. The difference between preaching and teaching is more in the delivery than in the preparation. Admittedly, sermon preparation can be somewhat more artful and crafted than teaching preparation, but this is due primarily to the more formal nature of the end product. But, imagine the results if teaching preparation were consistently given the structural attention of sermon preparation and yet retained its more personal and informal style of expression. The results could be strikingly effective. Let's consider, then, the following summary of Lloyd Perry's methodology.

• Step one, determine the *subject* of the lesson. The subject of the Bible passage ideally should be the subject of the lesson. To find this subject, Perry advises answering the question, "What is the one main center of attention of this whole passage?" See if there is a duty to perform, a precept or maxim to explore, a problem to solve, or an occupation, profession, or calling to pursue. Normally the subject is given in terms of a single word or at most a short phrase.

• Step two, select a *theme*. The theme of a lesson will be the particular aspect of the subject just discovered which is to be developed within the message. It is the function of the theme to divide the subject and to suggest relationships. For example, if the subject is "Discipline," a theme may be, "The Value of Discipline" or "Characteristics of a Disciplined Life" or "Disciplining Children," depending on the content of the teaching passage. As you can see, where a subject is normally one word, the theme will always be in the form of a phrase. Having identified the theme, you should then probe it in order to collect other material on the topic.

• Step three, formulate a *proposition*. The proposition occupies the focal point of the lesson outline. Perry says that it promotes "stability of structure, unity of thought, and forcefulness of impact." It announces the theme in a complete sentence. Essentially, it is a one-sentence declaration of the intent or core of the lesson. Each piece of raw research material you collect should be weighed alongside the proposition to determine its value to the lesson. If it contributes, keep it. If it does not, or if you are in doubt, throw it out. Should your teaching ever seem disjointed, lacking unity and focus, most likely you have either omitted or strayed from your proposition statement. A well-formed proposition should be an assertion of an evaluation or judgment, an obligation or duty, or an activity without a stated obligation (in this type the emphasis is placed on an inherent ability in the hearers).

● Step four, establish a *transitional sentence.* A transitional sentence is the hinge of the lesson; it is a rhetorical bridge between the core of your message, the proposition, and its development, the body or "main points" section. A transitional sentence is formed by progressing through three stages. First, apply one of the following six questions to the proposition: How can I? Why should I? When should I? Where should I? Where can I? Why is it? Second, include the proposition in as complete a form as possible. And third, select a *key word.* This step is critical! *The key word is the single most important element in generating order, clarity, and unity among the main points and, therefore, within the overall lesson.* The key word is a noun and is always plural. Some examples are: benefits, commands, incentives, etc. The key word characterizes the commonality among main points. Each lesson has only one key word; it always appears in the transitional sentence and never in the proposition.

● Step five, develop *main points.* Main points amplify, explain, or prove the proposition. Normally there will not be more than five and never fewer than two. It is best to have the main points in parallel grammatical form because they are easier to remember. It is also advisable to avoid figurative language since it is often ambiguous. The purpose of a given lesson can have an influence on the order of the points, but generally the order flows right out of the Bible text. And since they come directly from the Scripture, you should record the exact text in your statement of each main point.

● Step six, amplify the main points into *subpoints.* There should be at least two or three such categories under each main point; it is important that they be short in form, few in number, and similar in structure. The simplest way to form subpoints is to ask of each main point one of the six questions asked of the proposition in the forming of the transitional sentence.

● Step seven, formulate an *introduction.* Perry says that the introduction is the part of a lesson which clarifies the reason for that particular audience to listen to that particular teacher discuss that particular subject on that occasion. It consists of three parts.

First, there is the approach sentence. This is the first statement which comes out of your mouth and is generally the point at which your audience is won or lost. Therefore, it should be as short, direct, intriguing, and involving as possible. It should go out and capture the audience wherever they are and bring their attention to one common focus.

The second part is transition material between wherever the audience was when they were captured by the approach sentence and where you want to take them with the rest of the lesson. Sometimes it is a humorous story, sometimes a series of common experiences or observations; but its goal is always to identify gradually a frailty or lack in the lives of the people which will be filled by the content of the message.

The third part of the introduction is the explanation. It bridges between the transition and the main points which follow by shedding a biblical light on the frailty or lack which was uncovered. The explanation concludes with the transitional sentence. According to Perry, the complete introduction should occupy no more than 15 percent of the entire teaching time.

• Step eight, formulate the *conclusion*. The conclusion is a summarization of the lesson reemphasizing its relevance. It consists of two parts. First is the objective sentence, the first sentence of the conclusion. It usually begins with the word *therefore*, but in terms of components it is essentially the proposition plus a purpose which flows out of the collective weight of the main points. Second, a section follows which consists either of a recapitulation of the main points or a restating of the applications made within the main points throughout the lesson. Perry suggests that the teacher may want to challenge her hearers to accept the main points by appealing to altruism, aspiration, curiosity, duty, fear, love, or reason. But he also stresses that the lesson should be concluded on a positive note.

Having completed these eight steps, you should now give attention to two general items, the first of which you may have included as you went along. First, add in *illustrative material* wherever it is needed. These are the relevant illustrations I mentioned earlier. Perry advises inclusion of only one illustration per idea. Second, formulate a *title* which reflects the mood of the lesson, the nature of the audience, and the content of the message. Ideally it should not contain more than four thought-full words.

This process may seem cumbersome but, as with most systems of form, it soon becomes second nature. And when that happens, lesson plans begin to flow from virtually every source. You read a newspaper article and automatically you mentally arrange it into a teachable form. It's almost as though your mind is full of barrels labeled *Introduction, Illustration, Key Word,* etc., into one of which every new idea must be thrown. Then again, maybe this is just a teacher talking! Regardless,

155

formal systems are always more liberating in the long run than they appear to be at first hearing.

Let's Look at an Example

Expressing only the *theory* of an idea can make that idea sound more complex than it really is. In such cases examples are not only more beneficial but often even more accurate indicators of what the idea truly involves. Therefore, I would like to progress through an example of how a lesson plan goes together using Perry's eight steps. I mentioned Romans 12 earlier as a rich passage of Scripture; I believe it should serve us well as a sample text. For your own benefit, why not read Romans 12 right now so it will be fresh in your mind as we work with it. Let's apply the steps.

• Step one, determine the *subject.* We can see from the first word of verse 1, "Therefore," that Romans 12 begins a new section of Paul's letter the content of which is determined by what preceded it. In a nutshell, Romans 1–11 have methodically delineated the mercies of God expressed in the lives of Christians all the way from the helplessness without Him to the certainty of their future with Him. Then Romans 12 begins giving instruction on the nature and specifics of an appropriate day-to-day response to these mercies. An appropriate subject, therefore, would be "Response."

• Step two, select a *theme.* No doubt your completed study of the content of Romans 12 has shown you that there is far more material in the passage than can be covered in one lesson, so you have decided to divide the chapter in half at its most natural break and address verses 1-8. Wise decision! What aspect of the very general subject, "Response," is presented in Romans 12:1-8? Essentially it is the appropriate response of Christians to Christ's work of salvation on their behalf. There is your theme: "Christians' Response to the Work of Christ."

• Step three, formulate a *proposition.* This text seems to require a proposition which is a statement of obligation or duty. Romans 12:1 urges us to place ourselves at God's disposal as an act of worship for what He has done. Verse 2 follows with a command to allow the work of Christ, rather than our world system, to remake us. Verses 3-8 tell us what it would look like if all Christians obeyed verses 1-2. Notice that there is a progressive, unified nature to each of the responses Paul is suggesting, as opposed to a parallel, self-contained nature. That is to say, the *command* in verse 2 flows out of the *urge* in verse 1, rather than standing as a separate and unique command. And the *scenario* in verses 3-8 develops

156

the same thought. In such passages, the core truth is expressed right at the start and the rest of the text simply embellishes it. Thus, a possible proposition statement for Romans 12 might be, "The work of Christ requires a response of active worship." If the response called for in verse 1 was labeled an act of worship, and the responses of verses 2 and following flow out of it, then all of the responses taken together comprise progressive components of an act of worship which stands as the core truth of the passage.

• Step four, establish a *transitional sentence.* Remember that Perry suggested a three-step process. First, let's ask the question "How can I?" of the above proposition statement. How can I respond in active worship to the work of Christ? The answer will be the transitional sentence; but as we word it we already need to be including the proposition in as complete a form as possible, and also the key word. Let's try, "The work of Christ requires a response of active worship which consists of three *stages* according to Romans 12:1-8." The key word, *stages,* suggests the progressive nature of our text.

• Step five, develop the *main points.* By this point, however, they are all but developed as a result of choosing a key word for the transitional sentence. Since our key word is *stages,* it is not necessary that we state our main points in sentence form; a one-word title for each stage will suffice. (Had we chosen a different key word like "commands," for instance, it would virtually require the main points to be a sentence.) I alluded to the three stages of Romans 12:1-8 when we were formulating the proposition; our challenge now is to state them in some grammatically parallel form. I believe stages one and two can gain their title straight from the text: "Presentation," verse 1, and "Transformation," verse 2. And verses 3-8 suggest that stage three is the "Culmination" of individual acts of worship in the corporate experience of the church.

• Step six, amplify the main points into subpoints. This involves plugging your study notes into your newly formed outline. In the ordering of that material, I believe the best question to ask each main point is "How can I?" How can I present myself to God? How can I be transformed? How can I experience the culmination of my response to God in my church? It is interesting to note in the third stage that the culmination of our worshipful response to God for the work of Christ is the selfless exercising of our spiritual gifts in harmony with other believers. Teachers, you'd better be teaching!

• Step seven, formulate an *introduction.* The first consideration is determining an approach sentence. As stated earlier, this is the first statement which comes out of your mouth, and is generally where the point is won or lost. Therefore, it should be as short, direct, intriguing, and involving as possible. Consider the following as a possible approach sentence: "Our pre-Christian lives were still, lifeless pools into which Christ is received as a pebble from the hand of God." This immediately puts a picture in people's minds and draws them to a common focus. Everyone has seen what the entry of a stone does to a placid body of water. As you progress through the outlined portion you can develop this picture; and through the explanation you can create a context for the three stages of Romans 12 to be understood as the "ripples" which result from the entrance of Christ into our lives.

● Step eight, formulate a *conclusion*. The goal here is to tie any loose threads together. Taking your hearers back to the picture you created in the introduction is generally quite effective. "Therefore, the work of Christ agitates within us a response of active worship." This is a possible objective sentence.

Add to the subpoints illustrations which are relevant to your audience, title the lesson, and you are done. There are few experiences more rewarding than digging into God's Word and coming out with something truly meaningful which you can communicate effectively to other people.

I leave you with a paraphrased description of teaching from Warren Wiersbe. Teaching begins with a picture showing people where they need to be; then it turns into a mirror in which they see themselves; and finally it changes to a window through which they see God and His grace. This concept can revolutionize the way you teach and, therefore, transform the lives of your hearers. And if singles ministries truly exist to help the local church bring single adults to spiritual maturity in Christ, what more could you possibly desire?

L. Daryle Worley, Jr.
Pastor of Single Adults
The Moody Church
1609 N. LaSalle Street
Chicago, Illinois 60614

DEVELOPING SIGNIFICANT MINISTRIES

14. DEALING WITH GRAY AREAS

*"Baby boomers are returning to church, but they
don't necessarily have a system of morals and values
compatible with the average church community.
They frequently want to know what's wrong and
what's right and what is Christian. They have been
adrift without a moral compass, and yet now they
want to know that there is solid ground somewhere to
land on."*

Jim Berrier

What's wrong with a glass of wine at dinner?"

"How can a Christian singer allow her music to be played on secular stations?"

"Is it right for Christians to blockade abortion clinics?"

Sound familiar? These are just a few of the questions single adult leaders are routinely bombarded with as they attempt to give guidance to a generation of single adults from a kaleidoscope of cultures, religious preferences, and hereditary scruples.

We have endured a generation of moral and spiritual drought: No prayer in school, moral relativism, Norman Lear, Woodstock, Shirley MacLaine. We have gone from "God is Dead" to "God is Me." A generation whose battle cry was once, "If it feels good do it," may now be crying, "It still feels good, but I'm not sure I should." Indeed, Nancy Reagan preached, "Just say no" and Magic Johnson warned, "Just be safe"; but for the scores of other issues which may not be imminently life-threatening, we are often hard-pressed to give logical, balanced, biblically based answers.

The Ozzie and Harriet family of the 1950s where Dad works and Mom bakes cookies and they are only married once for a lifetime is very rare in the 1990s. Adult survivors of the baby boom who grew up in church espousing their parents' beliefs and values never to depart are an equally endangered species. What we are dealing with has been called the "Baby Boomerang." They are returning to church, but they don't have a system of morals and values compatible with the average church community. They frequently want to know what's wrong and what's right and what is Christian. They have been adrift without a moral compass, and now they want to know that there is solid ground somewhere to land on.

Church Fellowship

Sharing the love and life of Jesus Christ is a cross-cultural experience if you minister in a cosmopolitan arena, are on staff at a large church, or work with single adults. It might benefit us all to learn the basics of cross-cultural missions just to work in our own backyards. We have differences which require us to be flexible, teachable, and careful.

Solomon long ago proclaimed, "There is nothing new under the sun," and it is still true today. Much of Paul's teaching had to address the conflicts as cultures merged and people of diversified backgrounds were integrated into "one body." Reference to these passages will be foundational to our discussion of gray areas. Because this problem is so connected with the separation created between the extremes of legalism and license, it is necessary to develop a biblical base. The primary texts that must be understood are:

Romans 13:8-10	1 Corinthians 8:1-13
James 2:8-13	1 Corinthians 10:23–11:1
Colossians 2:16-23	Romans 14:1–15:2

Paul deals with specific controversies in the church, and the last three passages listed are the heart and soul of this chapter. The following paradigm is a four-tiered structure on which all understanding of right and wrong can be defined, tested, and applied.

1. The Law of Love   Higher in Authority
2. Biblical Absolute
3. Community Standard
4. Personal Conviction   Lower in Submission

When Jesus was asked, "What is the greatest command?" He replied, "Love the Lord your God with all your heart, soul, mind, and strength, and love your neighbor as yourself." "On this," the Son of God proclaimed, "hang the Law and the Prophets" (Matt. 22:36-40). In Romans 13:9-10 Paul said that whatever other commandments there may be are

162

summed up in one rule, "Love your neighbor as yourself. Love does no harm to its neighbor. Therefore love is the fulfillment of the Law." In 1 Corinthians 13 he stated that religious activity without love is meaning-less and worthless, and concluded that three things remain, faith, hope, and love, and that the greatest of these is love. James explained that breaking one point of the law makes one guilty of breaking all of it, because any offense violates the Royal Law (2:8-10). Therefore the high-est law in determining right and wrong is the Royal Law or what can be called moral law—love.

Though there are many areas the Scripture does not specifically ad-dress, there are plenty it does. Mark Twain once said, "It's not the things in the Bible I don't understand that bother me, but the things I do understand." There are still some of us who are committed to embracing the Holy Scriptures as the "inspired, infallible, unalterable Word of God." Commands such as "Do not commit adultery," "Do not murder," "Do not worship other gods," "Forgive men when they sin against you," and "Go and make disciples of all nations . . . and teach them to obey every-thing I have commanded you" are universal and absolute. They apply to all people of all the ages and transcend geographical, political, and sectari-an boundaries.

Community Standards and Personal Convictions

Jesus said, "Go and make disciples of all nations," and His followers responded. Consequently, the body of Christ includes people with a vari-ety of religious training, family tradition, political preference, cultural influence, racial bias, social custom, and community standards which can involve civil laws, ceremonial practice, family etiquette, social protocol, work ethics, tribal taboos, and more. We adhere to community standards if we want to remain a part of the community. By and large they are established and maintained by the community, whether it be family, de-nomination, government, tribe, corporation, or home Bible study group. The purest understanding of submitting to community standard for the sake of the Gospel is Paul's stand, in 1 Corinthians 9:22, "I have become all things to all men."

Every individual has certain specific issues that are simply a matter of conscience. This includes acquired conscience as well as innate con-science. The issue may be as casual as a personal preference or taste or as serious as a result of intimate personal communion and devotion to one's God. It may just be something I've learned I can live without, or a unique divine mandate from God. At any rate, it's safe to say that each of us has personal convictions that are between "us and God"; rarely do any two people match up perfectly with intensity and priority of personal convictions. Still, these convictions must be kept diligently.

Most of the time controversy over gray areas in the church community comes as a result of not defining the order of hierarchy from love to biblical absolute, to community standard, to personal conviction. Love should always preside over the interpretations of Scriptures; community standards are in submission to God's written Word; and personal convictions must yield to community standard. In fact, the majority of our conflicts lie in between the levels of personal convictions and community standards. Let me illustrate how lines of tension exist between each level.

First Line of Tension: Love/Biblical Absolute

Some might argue that love and biblical absolutes could never be in conflict with each other. But we need only look at the relationship between Jesus and the Pharisees to see that it is possible to keep the written law yet miss the Royal Law. When Jesus healed on the Sabbath, He had no desire to nullify the Law. Rather His purpose was to put the written law in perspective: any attempt to keep the written laws of God must be motivated by love. Any lesser motive reduces our choices to legalism and dead religion. This is spelled out in the Sermon on the Mount: "You have heard, 'Do not murder,' but I say whoever is angry or says 'Raca' or 'You fool' is guilty; or again, 'Do not commit adultery,' but I say if you look at a woman to lust after her you are already in adultery." And He continues: "Turn the other cheek," "Go the extra mile," "Love your enemies," example after example stating that a motivation of love is of greater importance than just keeping the rules (Matt. 5–7). God's Law of Love predates any written law given to man.

If we attempt to keep or teach any law that is not in submission to the Royal Law of Love, we will only succeed in becoming Space Age Pharisees. All too often we look at the Pharisee who prayed, "God, I thank You that I am not like other men—extortioners, unjust, adulterers, or even as this tax collector," and then add, "God, I thank You that I am not like this Pharisee."

"Woe to you Pharisees, because you give God a tenth of your mint, rue, and all other kinds of garden herbs, but you neglect justice and the love of God" (Luke 11:42). I was a young man in the middle of a painful divorce feeling the sense of failure, shame, and confusion about God's plans for my life. I remember always coming late to church and leaving

164

early, and sitting in the back row of the balcony to insure ease of entrance and escape. One night the pastor was addressing the subject of divorce when he made the statement, "I would rather be wrong on the side of showing too much mercy than wrong on the side of not showing enough." I'll never forget that turning point in my life. That pastor was stating his commitment to keep law and love in proper perspective.

Second Line of Tension: Biblical Absolute/Community Standard

Barbara Seuling's book *You Can't Eat Peanuts in Church and Other Little Known Laws* contains some humorous observations. In Gary, Indiana, it is illegal to attend the theater within four hours of eating garlic; in North Carolina singing out of tune is against the law; and you are not permitted to swim on dry land in Santa Ana, California. Though lighthearted and harmless, these laws remind us that we love to make rules, and those rules vary just as widely as people groups vary. When an individual crosses boundaries, he is sure to be introduced to new rules. They may often have been established long ago with legitimate reason, but now they seem foreign or amusing, and are frequently hard for the newcomer to swallow. Community standards are necessary to the fabric of society, but are always in danger of being put in too high a place of authority.

Jesus rebuked the religious churchgoers of His day for breaking the law of God for the sake of human tradition (Matt. 15:3). Paul warned against making human commands, traditions, and regulations equal to the law of God (Col. 2:16-23). Indeed, much of the strife and division in the church throughout history is a result of people elevating community standard to a place of moral absolute, and then condemning anyone who refuses to comply.

We can run into trouble today anytime we draw people from other backgrounds into our church community. If we assume everyone knows the rules, we may try to enforce codes about what clothes you can wear; what food you can eat or drink; what a Christian can watch on TV, listen to on radio, or do for recreation; how to vote; what kind of school to enroll our children in; if we should raise our hands in worship or be quiet or shout "Amen!"

I knew a church in the late '60s that was affiliated with a very conservative denomination. In a bold step, the pastor allowed the youth department to begin a coffeehouse on Saturday nights. Well aware of the community standards he himself grew up with, the pastor went before his congregation and said, "Pretty soon kids are going to be coming to church who won't look like you think they should. They may be barefoot and have long hair and not wear proper attire. But I want you to accept them just as Jesus would." That pastor was recognizing that community standards can be flexible and need not be enforced as biblical absolutes. His congregation responded and a church of a few hundred people exploded into a body of over 3,000 and is still thriving. Many of those "hippie kids" are in full-time ministry today.

To illustrate this a bit further, I was on staff at a church where normal attire included a coat and tie. I decided to drop in on a new fellowship down the street that was holding meetings in what was once a fitness club. I walked in and saw Hawaiian print shirts, shorts, and jogging suits. Even the people on the platform were dressed casually! I did a U-turn back to my car, lost the coat and tie, rolled up my sleeves, and went back in and had a great time. I adjusted to a community standard rather than distracting anyone by my custom. The same rule applies when a missionary goes overseas and learns to eat food and wear clothes and sing songs that are culturally correct in that community. It is important to recognize that community standards are not necessarily wrong. They may have evolved and survived because they work for a given set of circumstances. However, what is correct for one community is not an absolute for every other community. We as leaders must be diligent to do two things:

• We need to understand the standards in the community to which we are called. This is done by watching and talking and assimilating the standards of the community, and also by researching bylaws, doctrinal statements, historic records, and asking questions of those who understand the local history. Don't feel foolish for asking, "How do we view such and such here?" A friend of mine left a church in a beach community in California to take a position as youth pastor in a church in the middle of Texas. Upon arriving, he held an informal gathering with the parents in the church. When sharing some of his ideas for reaching the youth, one parent responded from the back of the room, "That stuff may work out there in the land of fruits and nuts, but it won't work here." He probably felt like saying, "Toto, I have a feeling we're not in California anymore." We must be familiar with community standards so that we don't unknowingly offend fellow believers, and also so we can become peacemakers by helping newcomers adapt to new surroundings.

• We must be painstakingly cautious to keep community standards in proper perspective. When community standards become too important, legalism arises, resulting in bondage, and ultimately squeezing the life out of spiritual relationships. I don't promote change for the sake of change, but we need to recognize when our traditions may no longer be

166

relevant or adequate to meet the needs of a spiritually hungry world.

A little girl was helping Mom make dinner. She watched with fascination as her mother cut the small ends off the roast, then seasoned it and put it in the roasting pan. She asked, "Mommy, why did you cut the ends of the roast off?" "Well, that's the way my mother did it and I've always done it that way." When Grandma came over for dinner that evening the little girl asked, "Grandma, why do you cut the ends of the roast off before you cook it?" "Well, that's the way my mother did it and I've always done it that way." A few days later they went to visit Great-grandma and the little girl couldn't wait to ask, "Great-grandma, why do you cut the ends of the roast off before you cook it?" "Well, I don't know why everybody else does, but I only had a little roasting pan and it wouldn't fit otherwise." What was once a practical rule had long since become just a tradition and could very well be laid to rest.

I wonder if some church families wouldn't benefit by taking a close look at some of our long held traditions which once had more meaning. In *Christ the Controversialist,* Dr. John R.W. Stott says:

> First, we must distinguish more clearly between tradition and Scripture. Most of us Christian people have a set of cherished beliefs and practices, probably inherited from our parents or learned in childhood from the church. Too many of us have accepted them uncritically en bloc. And evangelical believers are by no means free of this tendency. For example, our "touch not; taste not; handle not" has often been "smoke not, drink not, dance not." I am not expressing an opinion on whether we should or should not engage in these issues. What I am saying is that Scripture contains no explicit pronouncements on them. These prohibitions belong therefore to "the traditions of the evangelical elders"; they are not part of the Word of God.[1]

Third Line of Tension: Community Standards/Personal Conviction
"So whatever you believe about these things keep between yourself and God. Blessed is the man who does not condemn himself by what he approves" (Rom. 14:22). In *Decision Making and the Will of God,* Garry Friesen lists the following as issues he has personally encountered:

attending movies
going to a psychiatrist
watching television

women wearing two-piece
  swimsuits
mixed swimming

working for pay
  on Sunday
mowing the lawn
  on Sunday
fishing on Sunday
drinking wine
  in moderation
cooking with wine
attending stage plays
participating in sports
participating in
  contact sports
eating food in the
  church building
women wearing makeup
men wearing beards
men wearing hair over
  the ears
women having short hair
speaking in tongues

playing pool
playing cards
gambling for recreation
buying insurance
smoking
dancing
women wearing pantsuits
  to church
using a Bible translation
  other than *King James*
raising tobacco
playing guitars in church
listening to rock music
unmarried couples kissing
wearing skirts above
  the knee
playing the saxophone
  in church
taking sedatives

People who read this list tend to react with laughter and incredulity. On the one hand, they chuckle at the items that are "obviously" in the area of freedom. On the other hand, they can't believe that anyone could feel free before God to do the things that are "obviously" forbidden by principles of Scripture. And yet if we asked ten different believers of various ages and backgrounds from different parts of the country to separate those activities into categories of "permissible" and "not permissible," we would likely end up with *ten different* lists.[2]

I don't know of a more challenging area for a pastor or church leader to sort out than the area of personal convictions. It is a potential problem in preaching, teaching, counseling, witnessing, and running programs. As long as there is more than one person in the room, there will be different sets of personal convictions. A friend of mine used to say, "I'm in favor of us all having one mind—as long as we use my mind." But the beauty of Paul's repeated metaphor of the church being a body is that unity doesn't mean uniformity. Because we all are born unique and grow up in our own special environments, see through different eyes, meet our Savior in precious personal encounters, and mature at individual rates, we arrive in the church community with a great multiplicity of personal convictions and preferences.

Paul spent much time teaching New Testament believers to be tolerant of one another and honor each other's convictions. "One man's faith allows him to eat everything, but another . . . only eats vegetables. One man considers one day more sacred than another; another man considers every day alike" (Rom. 14:2, 5). Most of Paul's discussion in Romans 14 and 1 Corinthians 8 and 10 has to do with people who had been converted but whose souls were shaped by past activities and relationships. A fair comparison could be made between first-century Christians eating meat which was sacrificed to idols and some Christians of today approving of Hard Rock/Contemporary Christian Music. The problem lies in the link between ungodliness and an amoral element. It was not eating that offended certain believers, but that the food had been used as a sacrifice to a false god. Likewise, singing is not what offends certain saints today, but that the instruments or perhaps the sounds they produce are also used to promote ungodly ideas by secular artists. If Paul were addressing today's controversy he might say, "We know that a rock idol is nothing at all in the world and that there is no God but one" (1 Cor. 8:4).

To the notion that Christmas is a pagan holiday and decorating trees is a form of idolatry, a pastor I know replied, "As long as I can remember we've had a Christmas tree in our house, but not once has any member of my family ever bowed down to worship it." Again Paul might say, "Do not let anyone judge you by what you eat or drink, or with regard to a religious festival or New Moon celebration or a Sabbath day" — or Christmas or other holidays. He who regards one day as special, does so to the Lord (see Col. 2:16; Rom. 14:6).

One of the remarkable ironies about judging is that we insist on our own freedom where God has granted it, and then we turn around and rob others of their God-given freedom. A lady once shared with me how God had set her and her children free to go to movies, even though her husband refused to accompany her because of his upbringing. But before the conversation was over, she was criticizing the "worldly" style of the youth ensemble.

Remarking about a poster of a Christian band, a friend of mine asked, "Why do these guys always imitate the world?" I looked at him and responded, "Do you imitate the world of Wall Street with your three-piece suit?" We must each keep our own freedoms and restrictions and allow others to do the same. But at the same time, we must keep personal freedoms in line with community standards. For instance, I don't have the freedom to show up Sunday morning in tights with my Walkman and start doing aerobics during worship service.

I suggest that many of today's issues between fellow Christians can be resolved by using Paul's simple formula which balances on two basic platforms:

- The person without freedom is not to judge the one with freedom.
- The person with freedom is not to offend the one without.

Personal convictions cannot be made equal to community standards. It is simple, yet we miss it so easily so often.

Now please don't confuse Paul's teaching with the situational ethics prescribed in the popular poster of the Love Generation: "You do your thing and I do mine . . . I'm not here to live up to your expectations. . . ." God has called us to a far more radical concept. The church is to strive together as we each set aside our own rights, die to ourselves, and become servants of others. "We who are strong ought to bear with the failings of the weak and not to please ourselves. Each of us should please his neighbor for his good, to build him up. For even Christ did not please Himself. . . . When you sin against your brothers in this way and wound their weak conscience, you sin against Christ. . . . For none of us lives to himself alone" (Rom. 15:1-3; 1 Cor. 8:12; Rom. 14:7).

By God's design, the body of Christ is a complex organism comprised of many widely varied components, each unique from the others but vital to the whole; none is insignificant or expendable. "Let us therefore make every effort to do what leads to peace and to mutual edification" (Rom. 14:19).

Drawing the Line and Setting Guidelines

- I must keep my own personal convictions to myself.
- I must not judge others who do not share my convictions.
- I must not flaunt my freedom if I don't share their convictions.
- I must allow community standards to take precedence over my personal preferences.
- Community standards are not to violate biblical absolutes.
- Community standards are not to become equal to biblical absolutes.
- Biblical absolutes are always to be obeyed.
- All things are to be done in love.

If we as leaders embrace these guidelines and live by them, if we teach them to our single adults, if we counsel our people with them, and handle individual situations that arise by sorting out what is love—biblical absolute — community standard — personal conviction, we will effectively negotiate the gray areas and promote godly liberty among believers. Jesus said, "If you hold to My teaching, you are really My disciples. Then you will know the truth, and the truth will set you free" (John 8:31-32). I trust this teaching will bring freedom to many.

The following rules can serve as a checklist for gray areas. If you need to sort out some issue that is not clearly defined as a "thou shalt" or "thou shalt not," run it through this checklist. If you pass all ten with a yes answer to each question, you may proceed with freedom and confidence.

1. Is my motive unselfish? 1 Corinthians 10:24, 33; Romans 13:10; 15:1; Matthew 7:12; 1 Corinthians 13:4-7

Am I keeping the law of love? Love means choosing the highest good of others — unselfishly, unconditionally — no strings attached.

2. Is there a biblical absolute that applies? 1 Corinthians 10:23; 2 Timothy 3:16-17; John 8:31-32

Have I checked the Scriptures to see what they say? Am I being consistent with the truths revealed in the written Word of God?

3. Does this action edify the body? 1 Corinthians 10:23; Romans 15:2; 1 Corinthians 8:13; Romans 14:21

Will it fit within community standards? Will it build up or tear down? Will it cause peace or will it cause strife? Can I do it without causing someone to stumble?

4. Can I do it with faith? Romans 14:22-23; James 1:6; 1 John 3:21; Romans 14:5

Will I honor my convictions and keep a clean conscience? Or do I have doubts about it which I can't answer? When in doubt, don't. Don't be double-minded; wait until you're sure.

5. Can I thank God for it? 1 Corinthians 10:30; 1 Timothy 4:4; Romans 14:6; Colossians 3:17; 1 Thessalonians 5:18

Is it possible this is a gift from my Heavenly Father? Would He be pleased to·receive credit for this? Is it likely to find its source in God?

6. Does it glorify God? 1 Corinthians 10:31; Romans 15:7

Who will get the praise for this? Does it represent God as He is? Will any of His attributes be made known? Will it make others want to serve Him?

7. Does it imitate Christ? 1 Corinthians 11:1; Romans 15:7; 1 John 2:6

Will it produce Christlikeness? Would Jesus do it? Better yet, would I do it if Jesus were with me? Would I be embarrassed to be found out as a Christian while doing it?

8. Have I prayed about it? James 1:5; Philippians 4:6-7

If I haven't prayed, why not pray right now? "You have not because you ask not." Could it possibly be an answer to a previous prayer?

9. Do I have peace about it? Colossians 3:15; 1 Corinthians 14:33; 2 Corinthians 2:13; Philippians 4:7

Can I still hear the still small voice? Or am I in conflict and confusion? Does the thought of it leave me calm or does it produce anxiety? Do I trust God about it? Or am I trusting my own inclinations?

10. Am I following the Spirit? Romans 8:1-14; Galatians 5:16-25

Will it draw me closer to God or drive me further from Him?
Will it enlarge His kingdom or mine?
Will it satisfy the Spirit or gratify the flesh?
What kind of fruit or works will it produce?

Will it produce	life	or	death?
	freedom	or	bondage?
	righteousness	or	condemnation?
	pride	or	humility?
	blessing	or	cursing?

"The fruit of the Spirit is love, joy, peace, patience, kindness, goodness, faithfulness, gentleness, self-control; against such there is no law" (Gal. 5:22-23).

The Need for Grace

Even the most scrupulous system of determining right from wrong in gray areas is bound to have some imperfection. First, our Creator God is omniscient; we are created and finite. Second, only God is perfect; we are fallen. Third, no two fallen finite people are perfectly identical; each of us has a unique perspective. We fail to sail perfectly even through black and white areas. Why should we expect ourselves and others to navigate the gray areas without error? Now before anyone accuses me of "antinomianism," let me echo John's cry, "My dear children, I write this to you so that you will not sin. But if anybody does sin, we have one who speaks to the Father in our defense—Jesus Christ the Righteous One. He is the atoning sacrifice for our sins, and not only for ours but also for the sins of the whole world" (1 John 2:1-2).

Because of our own guilty consciences and the accusations of the adversary, it is hard at times to securely appropriate God's grace and assurance of forgiveness. Sometimes it's even harder to find grace and mercy from fellow believers. It grieves me to hear someone say, "The church is the only army that shoots its wounded." The only people Jesus could not tolerate were the intolerant.

In sorting out gray areas, be gracious, even if people don't espouse the principles you embrace. Be gracious if they agree but still fail to apply them perfectly. Be gracious because you yourself aren't always right. My pastor used to frequently remind our church, "You are never more like God than when you forgive."

The following verses remind us of our need to receive and to give grace.

• "I do not set aside the grace of God, for if righteousness could be gained through the law, Christ died for nothing" (Gal. 2:21).

• "For it is by grace you have been saved" (Eph. 2:8).

• "Blessed be to the ... Father of compassion and the God of all comfort, who comforts us in all our troubles, so that we can comfort those in any trouble with the comfort we ourselves have received from God" (2 Cor. 1:3-4).

• "Therefore, since through God's mercy we have this ministry, we do not lose heart" (2 Cor. 4:1).

• "Forgiving each other, just as in Christ God forgave you" (Eph. 4:32).

- "Forgive us our debts, as we also have forgiven our debtors" (Matt. 6:12).
- "For if you forgive men when they sin against you, your Heavenly Father will also forgive you" (Matt. 6:14).
- "I tell you, not seven times, but seventy times seven" (Matt. 18:22).
- "If any one of you is without sin, let him be the first to cast a stone at her" (John 8:7).
- "Judgment without mercy will be shown to anyone who has not been merciful. Mercy triumphs over judgment!" (James 2:13)
- "Love covers over a multitude of sins" (1 Peter 4:8).
- "Where sin increased, grace increased all the more" (Rom. 5:20).
- "Let us then approach the throne of grace with confidence, so that we may receive mercy and find grace to help us in our time of need" (Heb. 4:16).
- "He gives us more grace. . . . God opposes the proud but gives grace to the humble" (James 4:6).
- He said to me, "My grace is sufficient for you" (2 Cor. 12:9).

Jesus Is Still the Answer

As a minister to single adults, I look at the needs of our society and remember that "The fields are white unto harvest." But we will never reach a world of lost single adults with an outdated, irrelevant, insensitive, illogical, narrow-minded, uninspired, impractical representation of the Gospel. Twenty years ago we needed to satisfy an intellectually hungry world, so we brushed up on apologetics, creation science, and epistemology in order to feed them. Now we have a generation wrestling with AIDS, abortion, euthanasia, child abuse, addictions, and scandals. This time it's moral hunger. Case in point—Josh McDowell went from *Evidence That Demands a Verdict* to *Why Wait?* Just as we need to give sound answers about the validity of the Scriptures and the claims of Christ, so we need to help a puzzled people discern what is truly right and wrong, and then learn to live accordingly. Ultimately, the answer to the intellectual debates comes down to this: "Is Jesus really who He and His followers claimed He is?" The bottom line to the search for moral guidance is, "Can the teaching and example left by Jesus and His followers work today?" The answer to both questions remains a resounding **YES!** The singles ministry equipped to satisfy this hunger will reap a great harvest. Giving single adults clear answers to gray areas is a responsibility we cannot avoid. Let us commission ourselves and our people to honor personal convictions, recognize community standards, obey biblical absolutes, do everything in love, and be as merciful to each other as God has been to us.

Jim Berrier, Minister with Single Adults
Trinity Church
8750 Four Winds Drive
San Antonio, Texas 78239

Notes

1. John R.W. Stott, *Christ the Controversialist* (Downers Grove, Illinois: InterVarsity Press, 1970), 86.
2. Gary Friesen, *Decision Making and the Will of God* (Portland: Multnomah Press, 1970), 382.

15. DEALING WITH
DATING REALITIES

"Christian dating should have one primary pur-
pose — to glorify God. That is the first and best pur-
pose of all Christians. Dating does not glorify God if
it leads to sexual immorality or to treating others in
ways that are unkind, unloving, and inconsiderate
of the other's good."

Michael Platter

The dating scene has changed considerably in recent years, and the growth of the single adult population in the United States ensures that these changes are going to last a while. Dating is no longer just "kid's stuff" for teenagers experiencing puppy love, prom dances, and pimples. Now millions of widowed, divorced, and never-married adults have entered the arena, bringing with them a whole new set of concerns about dating: ethics, sexuality, and for some, Christian responsibility.

I suspect that many singles would love to close their eyes and wish the whole dating scene away, since it is an issue causing considerable anxiety. But it really cannot be avoided. Our society has for years encouraged the dating process as the *proper* way for an unmarried person to find a mate. This alone makes it a weighty issue. And, as if that isn't heavy enough, our peers have also piled on additional "baggage" by suggesting that one's dating life is a gauge of social desirability, physical attractiveness, and sometimes even of sexual prowess or preference. Given all of these pressures on a single person, the need for good teaching on the subject is clear. Although the realities of single adult dating are complicated, the valid concerns surrounding this issue are opportunities for growth and maturity, both for individuals and for single adult ministry.

What are our responsibilities as leaders when it comes to dealing with dating? Let's look at two areas which should be addressed in order to meet this issue appropriately. The first focuses on the type of teaching which can help single adults grapple with important questions. The second deals with how the single adult ministry group can best serve, in the light of the issues surrounding dating.

Scriptural Background for Dating

When it comes to proclaiming the Bible's teachings on the subject of dating, at first appearance it may seem that we have very little to work with. The Bible does not speak about dating, per se, because the different societies in existence at that time did not use "dating" as a method of selecting marriage partners. Prearranged marriages, multiple wives, payment for brides, etc., were common practices in Bible times. These prevailing courtship rites left no room for "Love, American-style."

However, the Bible does say a great deal about male-female relationships, and about Christian relationships in general. As we look to scriptural teaching in these areas, we can apply it to dating.

Let's take a look at some of the Apostle Paul's teaching regarding singleness, and also his concern for proper Christian conduct with the opposite sex:

> But I say to the unmarried and to widows that it is good for them if they remain even as I [unmarried]. But if they do not have self-control, let them marry; for it is better to marry than to burn. . . . Only, as the Lord has assigned to each one, as God has called each, in this manner let him walk. . . . Let each man remain in that condition in which he was called. . . .
>
> Now concerning virgins I have no command of the Lord, but I give an opinion as one who by the mercy of the Lord is trustworthy. I think then that this is good in view of the present distress, that it is good for a man to remain as he is. Are you bound to a wife? Do not seek to be released. Are you released from a wife? Do not seek a wife. But if you should marry, you have not sinned, and if a virgin should marry, she has not sinned. . . .
>
> I want you to be free from concern. One who is unmarried is concerned about the things of the Lord, how he may please the Lord. . . . And the woman who is unmarried, and the virgin, is concerned about the things of the Lord, that she may be holy both in body and spirit; but one who is married is concerned about the things of the world, how she may please her husband. And this I say for your own benefit; not to put a restraint upon you, but to promote what is seemly, and to secure undistracted

178

devotion to the Lord (1 Cor. 7:8-9, 17, 20, 25-28, 32, 34-35, NASB).

These selected passages from Paul's letter to the church at Corinth suggest some important starting points for a discussion of dating. First, Paul wants to reemphasize to his readers that it is all right to marry. He wants them to understand that the decision to remain single, in order to give more time and energy to Christ's work (as he himself was doing), is also perfectly valid. It is even the *preferred* choice if it is God's particular calling for an individual. But marriage still honors Christ, Paul says, and is a calling blessed by God.

• Perhaps it goes without saying, but this passage reminds me that if it is all right to marry, it must be all right to date as well. Some singles might feel that dating would threaten their relationship to God, and that they may be compromising on their "undivided devotion" to Christ if they start dating. But Paul is saying here that it is fine to pursue marriage. In our culture, dating is the way to do that. Singles should be reminded that though God may have called them to singleness now, it may not be His permanent calling for them. Those who want to date should feel free to do so, unless God definitely tells them no.

• In other parts of this passage (vv. 10-14, 39), Paul sends a second message about a Christian's relationship with the opposite sex: *God's will is that Christians marry Christians.* Paul's approach to dating and marriage is that the Christian is to be motivated by what will honor Christ the most. Since marriage to a non-Christian is unscriptural, dating a non-Christian is certainly a risky activity. We cannot use this text to definitely say that it is sin to date a non-Christian, but certainly there must be caution against allowing a relationship with a nonbeliever to progress toward deep love and commitment.

Another aspect of dating which arises from this passage is contained in the Scriptures directly preceding Paul's discourse in chapter 7. It is important to read because it sets the stage for Paul's teaching on Christian behavior between males and females.

Do you not know that your bodies are members of Christ? Shall I then take away the members of Christ and make them members of a harlot? May it never be! . . . Flee immorality. Every other sin that a man commits is outside the body, but the immoral man sins against his own body. Or do you not know that your body is a temple of the Holy Spirit who is in you, whom you have from

God, and that you are not your own? For you have been bought with a price; therefore glorify God in your body (1 Cor. 6:15, 18-20, NASB).

● Paul's third message is that sexual intimacy outside of marriage is a violation of God's law. This is one of the most critical concerns which single adult ministry must address. We live in a culture which has decided to cast aside God's laws regarding sexual purity, and Christian single adults are frequently tempted to buy into the values of their secular peers. But the Bible is clear on the issue: *sex outside of marriage is clearly a sin against God.*

Many single adults struggle with sexual issues in their dating lives. Not only are there strong, natural sexual desires which are encountered in close dating relationships, but these desires are sometimes more complicated when past sexual practices come into play. For example, those who were formerly married were accustomed to being able to pursue their sexual desires with their spouses. But following widowhood or divorce, these newly single people must now learn to restrain their sexuality during affectionate moments as experienced in dating. Yet, regardless of the sexual attraction during dating, the Christian stand is clear: God says no to sex before marriage.

Part of an approach to dealing with the issues of sex and dating should be an explanation of God's *positive* design for sexuality, as well as His restrictions. Scripture clearly shows that God plans for sex to be enjoyable and fulfilling (Song of Solomon 7:6–8:3). Since God created our bodies and their particular sexual functioning, He knows the conditions in which our sexual lives will be safest and most satisfying. Therefore, the rules which He has set forth in the Bible should not be viewed as attempts to stifle our sexual pleasure, but as explanations of the conditions in which sex is most fulfilling. He is the Master Designer; it is in our best interest to follow the "manufacturer's instructions." Those instructions tell us that sex outside of marriage is unsafe; it leaves people vulnerable to the increasing plagues of sexually transmitted diseases, and to the psychological and sociological pains of unwanted pregnancies, abortions, sexual dysfunction due to guilt, etc. Add to these effects some of the other social griefs in our culture related to rampant sexuality; child molestation at astronomical rates, widespread pornography, increases in homosexual and bisexual influences, date rape and work-related sexual harassment, the AIDS epidemic, and numerous other sexual problems.

Single adults need to know that God has created sexuality as a powerful force for personal pleasure and joy. But like any powerful force, the sexual urge must first be contained and then channeled in order to be useful. In this way it is like a river, a source of great power and productivity as long as it stays within its banks. But when it overflows the boundaries intended for it, floods cause widespread damage and destruction.

The bottom line for the Christian is that sexual intimacy is not to be part of the dating life of any single adult. Some of the factors in attaining the sexual self-control will be dealt with in the next section.

Beyond the Apostle Paul's three teachings mentioned above, other passages shed light on the Bible's expectations of Christian dating. Let's look at a few more verses from the New Testament:

> Let no one seek his own good, but that of his neighbor.... Whether, then, you eat or drink or whatever you do, do all to the glory of God. Give no offense either to Jews or to Greeks or to the church of God (1 Cor. 10:24, 31-32, NASB).

> For you were called to freedom, brethren; only do not turn your freedom into an opportunity for the flesh, but through love serve one another.... You shall love your neighbor as yourself (Gal. 5:13-14, NASB).

> And so, as those who have been chosen of God, holy and beloved, put on a heart of compassion, kindness, humility, gentleness and patience; bearing with one another, and forgiving each other, whoever has a complaint against any one; just as the Lord forgave you, so also should you.... Do all in the name of the Lord Jesus, giving thanks through Him to God the Father (Col. 3:12-13, 17, NASB).

Scripture places a priority on Christians showing kindness and love to Christian brothers and sisters, seeking the good of others before one's own good, and ultimately doing everything to God's glory. It's a tall order to fill, but God's grace is available to help us to live Christlike lives— even in dating.

Christian dating should have one primary purpose—*to glorify God.* That is the first and best purpose of all Christians. Dating does not glorify God if it leads to sexual immorality or to treating others in ways that are unkind, unloving, and inconsiderate of the other's good. This is not an easy task in dating, since emotions and attractions have a way of becoming intense and easily injured when men and women become close. Still, it is a worthy motivation to date in a way that truly honors our Heavenly Father.

Dating Which Glorifies God

Let me suggest a few ideas you may wish to pass along to those in your ministry to help them see dating as a way to glorify God and also to keep Christian kindness at the forefront of a relationship.

• Keep your date's interests and happiness at heart. The person you have chosen to date is someone God wants to be happy, to grow, and to be a well-rounded individual. Try to do the things which your date is likely to enjoy. Go to places and do activities which are positive and uplifting, and which you will both enjoy. Keep in mind that caring for another person's happiness involves more than just entertainment. It also includes contributing to his/her personal growth and to your own as well. Your date's growth can occur mentally, physically, socially, emotionally, spiritually.

Try some of the following activities which can keep dating interesting, full of variety, and growth-producing: visit an art museum, take a picnic in a state park and walk on a guided trail, play tennis, badminton, or racquetball, go to sports activities, watch "classic" movies on video, try a variety of regional restaurants and sample international dishes, attend a concert, go to a mall and visit shops you've not tried before, take a community education class together, go to a play, try cooking a new dish, etc., etc., etc.

• Don't expect your dating relationships to bring "Mr. or Ms. Right" your way. Some single adults mistakenly believe that if they wait long enough and look hard enough, the perfect person will magically appear. The sad thing about this view is that many singles forget to make productive use of this waiting time. Since our goal is to live to God's glory, we should be focusing on growth, whether we are in a relationship or not. One of the best quotes I ever heard at a single adult conference was this: "Stop waiting for Ms. Right and start concentrating on being Mr. Right!" And vice versa.

• Remember to "handle with care." One of the frightening aspects of dating is the possibility of a painful breakup. Since only one dating relationship will lead to marriage, most single adults have experienced one or more relationship breakups. As a Christian you are to care about your partner's feelings as much as you do your own. This means that you avoid making promises concerning commitments you don't intend to fulfill. Attempt to "break up" kindly, with no personal attacks and without undue criticism or gossip. Be cautious about claiming affection which you don't truly feel. Leading someone on leads to more pain in the long run than the painful truth at an earlier stage of the relationship.

• Handle sexual issues responsibly. Probably the most complicated aspect of dating falls under this category. The issue of sexual purity has already been discussed, but let me add some specific guidelines which have been helpful in establishing sexual control in dating:

1. Establish your sexual standards before you face the temptations of dating. Short of sexual intercourse, the Bible is not specific about where to "draw the line" in showing physical affection between males and females. But the general teaching of Scripture is clear — you are not to become sexually intimate before marriage. In fact, you are even told to restrain lustful thoughts in your heart and mind (Matt. 5:27-30). Since you are not to be sexually impure nor engage in lust, you have a responsibility to avoid subjecting your date to undue sexual temptation. You know where your personal "line" is when it comes to lustful thoughts and strong sexual desires. If you sense that your partner is coming close to his/her boundaries sexually, you have a responsibility to cool things down. These issues are not easy, but it is your goal to glorify God, and to help your Christian brothers and sisters to do the same. Know your limits, your strengths and your weaknesses. Talk about your sexuality with another person in an "accountability" situation, if this would help your self-control. Pray about your desire to honor God by not misusing or abusing His gift of sexuality.

Whatever you do, don't make the mistake of determining your sexual standards while in the passion of an intense romantic evening. And don't play the How-close-to-the-edge-can-I-get-without-going-over game. You are more likely to fail if you don't *prepare* to succeed in your sexual life.

2. Plan your dates to focus on other things than unrestricted intimacy. I remember the classic pun about a young man who asked a girl out by saying, "Hey, tonight let's go to a movie or something." Her reply was, "We'll go to a movie or nothing!" There is a nugget of wisdom in her answer. When there is no plan for the date, it is very easy for a couple to just spend time "making out" and struggling with sexual control. Some couples go through this weekend after weekend. They could avoid some of the intense temptation if they would carefully plan their dates for enjoyable social activities and leave less time for physical temptation. Certainly couples should still plan time for romance and affection,

but they should make sure that their dates include plenty of time for other activities which bring them together intellectually, emotionally, etc., rather than just physically. Because the experience of physical affection is so satisfying, it is often easy to let it take the place of conversation, discussion of values, relationship issues, etc. But this can be dangerous in the future — the enduring foundation of a good relationship is in the friendship, not in the sexual intensity.

3. Keep in mind who your date is. As a single person who has had to deal with these dating issues myself, I have found great strength in always recalling who it is I'm dating. I remind myself that I'm going out with a daughter of God. As a teenager, I remember how frightening it was to meet the fathers of the girls I wanted to date. I remember the fear I felt of what these men might do if I ever mistreated or hurt their daughters. I think it's wise for Christians to remember that whoever they are dating, that person is a son or daughter of God, and He is committed to the sexual purity and wholeness of His children. I would not want to incur His disappointment by mistreating a child of His for whom He has paid such a great price.

A Single Adult Ministry Response to Dating Issues
Since the issues involved in dating have implications for individuals as well as for Single Adult Ministries, I want to briefly address a few points which may need to be considered.

● Deal squarely with issues in Christian dating. Most single adults have a high interest in this issue. Take some time in your plan of activities to talk about dating ethics, dating problems, sexuality, etc. You may wish to have a speaker do a dating seminar, or you might read some good material on the issues and prepare your own seminar. Try tossing out some of the tough issues and questions to discussion circles or Talk-It-Over groups. Don't worry about not having all the answers; the issues are too broad and complicated for any leader to have complete answers; just deal with the questions.

● Concentrate on affirming your singles. Unfortunately, in the American culture, dating has been pictured as a game of the Have's versus the Have-Not's. Often women who are asked out on dates are seen as physically attractive and socially adept; women who seldom or never date are assumed to be undesirable physically or socially. The dating process and the values attached to it can often be cruel to those who are not dating much. Since our culture permits men greater social freedom in initiating dates, many women feel at the mercy of an unfair process, and may also feel self-conscious or bitter. A man who does not date may be the object of silent concern as to his sexual orientation, or be regarded as one who has never broken free of his attachments to his mother.

On the other hand, those who do date frequently may be seen as proud, easy, lacking in spiritual depth, or as having loose morals. Because our society has attached such "desirability" issues to the dating process, the fallout of hurt feelings or judgmental attitudes can be hurtful.

Be sure to affirm the worth and desirability of each single adult through positive messages of self-worth. Let them know that you and the group accept them, believe in them, love and value them because they are created in God's image and are worthwhile, no matter how the "dating scene" goes.

● Watch for wolves in the fold. In 1 Peter 5:2 we read, "Shepherd the flock of God among you, not under compulsion, but voluntarily, according to the will of God." Later in that chapter Peter reminds us that Satan prowls about like a roaring lion, seeking to devour the ones you have been called upon to protect (v. 8). One of the rough tasks of church leadership is caring for the weak and powerless among the flock of God, for Satan truly will try to hurt and injure them.

I find that in single adult groups there are a great number of people who have been hurt by painful relationships and broken commitments. I'm convinced that God dearly loves all His sheep, and is especially concerned that these hurt lambs of His be in a safe place where they can find healing. You want that place to be your single adult ministry. As shepherd to these hurting sheep, guard against things that could expose them to hurt again; and particularly guard against those "wolves" who are looking for easy prey. Most likely, they will enter your group dressed as sheep, and it may take you a while to recognize them. And you must be cautious against judging — even wolves may need a safe place to heal. Your goal is not to judge but to protect the weak and hurting.

Decide some policies in advance to help you guard your flock. For example, you may decide that your ministry will not have activities where "pairing off" is required (such as a formal sweetheart banquet). You will definitely need to consider a policy regarding keeping phone numbers and addresses confidential. For example, our group recently switched to listing only first names on name tags, in order to better protect women from unwanted phone calls from strangers.

● Decide what your group emphasis will be. What do you feel God is calling your single adult group to be? Do you believe that you are to be a social network for Christian singles? Do you sense that God is particularly leading your group to focus on nonchurched single moms? Have you felt that your group is supposed to be primarily a Bible study and keep a strong spiritual emphasis?

I'm convinced that God has a unique ministry for you and your group. I also believe that no *one* group is capable of ministering to the vast needs of singles in a large area—that it takes several groups fulfilling different roles to present a well-rounded ministry to a community. Find your specific calling, and do your best to meet the needs which seem to be God's direction for you. You may feel that God does not wish for your group to emphasize finding a mate, but instead to focus on plugging single adults into church ministry. And yet there are some single adult ministries who feel that God's leading is for them to help single adults pair off and find a possible romance. Both fulfill needs which Christian single adults have. Find your niche and fill it, and it will help to define ministry growth and spiritual growth.

● Encourage your singles to build friendships. Dating relationships come and go—often they seem to mostly go. And although dating holds some great possibilities for both individual and group growth, it is wise to encourage single adults to concentrate on forming good friendships. Friendship is much more stable in a person's life than romantic attraction. It is important that single adults are grounded in the love and commitment of friends, for friends tend to stand by through the easy and the difficult times, but dates often do not have such long-term commitment. Besides, the friendship bond is the basis of all good relationships; so if single adults constantly work on their friendship ability, those skills will eventually be helpful in relationship-building with a potential date— or mate.

Michael Platter, Minister with Single Adults
Springdale Church of the Nazarene
#3 Woodstock Drive
Fairfield, Ohio 45014

16. DEALING WITH HOMOSEXUALITY

"Any person being considered for a volunteer position has the right to know what will be expected. In addition to an outline of responsibilities in the job descriptions, you can prepare a brochure which states the behavioral expectations for leadership. This should not be limited, of course, to issues of sexuality, but should emphasize the importance of a Christian leader accepting the privileges and responsibilities of his/her work.

Warren Risch

For a change, everything seems to be running along smoothly in your single adult ministry. The volunteer leadership seems to be largely dedicated, enthusiastic, and effective in their respective areas of responsibility. An increasing number of single adults are becoming involved in the spiritual growth groups and Bible studies. The size of the ministry is also expanding. "Finally," you think to yourself, "the single adult ministry is truly coming into its own. This is really gratifying!"

Your moments of satisfied reflection are interrupted by the telephone. The caller, a member of the church, wants you to know that one of your single adult leaders has told a mutual friend that he has been a closet gay, but he now is preparing to openly declare himself as homosexual. "I thought you needed to know," says the caller. "We don't want this sort of problem at our church."

You thank the caller for the information and the phone call concludes. So much for the brief respite of tranquility in your singles ministry program. But this call will be less unsettling if you have taken the steps necessary to address this kind of issue before it becomes a problem. Unfortunately, as most of us have long since discovered, policies are usually developed after the fact and not in anticipation of a problem.

Your single adult ministry's position on homosexuality and heterosexuality will be reflective of the stand taken by your church and denomination. Many programs avoid having to directly face such moral issues by requiring anyone in a leadership position to also be a member of the church. Leaders are informed that they are expected to be faithful to the moral positions taken by the church. Should they find themselves in conflict with the church's stance, they would be expected in good conscience to step down from leadership. This, of course, does not mean that such an individual could not continue to be a member of either the church or the single adult ministry. (This position represents a majority of the churches.)

The real strength of requiring leadership to hold membership in the sponsoring church is that discipline issues will be consistent with established policy. If a problem should arise, it is to be expected that it will be dealt with in a manner that would not be different from any other program the church conducts. There should be no discrimination as to what is required of any church member, regardless of the church area represented. It is important to underscore this principle, because single adult ministry will frequently come under closer scrutiny than other programs. Leadership privilege, responsibility, and accountability should never be more or less for any group in the church. Occasionally, the governance of the church may need to be reminded of this truth.

Churches and single adult ministry groups that take the position of "leadership requires church membership" should have a clear procedure for dealing with violations of spiritual and moral positions. It would be well, however, to clarify with church leadership the expectations held by the body. These standards should be clearly understandable and not worded in a vague generality such as "good Christian character." You need to define what the standard means related to your church and denomination. The sexual expectations of behavior for married and single adults should be clear. Some churches miss the boat entirely in this regard by focusing all their concern about sexuality on the singles. The nature of the married relationship also needs emphasis.

In addition to a clearly understood position for church leadership, there should also be a procedure for addressing violations of such expectations. Once again you will want to make certain that such steps are well defined and understood by all parties concerned.

If and when such a process is used by your church, all proceedings should be carefully followed and documented. It is advisable to have legal counsel familiar with the process for dealing with leadership problems. A lawyer will certainly encourage you to document disciplinary and corrective steps that you may have cause to implement. This is not to suggest that legal counsel is necessary for actions related to violation of leadership requirements, but rather to review the process itself and be sure it is followed faithfully. We live in an age of litigation. Churches are increasingly targeted for suits related to alleged wrongdoing against church members. Clear leadership expectations, a well-defined and established process and careful documentation are necessary for fairness in church practice as well as to guard against unnecessary legal activity.

When Leaders Are Not Church Members

Not all single adult ministries will require that their leadership must also be members of the sponsoring church. When this is the case, it is usually based on two factors. First, the ministry is perceived as an outreach effort and not all the people involved in the program are necessarily at a personal place where they are able to make such a decision. Also, some may have a primary church home and may be using the singles ministry as an additional part of their spiritual life. Second, you will restrict your leadership pool if you require membership in your church as a necessary criteria. Many single adult leaders will argue that their programs consistently bring new members into the church. In the meantime it is not a good practice to waste leadership potential either because they are not ready to make such a commitment or because they are already members of other community churches.

In the event that your single adult ministry does not prohibit leadership from outside of the rank and file membership of the church, you will need to pay close attention to letting your volunteers know what is expected of them. You cannot take it for granted that your church's position will be reflected in a single adult's past religious experience or be held by other community churches.

A basic place to start this clarification is with your leadership board or committee. It should be clearly stated that the host or sponsoring church has expectations of what is required of Christian leaders. It is simply not realistic to assume that the singles ministry can disregard these beliefs and practices. Your single adult leaders will understand that this is a realistic expectation. Nevertheless, it is necesssary to clarify this relationship in order to avoid future misunderstanding. Incidentally, general minutes of your leadership council or committee should be documented and filed. This will be of great assistance should there be a need to restate the previous understanding.

In the period of time that you are initially clarifying the relationship of the single adult ministry with the church, it is advisable to have the senior pastor or a knowledgeable elder involved. This will accentuate the lines of communication and emphasize the nature of the working relationship.

The difficulty encountered by some churches is that their expectations for moral behavior as example are assumed rather than stated. "After all, everyone knows what the Bible teaches and we believe," some may say. It is not realistic to attempt to codify behavior to the extreme. On the other hand, it is equally unwise to make an assumption that everyone knows what the church believes. Your single adult ministry may play a significant role in helping the church leadership be clear about its beliefs for moral conduct for all members in positions of responsibility.

At this point it is necessary to mention that there are differing positions held by churches regarding homosexuality and heterosexuality. Some churches will maintain that based on scriptural teachings, all homosexuality is a sin. Other churches would argue that if a person admits to being homosexual but works to practice celibacy, he or she should not be denied access to leadership. Such churches would go on to argue that nonmarried adults, be they homosexual or heterosexual, should practice celibacy. Since they would not discriminate against a celibate heterosexual person, they feel it is equally unfair to do so with someone who confesses a wrongful condition and commits to remaining celibate. Still other churches, while agreeing with the second position, might carry it one step further and ask the individual to commit to a recovering homosexual support group such as *Exodus International* or *Where Grace Abounds.* The rationale for such a requirement is based on the belief that the practice of homosexuality is essentially a maladaptive sexual behavior. As such it would be seen as addictive and requiring a support program similar to Alcoholics Anonymous or other recovery programs for compulsive behaviors.

The important point in all of the preceding considerations is the necessity of being consistent with the position held by your church. This is crucial when your leadership requirements do not necessitate membership in your church.

Behavioral Expectations for Leaders
With the foundation for addressing any potential disagreement over the position of either homosexual or heterosexual activity well established by your leadership board or committee, you are prepared for your next step.

190

Any person being considered for a volunteer position has the right to know what will be expected. Some single adult groups have volunteer job descriptions that give a clear outline of what the individual will have to do in a given position. Also included may be special abilities or spiritual gifts appropriate for this volunteer position.

In addition to an outline of responsibilities in the job descriptions, you can prepare a brochure which states the behavioral expectations for leadership. This should not be limited, of course, to issues of sexuality, but should emphasize the importance of a Christian leader accepting the privileges and responsibilities of his/her work. The brochure needs to be direct and clearly stated. It should also indicate that there is an established procedure for adjudicating conflicts which may arise, should an individual disregard the standards set forth by the church and the single adult group. This process should not be spelled out in the brochure. It is sufficient for leaders to know that the church has taken its convictions seriously and has planned accordingly. This knowledge in itself will be extremely helpful to single adults considering leadership. They will be clear about what the church believes and what it calls upon its leaders to practice. That along with the understanding that a process for leaving and reviewing possible problems will allow honest and sincere persons to elect not to serve, should they be in conflict with the beliefs set forth. An individual who is not forthright with himself or herself will be fully aware of the probable eventual consequences of such a decision.

Some individuals may want to challenge the standards set forth by the church in its requirements for leadership. Rarely would such persons simply try to become leaders. They would instead, perhaps with several others, raise a strong objection to the "outdated and discriminatory" positions represented by the existing leadership requirements.

Do not allow yourself to become reactive or polarized in the face of such a challenge. You should underscore that these are the beliefs held by the church and the single adult ministry regarding requirements for leadership. All people are allowed to worship and participate in your activities (in the event that this is not true for your church, it is best to be clear about this immediately, but to hold leadership requires a different commitment.

Many single adult groups make a provision for a "leadership training" evening or day, in order to familiarize volunteers with program goals for the year, lines of communication and accountability, and other areas which will help people be more effective in their respective areas. This is also an excellent time to briefly reexamine the privileges and responsibilities of leadership. Once again, as in the case of the brochure, you are giving people the opportunity to choose not to serve if they should find themselves in conflict with the leadership requirements.

You expect specific behaviors for both homosexual and heterosexual regarding leadership qualifications. It is indeed fortunate if your church supports recovery groups such as *Where Grace Abounds* and *Exodus International.* Emphasize your dedication to helping people who are open to change through these groups. Be clear that you are concerned for helping reclaim life, not merely stating convictions. Perhaps you are also fortunate enough to be involved in some sort of mission assistance to people afflicted with HIV. You should also emphasize your concern for this area of need.

The single adult ministry and church that clearly communicates their expectations for leadership will weather any confronting homosexual (and heterosexual) behavior with only mild duress. The church and singles group that has not done its homework and implemented its policies will indeed be in for rough seas.

Each single adult ministry should evaluate its preparedness for managing the issues which have been raised in facing homosexuality and leadership in singles ministry. (See the next section of this chapter.) You may need to start at the beginning with clarifying the position held by your church. Remember the position needs to be clear and applicable. If you have this element in place, make certain that the process for review and decision-making is well defined and understood by the singles leadership body as well as by your church.

Given that you have done these things, you will want to provide ample opportunity for leadership candidates to know what the church believes and how it manages accountability. Once again, this should be emphasized in your leaders' orientation.

The single adult ministry or church that has done these things will still have a heavy heart in response to the conversation which introduced this chapter. Nevertheless, there will be a clear plan of action meant to address such a problem. Any actions taken should be done in the Spirit of the Lord, in accordance with the authority of the Bible, and with the intention of helping to reclaim the person caught in a homosexual dilemma.

What If There Is a Public Homosexual Demonstration?
In the event that your church is confronted, or perhaps more realistically targeted, by a militant homosexual individual or group, you should imme-

diately notify your pastor and the chairman of the board of this development. Such groups will go to great extremes to protest your right to establish and abide by the beliefs and practices set forth in your church. These extremists are not representative of most homosexuals.

Militant groups major in guerilla theater. They are out to make a statement, and they want as much publicity as possible focused on their cause. You are not obliged to assist them in achieving their objective. Such groups identify themselves by offensive names and have general disregard for property rights. This may mean invasion of the church premises and possible spray-painting of pink triangles (indicative of the practices of homosexual discrimination). On the other hand, such groups do stop short of causing physical harm. They would rather provoke your wrath in a manner that is timely for media coverage. This would demonstrate for all to see the punitive nature of religious people. Do not help them convey this message!

It is important that you take protective measures to minimize the impact of a planned disruption. Clearly the most significant period of risk is at the time you have a large public gathering. The Sunday worship service would be an ideal focus point for this activity.

A well-prepared single adult ministry group and church will develop a plan to deal with an attempted disruption of a worship service. Local public officials should be able to advise you as to your best plan of action. In an age of public demonstration, most communities have enforcement officers trained in responding to such situations.

Incidentally, lawful assembly does include the right to demonstrate one's opinion on a subject, but it does not include the right to carry this onto church property, to harass people attending a service or program, or to block the path of those attempting to enter or exit the building.

If such activity does occur, you can count on the news media having been previously contacted by the activist group. This too requires advance preparation. There should be one designated spokesperson for your ministry or church. Other staff should not be available for comment. They should simply indicate that the designated spokesperson is the one to talk with regarding this issue.

A prepared press release should be handed out to the media. This briefly outlines the church's position on homosexuality and also states that all people are welcome to worship and attend programs; however, those in leadership subscribe to the moral and spiritual convictions of the church.

The statement should not be overly long. It is not a doctoral paper.

The spokesperson may read the statement and then thank the reporters for their courtesy. It is unwise to be drawn into a debate with the protesters or the media representatives. Remember, both groups are looking for drama and excitement. Impromptu statements can be taken out of context and made to look inflammatory. It is more difficult (but not impossible) to do this when the only comments are from a prewritten press release.

Media representatives may later want to interview you or other staff. Once again the rule should be that one designated person represents the church. You are not bound to give interviews. The kind of excitement and interest of such events has a limited life span for the media, providing you don't choose to keep it alive. The activists would love for the debate to continue, but they need your cooperation in order to do so.

If your church leadership feels it must present its position on the homosexual issue, they should limit the interview time and avoid being drawn into making inflammatory statements. It is recommended that the church show a positive face regarding this issue.

Don't be surprised if your comments appear in the media in a less favorable light than you intended. Writers are looking for stories, and they are not usually going to receive personal attention or credit for an interview which does not generate some level of excitement or controversy. Avoid being drawn into an argument or protest over what a reporter has written. This will only extend the life of the issue and is a no-win situation. As one sage has said, "It is not advisable to argue with someone who buys ink by the barrel!"

If there is any comfort in such an experience, it should be in the knowledge that "this too shall pass." It is a window of opportunity for the activist involvement. Without other actions or reactions from your leadership, the individuals involved will move on to their next arena.

Warren Risch,
Pastor of Single Adult Ministries
First Presbyterian Church
1820 15th Street
Boulder, Colorado 80302

For Further Reading
Baker, Don. *Beyond Rejection: The Church, Homosexuality and Hope* (Multnomah Press, 1985). The story of one man's struggle with homosexuality and the path God took him on to find release—written from a pastor's perspective.

Beattie, Melody. *Codependent No More* (Harper & Row, 1987), Book and audio tape; *Beyond Codependency.* Help for the family of a homosexual person.

Carnes, Patrick. *Out of the Shadows: Understanding Sexual Addiction; Contrary to Love: Helping the Sexual Addict* (CompCare Pub., 1983). Includes information helpful to the homosexual addict.

Cook, Colin. *Homosexuality: An Open Door?* An understandable view of the homosexual conflict and its resolution. (Available through HA Book Ministry, Reading, Pennsylvania, 215-376-1146.)

Moberly, Elizabeth. *Homosexuality: Psychological Background and Theological Understanding* (2 audio tapes). *Psychogenesis: The Early Development of Gender Identity* (Routledge & Kegan Paul Limited, 1983). A major psychoanalytic study of gender identity. Discusses transsexualism and homosexuality from a psychodynamic point of view. *Homosexuality: A New Christian Ethic* (Attic Press, 1983). A significant book by an English author who has done years of research into the root causes of homosexuality. Includes challenge to the church.

Saia, Michael R. *Counseling the Homosexual* (Bethany House Publishers, 1988). Good information on understanding the gay community and their needs.

Schaef, Anne Wilson. *Escape from Intimacy: Untangling the "Love" Addictions: Sex, Romance, Relationships.* Thought-provoking and helpful.

Seamands, David. *Healing for Damaged Emotions* (Victor Books, 1981). Blends clear biblical theology, solid psychology, and practical common sense, guiding us to permanent freedom from our inner turmoil and damaged feelings (book and audio tape). *Healing of Memories* (Victor Books, 1985). *Putting Away Childish Things* (book and audio tape).

Wilson, Earl D. *Sexual Sanity: Breaking Free from Uncontrolled Habits* (InterVarsity, 1984). A Christian psychologist discusses sexual addictions.

Resource Organizations
Exodus International, P.O. Box 2121, San Rafael, CA 94912, (415) 454-1017

Where Grace Abounds, P.O. Box 18871, Denver, CO 80218.

Focus on the Family provides excellent resources on homosexuality and issues directly related to this subject. The ministry address is Colorado Springs, CO 80995, (719) 531-3400

17. DEVELOPING MINISTRY TO SINGLE PARENTS

"A successful program for single parents is one which has been tailored for the people in your ministry. This means that you cannot copy what another church has done and be successful. You should find out what needs exist in your own group and then set out to meet them."

Bobbie Reed

When I was a little girl playing house, there was always a daddy. I never dreamed I would be a single parent," Donna shared.

Many single parents can identify with Donna. Parenting is at least a two-person job and single parents face daily challenges which make them feel overloaded emotionally, physically, and psychologically. Most single parents approach their responsibilities with a serious determination not to fail. Our society accepts failed marriages, businesses, finances, ethics, careers, and almost any other kind of failure, but there is less tolerance of poor parenting. The pressure is tremendous.

Single parents must be mature enough and strong enough to take care of the needs of the children, in spite of sometimes feeling needy themselves. When too harsh discipline is handed out in frustration, and there is not that other parent around to say, "Well, now, Honey, maybe just this once," single parents have to learn to temper their own decisions and disciplines. When children aren't coping well with the change in the family structure, single parents often acutely feel the need for the support of a spouse and fellow parent.

In order to continue to function as a family, single parents must learn to change their to-do lists. Some tasks will just have to be eliminated, others completed less frequently, while still others can be shared with the kids. Attempts to do it all and be Superman or Wonder Woman will only wear out the parents.

Facing the challenges of parenting, and failing at times to succeed in all the ways they want to, can result in a serious loss of self-esteem for single parents. They often feel as if one small setback labels them a total failure. During such times, the children tend to sense the lack of confidence and leap at the chance to take control of the family.

On the other hand, there are moments of joy, times of family closeness, and exciting occasions in the single parenting experience:

–a special closeness with the children

–being able to raise them *your* way

–seeing them make progress in their own growth toward maturity

–sharing your faith and worshiping together

Wherever the single parents in your church are in their journeys, you can help.

Ways to Minister

• Redefine the term "family." In some churches the term "family" is still limited to those groupings which have two parents in the home. However, researchers say that one out of every two children born in the 1980s will spend some time living in a one-parent family. A family can be one parent and his/her children. If we accept this reality, our programs may also undergo some changes. Mother-Daughter or Father-Son activities might become Parent-Child functions, or provisions might be made for sonless men or daughterless women to be surrogate mothers and dads for the occasions.

• Provide respite. Many single parents have no family in the area, do not have ex-spouses who take the children away for visits periodically, and cannot afford childcare for anything more than the time they are at work. They have virtually no free time away from the children.

Reading a book, taking a nap, running errands alone, cleaning house without being interrupted to play judge between two siblings, or listening to quiet music are often only fantasies for single parents. One of the greatest rejuvenators you can give the single parents in your ministries is an afternoon or evening alone.

In one church four men provide free respite for the single parents by taking the children on a four-hour outing once a month. One mother who takes advantage of this offer admits to spending most of her free afternoons just sitting alone in her house listening to the quiet or taking a nap. Often married couples are willing to take single-parent children for Friday nights or a Saturday, if they understand just how much their gift will be appreciated.

• Check your program. Single Adult Ministry leaders will want to ensure that there is childcare provided for single adult functions. Often those who need the workshop or fellowship the most can afford it the least. Given the choice between paying $5–$10 for childcare to attend a Bible study and using that money to pay for food, the single parent will usually choose the groceries.

The single adult calendar needs to be balanced to include free activities as well as some for which there is a charge. Each month include at least one event where children are welcome and there is opportunity for family interaction.

• Develop support groups. One of the more successful and helpful ministries for single parents is a weekly or biweekly discussion group where they can talk about what's happening in their lives. Although the discussions are on assigned topics, members are encouraged to be open about their struggles and their successes. From this sharing, a sense of community develops and the body of Christ is edified. Shared struggles remind group members that they are not the only ones with problems. Sharing what God is doing in their lives provides courage and strengthens the faith of other parents.

• Teach parenting. Unfortunately, many of us learn to be parents through on-the-job training or years too late. It is very helpful to provide workshops or a short-term weekly study series on disciplining children, avoiding power struggles, or ways to effectively communicate with children. You can usually find good speakers/teachers at a local community college. Several video series are available. Plus, it is amazing how parents can mentor other parents.

• Organize resources. Many single adult ministries have found creative ways to provide practical assistance to the one-parent families, such as an organized clothing exchange, or advertising "needs" and "haves" to indicate who has extra furniture (clothes, books, etc.) and who needs some. One ministry put together a newsletter where single parents advertised services they could provide for a small fee and distributed it to the entire church. Work exchange days are always a big hit, as singles swap their skills (sewing, cooking, painting, car repairing) with one another. One inventive singles pastor solicited services from within the church and the community for the single parents in his ministry. He was able to provide free dental exams, tune-ups, haircuts, legal work, and a number of other very valuable services for single parents. One of my favorites is the "recycled Christmas" where single parents bring toys their children have either gotten tired of or outgrown and exchange them for "new" toys to give their children for Christmas.

● Assist with opposite sex role models. Single mothers raising sons and single fathers raising daughters have a need for opposite sex role models for their children, particularly if there is little or no contact with the other parent. Men report that there is little difficulty finding women role models and mentors for their daughters, but mothers often have to struggle to locate male role models.

Single adult ministries can help by recruiting male Sunday School teachers, childcare workers, children's ministries workers or helpers. Or, families in the church can be encouraged to "adopt" a one-parent family for periodic outings and gatherings so there are role models available. A "big brother" type program can be instituted with either married or single men participating. Often helping out this way can ease the pain a noncustodial father has over not being able to spend as much time with his own children as he might like to.

● Give hugs. The friendly touch of another adult says a lot to each of us. There's nothing like a bear hug from a friend. It says "I care," "I understand," and "I'm there for you." Build a time of hugging into your weekly program.

There are many ways to give "hugs," and we need to remember that some people are not comfortable either giving or receiving actual physical hugs. Find other ways to "reach out and touch" the lives of the single parents in your ministry. Greet them with warmth and acceptance. A friendly smile, a listening ear, a sympathetic nod, a shoulder to cry on, a funny card, or a thoughtful note in the mail can be the highlight of a single parent's week.

The effective leader will become a friend and make time available for the single parents who need extra assistance, but will also begin to develop that kind of help from within the group and let members minister to one another.

● Minister to the children. The old myth that all children of single-parent families will be discipline problems must be abandoned. Some will and others will not. However, most children of divorced parents could benefit from a ministry which would help them understand and cope with the changes in their families. Curriculum is now available to set up such a program. Children learn to identify and deal with guilt, anger, fantasies of reconciliation, and fears.

● Understand and accept. Single parents respond in different ways to the reality of parenting alone. They experience a variety of conflicting emotions depending on the situation and their energy levels at the time.

Some are so overwhelmed that they believe, *"I can't do anything!"* They feel defeated, depressed, useless, inept, and appear nearly immobilized until they can learn to just take things one step at a time.

Others rise to the challenge with an attitude of *"I'll do it or die!"* And they nearly work themselves to death trying to do everything—alone. They refuse to curtail any activity or chore and work at fever pitch, getting little sleep, rest, or relaxation. These parents need to be taught to focus on essentials, and to build in time to relax and enjoy life.

A third response is *"I'm surviving!"* These single parents are hanging on by their fingernails, up one day and down the next. Once they find their balance, and build their confidence, their lives begin to smooth out.

The ideal approach is *"I'm doing my best!"* There are no perfect parents. We all do our best with the time and energy we have. We all make mistakes. We can actually enjoy parenting sometimes when we let go of unrealistic expectations and simply do our best.

If leaders understand that these different responses are normal, and can in a nonjudgmental way assist single parents toward the fourth approach to the parenting experience, they will be of tremendous support and help to the single parents they seek to serve.

Getting Started

A successful program for single parents is one which has been tailored for the people in your ministry. This means that you cannot just copy what another church is doing and be successful. You should find out what needs exist in your own group and then set out to meet them.

Invite single parents to a planning session and have them share their needs, their dreams for a ministry, their visions for serving, and their ideas. If there is no defined need, don't start a ministry just for the sake of starting one. If there is no one willing to commit to leading the ministry, wait until God raises someone up to be the leader.

When a need has been defined, and people are willing to make commitments to minister, you are ready to begin an exciting new expression of Christian love in your group.

Dr. Bobbie Reed
Single Adult Ministry Consultant, Author and Speaker
7484 Carrie Ridge Way
San Diego, CA 92139

For Further Reading
Books by Bobbie Reed
Single on Sunday
I Didn't Plan to Be a Single Parent
Step-Families
Single Mothers Raising Sons
Too Close, Too Soon (with Jim Talley)
Prescription for a Broken Heart
Christian Family Activities for One-Parent Families

Curriculum for Children of Divorce Ministries
God Heals My Owies
God Heals My Hurts
Both are by Jim and Barbara Dycus, and available from them at 1199 Clay Street, Winter Park, Florida 32789

Curriculum for Single Parents by Bobbie Reed
Single Parent Journey, Warner Press, 1992

18. DEVELOPING MINISTRY TO CHILDREN OF DIVORCE

"If the church is a Christian family doing the work of the Lord, then one of its roles is to "be there" for families who do not meet the traditional model of family, as well as for those who do . . . to "be there" in attitude as well as in activities."

Kay Collier-Slone

In the early 1960s, a Sunday School class of three- and four-year-olds were enjoying the day's lesson which was entitled, "God the Father loves you just as your earthly father loves you." The teaching series provided a drawing to color, with a ghostly image of God hovering over an intact earthly family . . . the requisite two or maybe three children, mother, father, cat, and dog. Then the sharing time began, with children telling their experiences of fatherly love.

Tow-headed Mark spoke suddenly, his small face clouded. "My daddy doesn't love me. He went away."

In those days, divorce was still rare enough for the teachers not to have been concerned about the title and thrust of the lesson, or the picture. The lesson would hold true for most of the class. Divorce was still enough of an oddity to be an embarrassment, and Mark was one of those children caught in the limbo of a family on its way to divorce.

At the end of the twentieth century, Mark's story is not unusual. And in Sunday School classes, youth groups, choirs, and in individual encounters, the children of divorce, from the smallest to the oldest, need to be given the attention, support, and assistance of the family which will not be broken . . . the church.

Periodically, someone in a church will say, "But aren't there private agencies and counselors to do that kind of work?" Certainly there are. But if the church is a Christian family doing the work of the Lord, then one of its roles is to "be there" for families who do not meet the traditional model of family, as well as for those who do . . . to "be there" in attitude as well as in activities.

Never again will this be an "occasional" issue, or outside the norm. With the single adult population hovering near the 48 percent mark, church populations should reflect that figure in numbers of singles, single parents and, therefore, children of divorce. Numbers, however, do not mute the feelings that go with divorce, for both adults and children. And in this issue, there is no comfort in numbers, nor do the numbers "normalize" the experience of divorce itself. Each adult and each child still must go through the experience for him/herself.

It is also important to remember that the church offers its responses based upon faith, upon the Gospel. In secular settings, any spiritual base or content will be accidental rather than intentional.

Who Are the Children of Divorce and What Do They Need?

Children of divorce may range from infants through adults. This chapter will be limited to the preschool through college years. It is important to note, however, that issues of divorce which occurred in an adult's childhood and were never attended to are often at the root of adult issues concerning relationships, self-esteem, and other aspects of life.

Judith Wallerstein, Ph.D., heads the Center for Families in Transition in Corte Madera, California, which counsels more divorcing families than any other agency in America. She has produced the first major longitudinal study of divorce conducted to date, based upon fifteen years of work with sixty middle-class families. The resulting picture of the long-term emotional, economic, and psychological effects of divorce on adults and children tells us clearly that divorce is not a short-term crisis, but a profoundly life-changing event for all concerned. In her book *Second Chances*, Wallerstein says:

> In most crisis situations, such as earthquake, flood or fire, parents instinctively reach out and grab hold of their children, bringing them to safety first. In the crisis of divorce, however, mothers and fathers put children on hold, attending to adult problems first. Divorce is associated with a diminished capacity to parent in almost all dimensions — discipline, playtime, physical care and emotional support. Divorcing parents spend less time with their children, and are less sensitive to their children's needs. At this time, they may very well confuse their own needs with those of their children.

204

Wallerstein goes on to point out that divorce is also the only major family crisis in which social supports fall away. "Friends are afraid they will have to take sides," she says. "Neighbors think it is none of their business. *Although half of the families in our study belong to churches or synagogues, not one clergyman came to call on adults or children during the divorce.*"

Research continues to shed light on the experience of divorce in the lives of children and young people. Studies indicate that:

• Much of the damage of divorce happens during the predivorce conflict, and not strictly as a result of the divorce. Therefore, some of the most severe problems may be present before the fact of divorce is known to the church, or even to the child.

• There are ranges of responses in all age-groups. Some children show distress immediately—during divorce proceedings or in the subsequent changes which upset their lives and routines (moves, change of schools, one parent leaving, separation from siblings, dating and/or remarriage of a parent). Others may appear to weather the situation with minimal distress, but in young or later adulthood, they manifest symptoms traceable to this turbulent time.

• The child or young person does not have to be clinically "disturbed" or "unstable" to feel pain about this issue. Rarely does a child of divorce go through the experience without needing (but not necessarily asking for) some help.

CHILDREN OF DIVORCE ARE CHILDREN WHO . . .

• Are experiencing two major losses . . . loss of an intact family, and loss of the daily presence of one parent.

• Along with the developmental tasks of their individual age and stage, now have a complete other set of developmental tasks having to do with grief, transition, and recovery.

How Might Children of Divorce Differ from Those from Traditional Family Units?

• Children of divorce may be on a visitation schedule with the noncustodial parent which does not allow regular class attendance. Awards and emphasis on "perfect attendance" or examples which equate interest and/or commitment with attendance may force the child/young person into nonattendance or reluctance from embarrassment or feeling "out of things."

• The issue of religion may become an issue of contention between the parents, and may be further complicated by remarriages, moves from the neighborhood, community, etc.

• The stress of single parenting may mean that younger children are irregular in attendance, or are unable to participate in certain events. The older child may be without funds, or be assuming home responsibilities not usual for his/her age.

• They may have repressed many feelings of pain and anger but live on an emotional "edge," may be considered "moody," or have "shut down" emotionally.

• Children of divorce may have different names than the custodial parent, or surnames which differ from their siblings.

Are There Differences by Ages and Stages?
While there are commonalities in responses to divorce, there are also predictable responses at specific ages. It is important to remember that every child/young person will respond uniquely, depending on personality and particular circumstances. The following guidelines, however, are helpful to teachers/leaders in developing a sensitivity to possibilities in behavior.

• Preschoolers

Issues: Fear of abandonment; confusion.

Behaviors: Reluctance to let custodial parent out of their sight; regression to earlier behavior, such as lack of bladder control, thumb-sucking, clinging to security items; sad, withdrawn; hitting, throwing fits to release anger.

• Early school years (roughly 5–8)

Issues: Preoccupation with feelings of loss and rejection; fear of replacement in the affection of the absent parent; conflicted loyalties; guilt.

Behaviors: Sudden tears; crankiness; lack of concentration; change in school performance.

• Middle school years (roughly 9–12)

Issues: Awareness and anxiety that their practical and emotional "base" has been disrupted; concern for personal future; feeling insecure, out of control, powerless; angry at whichever parent they fault; grieving, lonely, confused, and possibly overstimulated by parents' dating/sexual lives.

Behaviors: Inappropriate caretaking for the family; physical symptoms such as headaches, stomachaches, and other stress-related ailments; changes or disruptions in peer relationships; delinquent behavior; manipulative behavior; change in school performance.

● Adolescence/teen/college

Issues: Vulnerability to losing base of strong family structure which they need to set their own emotional, sexual, and other impulses; fear of repeating their parents' mistakes; not sure where home is (particularly if away at school); concern for their personal future; angry; grieving; aware that society thinks they are too old to need help or be disturbed, and attempting to live out that expectation; confused and often angry/jealous at parents' dating/sexual lives.

Behaviors: May spend more time away from home; may move into premature sexual activity in search of warmth, closeness, identity; may assume more home responsibilities; may exhibit inappropriate caretaking behavior; changes in peer relationships, school performance; physical ailments. (It is important to note that though this age-group acquires greater strength and independence through the crisis of divorce, many sacrifice important aspects of the teen/college experience, and become "old before their time."

What Is Needed for the Single-Parent Child/Young Person?

These children and young people need an *aware, prepared, accepting, and loving environment.* These words are listed in an intentional order. A church must be *aware* of statistics, of research, of the new facts of life in this society before it can be *prepared.* If it is not *prepared,* then, at some level, it is not *accepting* reality and, therefore, the *people* of the reality. Without feeling *acceptance,* no one can feel *loved.* In the past, issues of divorce have been dealt with piecemeal, as deviations from the norm, individual crises which could be handled as the "exceptional" situation in the parish.

In a recent single adult class on Loneliness, a woman new to both secular and church communities as a single parent, said that she felt "out of it" at the church. "There is nothing here for a family like mine" — divorced, with young school-aged children. A widow and long-time church member spoke of how the church had been like a surrogate family after her husband's death.

Which of these two stories accurately describes this parish church? Both are realities, spoken out of two radically different experiences.

The widow and her family moved into the church community as an intact family, and were known well there for many years. After the death of the husband and father, many people reached out to them in love and concern, in very practical as well as spiritual ways. There was, indeed, the experience of "just like a family."

For the new family, there was no history with the church as a "traditional" unit . . . of knowing and being known. The church offered no activities, support groups, or classes attentive to the needs of single parents. There seemed no way to develop a network, no way to sense "family." The environment felt more like form than substance in this phase of the family's life.

Reminder: There is a difference to how the church looks, feels, and is represented to oldtimers and newcomers, to those who are familied and coupled, and to those who are alone. There can also be a difference to how a long-familiar church looks, feels, and presents itself when a family configuration changes.

Where to Begin
As we move from the general to the particular, we begin by
- *Being aware* and showing an *attitude* of *awareness* and *preparation* which speaks of *concern*.
- *Educating* clergy, staff, congregation.
- *Helping* parents help themselves and thus help their children.
- Specifically *helping children.*

Does your church program advertise activities which indicate an awareness of families of divorce/children of divorce?

Does your church bulletin/directory/other printed material list a resource for single adult ministry as well as for Christian education and youth activities?

Do the activities listed as regular offerings of the church indicate that "familied" and "coupled" are part, but not the total, population?

Are there support groups/education activities listed?

The church's program and promotion make a statement. Parents and children will not feel they can turn to their church in time of stress if it does not indicate both *awareness* and *preparation.* Families in stress do not always have the emotional energy or the time to search out resources. The activities listed, and the way they are targeted, is an indicator of where the church's time, money, energy, and ministry are directed. Already established members of the church who find themselves "suddenly single" will view their church from quite a different perspective than when they were coupled. One young woman who grew up in a church, married and was raising her children there, moved her membership to a church "where there were real efforts to help children of divorce, and people going through divorce." For both the prospective member and the long-time member, single-parenting will be impacted by what programs are available, and how they are promoted and presented.

Have your teachers, youth leaders, and single adult leaders been trained in awareness and sensitivity to families who do not fit old norms?

Are these leaders trained in an overall approach to ministry in which Christian education, youth, and single adult leaders minister from a unified understanding of personal and Christian formation, rather than a remedial approach?

Those who have never experienced divorce themselves or with anyone close to them may have "head knowledge" of what the experience is all about, yet miss some of the ways in which the very environment of the church, its language and its activities, can be hurtful to children and adults of divorce.

One clergyman told of having his consciousness raised by a child who quite innocently told him, "The family Advent service made us cry." The puzzled pastor discovered that it was the absence of a "Reader number three" in this dad and son family unit which had proven very painful as they attempted to use the church-provided Advent guides for families.

"It made me start looking at our resources," he said, "to try to deal with preparing our teachers to be sensitive." Teachers and leaders who have been trained in this manner will be more thoughtful in planning and considering resources, using books and pictures, movies and videos which show single-parent homes as normative as well as problematic; recognizing and choosing examples which depict a wide range of family configurations. It is also important when asking parents to help with an activity or outing, or having "family pictures" taken for the directory, to know that from one to four "parents" may show up, and the experience may cause pain for a child. As one teen whose parents had been long divorced said, "I just wish my family could be 'normal' — happy — *together.*" Another junior higher said, "I wish my mom could drive the carpool or chaperone sometime, but she has to work." One child may be sensitive to having both natural and stepparents present for church functions; another may be in pain because one of the natural parents is missing. Children are also sensitive about the use of correct names. The church needs to know a mother's last name, if she is remarried, and be able to call the stepfather by his name. In referring to parents in blended families, it is important to acknowledge the correct relationships. When in doubt, ask.

While building a ministry for children of divorce may involve a number of aspects, some of which are appropriate only for large, multi-staff churches, there are others which can be accommodated by smaller churches and can be immediately facilitated. Still others require long-term planning and financing. Awareness and sensitivity training at all levels, for all sizes of churches, is immediately accessible.

Immediate Help for Children and Families of Divorce: Awareness Training/Environment and Attitude Adjustment

All clergy, teachers, and church leaders need to have facts about the new normative states of singleness/single parenting/children of divorce. In this day and age, it is critical that all church leaders assume that some of the students in each group/class are not living with both natural parents. They need to take basic steps in identifying those students, and adjusting the classroom/group to this new norm.

● Clergy, teachers, and leaders need training in concepts of crisis, loss, and grief, to fully understand the length of time and other aspects of the process.

● They need to be introduced to standards of inclusivity in resources and materials, so that they can knowledgeably avoid the use of those which might be painful to children of divorce.

● They need trained resources to be available to answer "how-to" questions as the most effective ways of dealing with problems that arise.

● The church needs to regularly have families fill out registration forms and yearly enrollment updates which will provide a "report" on family status, correct names. This information would go to the teacher when he/she receives a list of participants.

● When there are materials to send home, or gifts or pictures made for parents, there should be sufficient supplies, and an opportunity for self-selecting which allows students to make duplicates, or receive duplicates,

when necessary, without having to specially request them.
- The church can offer classes for children and young adults on topics such as self-esteem, loneliness, and solitude.

Long-Term Goals
In planning long-term goals, a church needs to consider its facilities, resources, and leadership, as well as community resources. Long-term goals might include:
- A day-care program available through the week, at minimal cost.
- Mentorship programs, which offer same-sex, opposite-sex role models and helpers to single-parent families.
- Children of Divorce groups, with trained leadership helping youngsters through the experience. (Designs and training available by age-group.)
- Organized efforts for carpooling, surrogate parenting, etc. which will allow children to participate fully in regular programs of the church, regardless of home circumstances.
- Integrated efforts at curriculum which includes ongoing work on issues of self-esteem, loneliness/solitude, grief, preparation for individual as well as married adulthood, personal wholeness, internal satisfaction.

The long-term results should be young people who grow into adults more prepared for healthier living, individually and in family.

Helping children often begins with helping the parents. Divorced and/or grieving parents are often out of control, dazed, barely surviving. This state lasts much longer than is generally recognized. The effect is often as if there is no adult person in the home at all. By the time observable symptoms emerge in the child/young person, or a parent seeks help, considerable damage may have been done to the child. The church can help by offering:
- Mediation training to help parents learn new ways of communicating/ relating to each other which will not be so damaging to the children, regardless of their ages.
- Classes in single parenting which offer practical help as well as support.
- Teaming with neighboring churches to bring in community resources trained in special areas of need.
- Plan a special reference section in the church library with books on divorce, divorce recovery, custody, continuing parent relations, children's issues, etc. Keep several copies of each book on hand so that individuals who cannot afford to purchase these resources will have them available.

Children of divorce should have a very special place in the church family. The corporate body can offer a sense of continuity, of structure, of unbroken tradition, of stability and hope at a time when the children's lives seem devoid of these qualities. Such ministry will not only help and sustain the children of divorce through the crises in their families, but will provide a model of family for the rest of their lives.

Kay Collier-Slone, Ph.D., Director of Single Adult Ministries
The Episcopal Diocese of Lexington
P.O. Box 1600
Lexington, Kentucky 40586

For Further Reading
Berger, Stuart, M.D. *Divorce Without Victims: Helping Children Through Divorce with a Minimum of Pain and Trauma,* New York: Signet Books, 1983.

Berman, Claire. *A Hole in My Heart;* New York: Simon and Schuster, 1991.

Bienenfeld, Florence, Ph.D. *Helping Your Child Succeed after Divorce:* Claremont, California: Hunter House, 1987.

Diamond, Susan Arnsberg. *Helping Children of Divorce: A Handbook for Parents and Teachers;* New York: Schocken Books, 1985.

Kline, Kris and Pew, Stephen, Ph.D. *For the Sake of the Children: How to Share Your Children with Your Ex-Spouse in Spite of Your Anger.* Rocklin, California: Prima Publishing, 1992.

Ricci, Isolina, Ph.D. *Mom's House, Dad's House; Making Shared Custody Work: How Parents Can Make Two Homes for Their Children after Divorce.* New York: Collier Books, 1980.

Virtue, Doreen. *My Kids Don't Live with Me Anymore: Coping with the Custody Crisis.* Minneapolis: CompCare Publishers, 1988.

Wallerstein, Judith S. and Blakeslee, Sandra. *Second Chances: Men, Women, and Children a Decade after Divorce.* New York: Ticknor and Fields, 1989.

19. DIVORCE RECOVERY—
INDIVIDUAL COUNSELING

*"The divorced person can feel like a sinner. To stand
before God, family, and friends, and vow to remain
married—this does not allow for divorce. The goal of
marriage is not simply to remain together, no matter
what, but to commit to love each other. To divorce is
to miss the mark."*

Frederick G. Cain

Divorce recovery is not one process but many. Some of these processes
occur simultaneously, others in a series. These processes of divorce
usually take from two to five years to run their course. The first three
areas where a divorced person must cope are pain, guilt, and anger.

Though marriage can be painful, destructive, and even life-threatening,
the concept of divorce is more agonizing. It is death—the death of a
marriage, the death of a family—both nuclear and extended, the death of
a couple's hopes and dreams, and the death of their future together.
Divorce is a painful death and leads to grief.

The divorced person must grieve for all that is lost: marriage, family,
identity, hopes, dreams, house/home, friends, church, and anything that
was a part of the marriage. Much of this grief is immediate, but some
may linger, and other losses may not come into a person's awareness
until long after the divorce. Counseling the divorced person means helping him/her work through pain and grief.

Divorce is an affront to one's self-image and self-esteem. The stigma
society attaches to divorce, while not as odious as it once was, marks an
individual as "not quite right." Having society attach this stigma to one's
self-image is defacing and destructive. Counseling the divorced person
helps him/her reconstruct damaged self-image and self-esteem.

Pain causes wounds that must heal, and healing takes time; therefore,
recovery from divorce is not quick. Healing an illness sometimes takes

the trained hand of a physician. Healing after a divorce may take the skills of a minister, counselor, or psychologist. Counseling the divorced person includes helping him/her seek the healing grace of Jesus Christ in all the processes involved in recovery from divorce.

Emotional Issues

The divorced person feels great guilt. S/he can feel guilty about not being a good spouse, about letting relatives and friends down, or many other aspects of the divorce. Some of the guilt may be justifiable, some may be neurotic. This latter kind of guilt does not lead to change in one's life, but just causes pain. Counseling the divorced person helps him/her abandon the neurotic guilt and resolve the real guilt through repentance, forgiveness, and sometimes restitution.

The divorced person can feel like a sinner. To stand before God, family, and friends and vow to remain married — this does not allow for divorce. The goal of marriage is not simply to remain together, no matter what, but to commit to love each other. To divorce is to miss the mark (*hamartia*) and not achieve the goal of marriage.

The divorced person has sinned; but since we are all sinners, the divorced person should not be singled out. The problem in calling divorce a sin is defining just what divorce is and when the sin occurs. Is the sin in getting a divorce? In falling out of love? In marrying the wrong person? The problem is not necessarily that divorce is a sin, but that sinful behavior in an interpersonal relationship between two imperfect persons in an imperfect marriage can lead to divorce. Consequently, the problem is not necessarily with divorce, but with the marriage. Counseling the divorced person helps him/her learn to replace destructive patterns in interpersonal relationships with healthy patterns.

Guilt and anger meet when blame is assessed. The divorced person may blame self, ex-spouse, parents, and family and friends who encouraged a marriage proven to be unsuccessful, and even the church for not preparing him/her for marriage. Over the short period, blaming can be healthy. It helps the divorced person sort through what went wrong in the marriage and see what issues need work and resolution. Blaming also vents anger. But over the long period, blaming is destructive; healing and growth cannot occur in a person who is stuck in blaming. Counseling helps the person move through the blaming process and into the process of asking the questions: "How can I develop a healthy interpersonal relationship?" and "If I marry again, what do I need to change about myself to be a good spouse?"

214

Divorced people struggle with anger. Everyone on whom the person blames the divorce is an object for anger. An angry person needs to release the anger, resolve its cause, forgive the person(s) involved, and move on with life.

Identity Issues

There are two kinds of divorced persons. One type is the person who (for example) divorces an alcoholic and marries a drug addict, who does not resolve the problem issues. The other type works through the issues that caused the divorce and the situations following the divorce, and is then free to marry without an encumbered past. The divorced person who does not work through the pain, guilt, and anger of divorce condemns him/herself to never having a successful interpersonal relationship with a person of the opposite sex. The divorced person who does work through the pain, guilt, and anger of divorce and then chooses to marry again will have a strong and healthy marriage.

The divorced person needs friends to help him/her through the processes of divorce. He or she especially needs a friend who can fully understand and clearly identify what the divorced experience and the processes of recovery. This friend can let the divorced person know s/he is not alone or unique in the suffering of divorce, and can act as a guide through the processes of recovery. Ideally, this special friend should be the same sex as the divorced person, for two reasons. Men and women differ in how they experience and process divorce. Also, when a man and a woman share their most intimate pain, thoughts, fears, hopes, and dreams, the tendency is to become romantically and sexually involved. The person in the throes of divorce needs an understanding friend, not a sexual partner. A single adult ministry group is an excellent place to make such friends.

Some divorced people need to work on developmental issues. If a divorced person went from dependence on parents to dependence on a spouse, s/he has probably not experienced or discovered adult maturity. This person needs to resolve identity issues and discover who s/he is as an independent adult. This person also needs to learn how to act as an adult and how to take care of him/herself. Counseling the divorced person can help him/her work through unresolved developmental issues.

The divorced person must structure a new future. In the autumn, leaves fall from the trees. Nature composts them, making mulch and fertilizer for the spring flowers. The garbage of divorce needs to become compost for a new life. The divorced person needs to envision a new future for him/herself and then spend time in dreams and hopes. Only after this can plans be made and carried out based on these dreams and hopes. This is a time of becoming new and a time for reconstructing one's self-concept. The divorced person in this "newness" process may need to make symbolic changes to state s/he is new; a new house, car, hairdo, job, or name. Counseling should not end until the divorced person discovers a new life and is ready to face the future.

Some of the processes of recovering may be long term because certain issues may come up several years after the divorce. These issues may stir up old pain, guilt, and anger, or may create new pain, guilt, and anger. The divorced person must face and resolve these issues as they come. A part of counseling is to teach the divorced person how to cope with these problems.

Family Issues

Counseling a divorced person may go beyond talking with one person. No one has fallen out of the sky or is without attachments. We are born and raised in families. Every divorce occurs in three family systems, the couple's family and each spouse's family of origin. The counselor needs to be aware of others connected who are in need of counsel.

Divorce is hard on children. They must be assured they are not the cause of the divorce. Love of parents or others must be identified and affirmed. Children can regress when their parents divorce and act as if they are younger than they are. They need personal or family counseling to resolve issues of the divorce affecting them and to learn to cope with the stress in their lives. When a child is having behavior problems as a result of his/her parents' divorce, the parents are best counseled together.

Divorce is not one issue in a person's life but a multiplicity of issues. Resolving a divorce is not one process but many. Counseling a divorced person assists that person through all the processes of divorce.

Frederick G. Cain, Pastor
Rosedale/Bridgeton United Methodist Church
P.O. Box 181
Rosedale, Indiana 47874

20. DIVORCE RECOVERY — SMALL GROUP MINISTRY

"The tasks of divorce recovery are serious and complex; they are like deep, multiple trauma wounds, and as such, they take time to heal."

John Splinter

There are many reasons why our church developed a fourteen-week, small group approach, divorce recovery program. Indeed, all of the "healing" programs which we run (for victims of sexual and physical abuse, for children of divorce, etc.) now use the small group format. This chapter will provide a framework of understanding the history, benefits, and problems in this approach.

A Brief History

We call our divorce recovery program Second Chapter. After surveying virtually all of the available divorce recovery programs, we decided there was none which met our standards. We wanted to have the very best, the top of the line approach to this ministry. We found that to get what we wanted, we had to create it.

• Why fourteen weeks? We chose a fourteen-week program, rather than opting for a shorter approach (four or six weeks), or using a weekend divorce recovery approach. The reason for this came from the group which helped create the program. All of them were divorced, and all were professionals of one type or another. Three had advanced clinical degrees.

These individuals uniformly said that their personal quest for healing following their divorces took them a long time — many months and in some cases even many years. Given the level of trauma which divorce usually causes, it is not realistic to expect people to absorb within a short period of time a lot of head knowledge about "how to recover from divorce."

When the spirit is deeply wounded, it is usually a quantum leap from head knowledge to the application of that knowledge. The tasks of divorce recovery are serious and complex; they are like deep, multiple trauma wounds, and as such they take time to heal. They are not like a broken bone which, if set correctly into a hard cast shortly after the break, will heal itself within six weeks. Rather, they are more like severe, uneven, and infected gashes and punctures which need ongoing attention and regular cleaning over a long time.

While shorter divorce recovery programs can be helpful, it was our opinion that they are not capable of getting as deeply into the wound or providing as complete a healing as are longer programs.

• Why small groups? The clinically trained members of the Second Chapter committee pointed out that the more time spent in small group interaction, the better the participants' healing would be. These small groups had to be closed to outside participants, completely confidential, and run by lay (but trained) individuals who had themselves been divorced.

One evening at our weekly Second Chapter committee meeting, a member presented a doctoral dissertation which confirmed everything we'd been discussing—from the fourteen-week length to the closed, small-group approach. It iced the cake for us, and the Second Chapter Divorce Recovery Project was officially born.

How Groups Are Run

• Two leaders per group. Each group is built around two leaders, one male, one female. All leaders have been through divorce, most have been through Second Chapter, and all are required to be at least two years away from their own divorce.

• Meetings in leaders' homes. Groups meet in the homes of leaders two and one half hours weekly.

• Mixed groups, closed groups. Groups are mixed, with males and females in all groups. We do it that way because we believe it's important for both sexes to see each other struggle through divorce. It gives them a better understanding of what their ex-spouse is going through, and it destroys the tendency to generalize ("All men are jerks; all women are dependent, etc."). Once formed, groups are closed. No visitors.

• Firm ground rules. There are a few ground rules which are firmly maintained, such as, no dating among group members, absolute confidentiality, respect of group leaders.

• Methods.

1. Each person is given a *Second Chapter* book and is expected to read one chapter a week. That chapter becomes the focus of the week's study, conversation, and out-of-group activity. (Rather than starting the weekly meeting by listening to someone lecture for an hour, we require that participants read the weekly chapter. Almost all participants do so, religiously.)

2. Each group meeting is begun with a short time of prayer, usually led by one of the leaders.

3. Although the group is free to discuss anything, most of the focus of the meeting revolves around the Discussion Questions provided at the end of each chapter. In this way the material is handled sequentially.

4. Group members are encouraged to accomplish the Action Items in each chapter during the rest of the week, and to discuss how these helped in divorce recovery, at the next meeting.

5. Meetings end with a short prayer time.

● Cost. We charge $100 for each person. That fee accomplishes three important things:

1. It increases the level of commitment to the group. They've paid for something and now they want to get their money's worth, so they attend every meeting.

2. It increases the expectation level of the participant. Having paid $100, they now expect the program to be more professional and powerful; and as their expectation level increases, so also does their active participation, and their healing.

3. It pays for a full-time program director. Individuals who cannot afford the full fee are helped on an individual basis; nobody is ever refused. When people have gone through Second Chapter one time, they can go through it free as many times thereafter as they want or need. We've had several people take the course twice, and one person went through it three times.

Some Reasons in Favor of Using Small Group, Longer-Term Divorce Recovery Methods

Here are a few of the distinct advantages of using the long-term, small group approach to divorce recovery.

● Cognitive processing alone is insufficient. Following divorce, many people attempt to ease their pain through reading several books about the subject. Although such reading is informative, it seldom helps ease the suffering. Healing generally does not come through cognitive input.

Shorter divorce recovery programs are limited in their effectiveness;

by their nature, they either provide a heavier dosage of cognitive material or limit the scope of material to be covered. This is true because they have less time in which to provide their information. There is, in fact, a very popular weekend divorce recovery program. People who have taken the class have told us that after the first two or three hours they were on such emotional and cognitive overload for the rest of the weekend that they couldn't absorb most of what was presented. Divorce recovery doesn't happen quickly, nor is cognitive information the key element in divorce recovery.

● Content vs. process approaches. Obviously there must be a blend of content and process in any learning or healing endeavor. However, shorter programs must, by their very nature, focus more upon content, giving people quick solutions regarding "how to recover." Longer approaches allow for more process orientation, focusing upon issues — where the pain is, why it's there, when it hurts most, thoughts on how to grow past it, group support in one's efforts to heal and grow, etc. The longer approach also better allows for more individuality — "Bill, you're struggling with anger and bitterness. Jane, you seem to be struggling with sadness and fear. Terry, right now you're pretty deep into depression, aren't you?" — rather than rapidly offering canned solutions which are supposed to fit everyone's circumstances.

● By relationships wounded, by relationships healed. It is the ability to share one's pain with another person, while slowly and gently learning of solutions which can help mitigate or ease the pain, that most effectively helps the healing. We know that the healing process is highly relational and interactive in nature. In the field of family systems theory there is a phrase, "By the family wounded, by the family healed." Small group divorce recovery uses the group to act, in some ways, as a "family" to which each person belongs. The wounds of divorce are relational and spiritual in nature. The small group provides relationships within a very gentle spiritual environment, for the purpose of healing.

● Relationships don't happen quickly. It takes time to build or rebuild relationships. Divorce represents a shattering of what was probably one's most closely held intimate relationship. Since the wounds of divorce are relational and spiritual in nature, it stands to reason that one does not quickly rebuild such relational/spiritual items as trust, hope, and love; nor does one quickly rebuild the openness and willingness to heal so necessary to sustain future relationships. It takes time, within the caring and supportive environment provided by a surrogate "family," to accomplish deeper levels of healing and rebuilding.

• Bonding and self-examination. Healing after divorce usually involves lots of self-examination, and that process is accomplished best within a community of bonding and support. Such is the small group. Being together as a group on a regular basis, sharing the wounds of divorce, learning to be open and vulnerable with one's own responsibility for the divorce, watching each other struggle toward renewed wholeness, watching each other fall from time to time, yet giving and receiving the support and caring that comes from the depth of each group member's heart. These are all powerfully healing factors.

• Small groups and body ministry. When presented within a format of gentle spiritual acceptance and love, the small group actually represents the body of Christ as it expresses grace, forgiveness, reconciliation, compassion, and more. Most people going through divorce experience some sense of alienation from the church, at least temporarily. The small group can be an effective means of experiencing the love and healing of Jesus Christ, while the individual is emotionally or spiritually separated from the larger church.

• Small groups have real flesh and bones. One method of doing divorce recovery involves an individual standing in front of a group of divorcing people and teaching methods of healing, followed by an hour of discussion in groups.

It is our belief that it's far more effective to enter into the trenches with those who are wounded and touch their wounds with the love of Christ. Small group divorce recovery is flesh and bones, hands on, "We're right here with you" ministry. We do not want distance between the medic and the wounded.

The process is often very painful for the leaders themselves, as they watch their "babies" struggle through recovery, but it's far more effective ministry than the lecture approach.

• Small groups provide nurture and time. Almost any clinically trained person will agree that two important components of healing are nurture and time. Although the small group can't provide all of the nurturing needed for healing, it does give a large portion of it. And then it just takes time—time together with people one trusts with the deepest hurts.

To develop the depth of trust and support needed to begin healing within divorce recovery usually takes several weeks. We have found that many people just *begin* to open up to their group after the sixth or seventh weekly meeting, and yet that's when many programs end.

• Confidentiality is almost assured. Another benefit of the small group approach is that confidentiality is more easily assured. Everyone's in the same boat, so to "spill someone else's beans" is usually not even a consideration. This is in contrast with some divorce recovery programs in which the recovering person is with a different group of people every week.

• The leaders become paths toward healing. Many people lose hope when going through divorce. Within the small group approach, they have ample opportunity to look at, question, and evaluate the lives of the leaders who take them through the program. All of these leaders were themselves divorced, and the knowledge and observation that the leaders have gone through the pain, and are now whole, happy, and productive, offers growth and hope.

• Ongoing ministry after the group is finished. One of the most powerful reasons we use the small-group long-term approach is that the relationships formed continue on. The group frequently becomes a major part of the individual's support network for the next many years. In other words, people don't just "go to a divorce recovery program" and then walk away. They usually stay connected.

When that connection is to people who are also active within the church, the long-term nature of this approach frequently ends up drawing participants back to the church—or in many cases, to the church and Christ for the first time. In fact, our divorce recovery program is one of the strongest tools for evangelism in our church.

• Ongoing leadership development. The long-term nature of this approach to divorce recovery means that leaders have to make a substantial commitment. This is a decidedly positive aspect of our ministry. We have found that as leaders make deep and long-lasting commitments, they grow, mature, and usually become even more deeply committed both to the ministry and to Christ.

When we don't ask anything of our people, they don't give much. When we ask a lot, they have to make a decision. If they decide to give a lot, then everyone benefits—the participants, the leaders, the specific ministry, and the church body. The larger church benefits in that when the leaders feel they've done divorce recovery for enough years, they are already in a Christian service mode, and usually seek to direct their energies into some other church ministry.

• The leaders benefit the most. At the end of every Second Chapter program, we ask each participant to evaluate the program, the leaders, the written material. For the most part we receive a grade of 90 to 95 percent; the program is tremendously well received.

However, as much as the participants benefit, the leaders usually gain more. In leading others through the swamp of divorce recovery, they reinforce their own paths of healing. In praying for group participants' healing, they are led to the Lord for their own wholeness. Our leaders over the past six years have come away from leading these small groups saying that they grew far beyond their expectations as a result of leading others.

Many said that initially they were very hesitant to lead, for fear it would lead them back into the emotional pain of their own divorce. This has not happened. Through leading others, they have found healing for unresolved issues in their own lives.

Pitfalls to This Approach

Any divorce recovery program will have its own strengths and weaknesses. Here are the issues which have surfaced within the past six years of our using this approach.

• Leadership development takes work. It takes more time and energy to get a program like this up and running. It takes time to recruit and train leaders. Some people are not willing to commit to a fourteen-week ministry, so it is important to handpick the leaders, rather than asking for "anybody out there who wants to lead a divorce recovery group."

We shoot for the very brightest and best leaders we can find. We seek people who are committed to the Lord, who have healed, and who have a lot on the ball. Over the long haul, this approach builds a powerful and effective ministry. Several psychologists, psychiatrists, and attorneys in town regularly refer people to our divorce recovery program.

• Deeper ministry requires better training and support. The fourteen-week small group approach runs much deeper than a course of fewer weeks. People share in more depth and painful wounds are exposed. Consequently, it takes thoughtful training and support to use this approach.

We provide small-group-dynamic training for all of our leaders. We also provide training to all our leaders to help them recognize individuals who might be suicidal, and to know what steps to take.

We then provide a trained clinical person as a backup, on call twenty-four hours a day for emergencies. In six years we've had two potential suicides which were averted through trained intervention of our lay leaders. They have frequently called on the clinical support person for insight or suggestion on how to handle specific participants.

• Slower growth rate of ministry. This approach won't "explode" a ministry into instant stardom. It takes time to build this kind of ministry.

On the other hand, one church decided to use this approach, and in the first divorce recovery session started their program with over 100 participants. Usually, however, the growth of this approach is slower. The long-term payoffs are much greater, but the initial growth rate is usually a little less aggressive.

Summary

If we had it all to do over again, if we were just starting a singles ministry and were trying to figure out how to do the very best divorce recovery ministry possible, we would do exactly what we have done. We'd go for long-term, small-group, closed-group, step-by-step, mixed-group (male/female), lay-led divorce recovery.

John P. Splinter,
Minister with Single Adults
The Central Presbyterian Church
7700 Davis Drive
St. Louis, Missouri 63105

21. ORGANIZING A DIVORCE RECOVERY WORKSHOP

"Facilitators are a key to the program. Choosing divorced facilitators will allow participants to feel more comfortable, especially those who are most recently involved in the divorce process."

Andy Morgan

Once the decision has been made to develop a divorce recovery program for your church and/or community, the next question is the kind of program you are going to use. The options are many. Weekend programs, or programs ranging from six weeks to sixteen weeks, meeting once a week. In deciding which format you would like to develop, you need to define your goals by what you would like to see accomplished. What are the needs? What do you feel uniquely qualified to do?

It is my belief that the best divorce recovery program is one owned, organized, facilitated, and taught by local people. By not making it another thing done for you but something you do for yourselves, you benefit from knowing that you have done something significant for the building of the kingdom in your community. At first the quality may not be as good as having outsiders come in and do a program for you, but ultimately, the health and well-being of your group will be stronger.

It doesn't matter how large or small your group is—you can have a divorce recovery ministry in your church. If you only have three people, you can have a program. If you know three people who have experienced divorce or the end of a long-lasting relationship, then consider purchasing a divorce recovery video series and start there. Invite some people to your home or to the church to watch the videos and then go over the workbooks or discussion questions that accompany the divorce recovery videos. It is important to remember that you don't have to have large numbers to have effective ministry.

The type of divorce recovery ministry discussed in this chapter meets once a week for eight weeks. The evening begins with one hour of teaching. Next the group breaks into smaller groups for discussion. Due to the nature of divorce recovery, discussion groups work best when they have an average of ten participants with a male and female facilitator. An evening might be frameworked as follows:

> 6:30 P.M. Registration and coffee
> 7:00 P.M. General session
> 8:00 P.M. Break
> 8:15 P.M. Small group discussion or "talk it over"
> 9:15 P.M. Dismiss

• It helps to end all the discussion groups on time. Starting and ending on time tells the participants that their schedules are important.

• It provides a time when facilitators can discuss any immediate problems (while still keeping the group's confidentiality).

• It allows facilitators a time to recover if their groups were especially emotional.

The book I use as a text is *Growing Through Divorce* by Jim Smoke. I personally believe this to be helpful for the journey through divorce recovery. It is good to have participants reading something during the week, to keep their minds focused on recovery. To supplement the book, I provide handouts for each session. There are many different workbooks and materials available that make excellent supplemental material.

As you plan and develop your own divorce recovery workshop, you may want to consider the following sequence.

Eight to Ten Months before Your Workshop

• Pull together a ministry team to brainstorm. This can be five to ten people who have gone through divorce and have a burden for ministering to others who have. Make sure that your leadership team is made up of a variety of people, i.e., custodial and noncustodial parents, individuals who were married less than ten years and those married over twenty years, male and female, etc. By pulling together a team of leaders, you have already expanded the number of people who will have some kind of ownership in the divorce recovery ministry.

• Decide what kind of divorce recovery program you desire to have in your church; i.e., weekend, six, eight, or twelve weeks. Is it going to be taught by someone or are you going to use one of the video series that are available?

• Start gathering material from others who are doing divorce recovery. Develop a network of support from other organizations.

Six to Eight Months before Your Workshop

• If you are going to have a speaker vs. a video series, determine your main speaker. If you are going to use a video series, start reviewing different videos to see which one you would like to use.

• Establish your dates. I have used an eight-session program, preferably running on a weekly basis. The last session may be in a banquet or dinner format, even a potluck dinner with music, special guests, and the speaker presenting the last session. I recommend the eight-week program, realizing that many people feel that they need more time. Indeed, recovery takes longer than eight weeks, and for that reason I always try to find other support systems, i.e., counseling centers, support groups, single parent groups, etc. within the community or church to help facilitate the recovery process.

I recommend the eight-week program be in conjunction with other programs or support ministries within the church, i.e., singles ministry, Sunday School classes, week night fellowships, Bible studies, etc., so that when the program is over the people have many other options to choose for continued healing and growth. When there aren't other opportunities for continued small group interaction, then a longer divorce recovery program might be beneficial.

• Establish your location (church building, etc.). When selecting a room try to make it as warm and friendly as possible, providing a safe place for sharing.

1. Reserve a main lecture room for the opening sessions. This needs to be a room that will hold your expected participants comfortably. Don't have a room that is too small, and at the same time, don't have a room that is too big. You don't want people to feel lost in the room.

2. Reserve "breakout" rooms for the small groups. These rooms should hold ten to fifteen chairs in a circle arrangement.

3. If you plan to have child care available, you will need rooms for this. (Child care is recommended.)

4. Determine your sound system requirements (will you tape each session, do you need microphones, etc.). The participants need to hear the main speaker clearly. Your sound system can either enhance your program or make it very difficult for people to follow the speaker.

• Determine the cost of the workshop. When doing divorce recovery, I state that the charge is on a "donation" basis and that scholarships are available to those who cannot afford to pay. The donation should cover honorariums (for the speaker), books and materials you will hand out, refreshments (if provided), scholarships, child care, advertising, etc.

227

• Determine the ways you will promote your workshop. What audience are you trying to attract? If you are trying to reach out to the non-Christian community, putting flyers in your local Christian bookstore is not going to attract many non-Christians. A better place to advertise might be in the "personals" of your local paper. Know your audience and target your advertising.

1. Promotion through your own and other churches (using inserts for the church bulletin), can be a very inexpensive way to get advertising into the Christian community.

2. Newspaper promotions (not just on the church page).

3. Radio promotions (public service announcements).

4. Cable TV promotions (public service promotions are often free).

5. Flyers at bookstores, counselors' and lawyers' offices, human resource departments at corporations, mental health clinics, and AA are some places you can promote the divorce recovery program. Get together with your brainstorming team and see what other ideas you can develop.

6. Word of mouth promotions — start promoting early!

Many of the participants will come from word of mouth advertising. Make sure to develop a good ministry team that networks with others. Make the quality of the promotional material equal to what the average person sees every day. Quality advertising sends the message that what you are doing is important.

Three to Four Months before Your Workshop

• Design a brochure and registration form. Print copies for eight to ten times the number of anticipated participants. This larger quantity enables you to distribute your brochures at other places. Also, printing costs for 750 or 1,500 is practically the same. Make sure the brochure contains phone numbers where people can call for information. Answer the basic questions of *who, what, where, when,* and *how much.*

Write to other churches to see what kinds of brochures they use and then design your own. (A list of churches using this model is at the end of this chapter.)

• Select your facilitators. Establish the number of facilitators you will need. Try to have two per group.

1. Use facilitators who are legally divorced. Facilitators are a key to the program. Choosing divorced facilitators will allow participants to feel more comfortable, especially those who are most recently involved in the divorce process. This also avoids the subtle message that only married

people are qualified to teach, lead, and facilitate.

2. Use facilitators who have gone through a divorce recovery program, or who are in the process of healing. If they have not gone through a divorce recovery program, I would recommend having them read *Growing Through Divorce* before facilitator training begins.

3. Only use facilitators who are committed Christians. Many of the principles brought out in the programs have their basis in the Scriptures; you will want people who are in harmony with the material, instead of those who constantly disagree and state their own opinions.

4. Have the facilitators complete an application form. This will not only help you but will also convey the message to volunteers that this is serious business for servant leaders.

5. Inform your facilitators of their need to commit to the *set number* of training sessions before the program begins. It is important for the facilitators to be a part of the training session, so that a team is developed that takes their role seriously. Usually people will only rise to the level of commitment expected of them. The more you expect from leaders, the more responsible they will be. Do the ministry and your volunteers a favor and let them know what you expect and the importance of their role. Have a variety of good training materials available. When training, emphasize the importance of listening, asking appropriate questions, and providing a safe place for people to share their experiences.

6. Make sure each facilitator is willing to commit time to be present for each workshop session.

• Determine who will train your facilitators, and prepare the training materials. Prepare handouts for your training material and try to make your training user friendly. Be careful not to overwhelm your facilitators with excess materials and responsibilities. I emphasize that the primary job of facilitators is to be good listeners.

Eight to Ten Weeks before Your Workshop
• Start distributing your promotional brochures to other churches, counseling centers, lawyers' offices, other single adult groups, local cable and radio stations, and anywhere else that your brainstorming team decided to advertise.

• Take registrations from participants.

• Have training sessions for your facilitators. I have traditionally used two training sessions. The first session can be two to four weeks prior to the beginning date. Have the second session the week prior to the beginning of the workshop.

- Recruit other volunteer help. People are needed to:
    1. Assist with registration and greeting each night (hosts/hostesses). Your hosts and hostesses can have such an important impact on the overall ministry. They should treat all the people with dignity and sensitivity and remember what the participants may be going through. Divorce recovery should be a safe place.
    2. Assist with refreshments, if provided.
    3. Serve at a book or tape table, if provided.
    4. Run the childcare program.
    5. Run the sound system. This is a very important part of the program.
    6. Help with room setup if you don't have a custodial staff to do that.

One to Two Weeks before Your Workshop

- Start assigning participants to groups (strive for 10-12 people per group, but you may leave the groups smaller at this time to allow for walk-ins the first or second night). Try to group people together based on their backgrounds:
    1. Number of years married. Suggested groupings: 0–8 years, 9–18 years, 19–26 years, 27+ years.
    2. Participants who have no children.
    3. Participants who have been divorced more than once.
    4. Divorce has been final over five years.

These groups may have to be adjusted based on the size of your workshop. It is not imperative to divide your group into these categories, but as your group grows, these categories can help make it easier for discussion in the groups.

- Assign facilitators to groups. Where possible, match facilitators' backgrounds to the type of group, although this is not absolutely necessary.
- Reverify all rooms to be used. Make sure custodians are aware of your arrangement needs! Custodians may be your best "friends"!
- Organize a prayer meeting to commit the ministry to the Lord.

Opening Night

- Arrive early and check all rooms for tables, chairs, lighting, signs, and other setup items.
- Test sound system setup.
- Have workshop materials ready for people who are preregistered.
    1. Each person should be given a packet with name, group assign-

ment, and group meeting location written on the front. This helps make the participant feel welcome. Remember, this is not the place they really *want* to be.

2. The packet should include handouts, outlines, ground rules, name tag, etc. (Note: Most people prefer to write their name on the name tag.)

3. If you are planning to give each person a book, make it available at this time.

● Have registration materials available for "walk-ins." You might anticipate doubling the number of preregistrations with walk-ins the first night (so if you have fifty preregistered, you could conceivably have up to fifty more people the second week).

● While the first main session is in progress, that is a good time to be placing the new registrants into small groups. Be sure that you have allowed available space in the groups to accommodate these people.

● When the speaker has completed the first main session, dismiss those people who have their group assignments. Then read off the names of new registrants and their group assignments.

Do not place new people into small groups after the second week! Bonding has occurred in the groups by this time, and new members will detract from the trust relationship. New groups may be formed.

It is also important to determine at what point newcomers are encouraged to only audit the general session and then consider signing up for the next workshop series.

Some churches using this model of divorce recovery workshops are:
● Calvary Church, Grand Rapids, Michigan
● Single Point Ministries, Ward Presbyterian Church, Livonia, Michigan
● First Presbyterian Church, Aurora, Illinois
● Arlington Heights Evangelical Free Church, Arlington Heights, Illinois
● Willoughby Hills Friends Church, Willoughby Hills, Ohio

Divorce recovery audio tapes, video series, participant workbooks, leaders' manuals, and the divorce recovery program on computer disk are available through Polestar Ministries.

Andy Morgan
Polestar Ministries
RR 2, Box 84AC
Sheridan, Illinois 60551

22. SINGLE ADULTS AND DEATH

"All of us are going to die. The only questions are about details. Single adults must come to terms with their own deaths, as well as the deaths of family members and significant others."

Harold Ivan Smith

There are approximately 66 million single persons in the United States; one in every three adults. Moreover, because of the marriages/divorces/deaths, an incredible number of people will be single for some period of their adult life.

After thirteen years of full-time ministry with single adults, I have concluded that the *only* taboo topic among single adults in ministry settings is the discussion of death. There are several reasons for this.

First, single adults do not want to be reminded that they could die before they marry; they would feel cheated. Therefore, I focus on goal-setting when I meet with single adults. I have adapted an exercise, developed by Sidney Simon, in which the participants draw a straight line on a sheet of paper. On the left end of the line they write the year of birth; on the far right end, they write the year of their anticipated death.[1] Without exception, the response has been disbelief, expressed through laughter, moans, or noisy chit-chat. Some think I am joking.

"I hate to break the news to you," I interrupt, "but unless the Lord comes back first, you *are* going to die!" Two common responses follow. Some cannot complete the rest of the exercise to define "How I want to spend the rest of my life"; others, however, are energized by the reality.

A second contributing issue is that many single adult organizations emphasize program rather than ministry. In fact, some cannot be correctly labeled single adult *ministries* because faith is secondary to program goals. The emphasis is on singleness and social activities. Leaders plan "upbeat" and "positive" programs to draw crowds, since attendance is a

233

key criterion of success. Death is definitely a downer.

Third, some leaders are nervous about the issue of death, since some adults have been singled through the death of a mate and this topic might make them uncomfortable; it might "knock the scabs off their unhealed grief." In many single adult ministries, underlying tensions exist between the positive value assigned those who lose a mate through death and the negative value assigned those who lose a mate through decision/divorce. Repeatedly, widowed participants complain that there is nothing specifically on the program for them.

Fourth, some leaders are afraid that if programming attracts too many widows/ers, it may affect the age configuration and balance, since widows, in particular, tend to be older; widowers remarry. Ageism is a common and acceptable prejudice in single adult ministry.

Fifth, I believe that death-associated fears, rather than the fear of death per se, trouble singles. The fear of helplessness, fear of being alone or deserted, fear of being a burden, fear of humiliation or loss of dignity, fear of others having to "take care of me," fear of running out of money for treatment/funeral expenses — all are strongly felt by single adults, particularly those without family.[2,3]

It is important that the subject of death ceases to be a taboo in single adult ministry, thereby opening single adults up to "the fullest possible spiritual formation"[4] in anticipation of life's most rigid finality.

A Biblical View of Death Anxiety

Vance Havner observed, "If a man cannot turn to God in the hour of his deepest need and come boldly to the throne of grace for help in such a time, then the Gospel means nothing."[5]

Scripture contains hundreds of references relating to death and to death anxiety. However, all should be filtered through one key passage, "Brothers, we do not want you to be ignorant about those who fall asleep, or to grieve like the rest of men, who have no hope" (1 Thes. 4:13). Yet, many believers grieve with little awareness of the hope of our faith.

• Old Testament. Death came upon earth as a result of the Fall. Pointing out the tree of the knowledge of good and evil, God warned against eating its fruit, "for when you eat of it you will surely die" (Gen. 2:17). After the Fall, God said, "By the sweat of your brow you will eat your food until you return to the ground, since from it you were taken; for dust you are and to dust you will return" (3:19). If Adam wondered what death was, he soon discovered its horror when his son Cain killed his brother, Abel (4:8). Adam himself died after 930 years of life (5:5).

To the Jews life and death were not separate entities, but two sides of a coin. The Israelite "viewed death as the ultimate and undesired weakening and loss of vitality."[6] He considered death at advanced age as natural. "With long life will I satisfy him," the psalmist reported (Ps. 91:16). "The length of our days is seventy years — or eighty, if we have the strength"; yet the psalmist lamented, "their span is but trouble and sorrow, for they quickly pass, and we fly away" (90:10).

1. Death evoked strong emotion. When Sarah died at age 127, Abraham "wept over her" (Gen. 23:2). Later, Joseph "threw himself upon his [dead] father and wept over him and kissed him" (50:1). When the Shunammite's son died, the mother went to Elisha and demanded that the prophet raise him from the dead (2 Kings 4:27-28).

2. Death was prepared for. Jacob, "when the time drew near for Israel to die," called for his favored son and made Joseph promise not to bury him permanently in Egypt. "When I rest with my fathers, carry me out of Egypt and bury me where they are buried" (Gen. 47:29-30). On his deathbed, Israel blessed the two sons of Joseph. Then he gathered in his entire family and prophesied their future (49:1-28).

3. Dying produced spiritual anxiety. King Hezekiah, sick "and at the point of death," was visited by the Prophet Isaiah. "Put your house in order, because you are going to die; you will not recover" (Isa. 38:1-2). Hezekiah "wept bitterly" and pleaded with God to spare his life. God relented and added fifteen years. Hezekiah's anxiety was evident, "I said, 'In the prime of my life must I go through the gates of death and be robbed of the rest of my years? . . . Like a shepherd's tent my house has been pulled down and taken from me' " (Isa. 38:10, 12).

4. A premature or early death was feared. Even though Absalom had led a rebellion against his father, David was shaken by his untimely death. "O my son Absalom! My son, my son Absalom! If only I had died instead of you — O Absalom, my son, my son!" (2 Sam. 18:33) During his lifetime, Absalom had an anxiety about being forgotten and erected a monument to himself, saying, "I have no son to carry on the memory of my name" (2 Sam. 18:18), even though we have record of three sons and two daughters being born to Absalom (2 Sam. 14:27; 2 Chron. 11:21).

An example of the death of an unmarried woman is found in Judges 11, when Jephthah the Gileadite vowed to sacrifice the first person that came out to greet him when he returned in triumph from the Ammonites. Much to his horror, his daughter — his only child — met him. She accepted his decision, asking only for "two months to roam the hills and weep with my friends, because I will never marry" (11:37). As a result, the young women of Israel annually commemorated the sacrifice (11:40).

• New Testament. The reality of death comes early in Matthew's Gospel, when Herod ordered his soldiers to kill all the males under the age of two (2:16-17).

In Jesus' life and ministry we discover His attitudes toward death.

1. In the story of Jairus' daughter, Jesus demonstrated His power over the *dying*. When Jesus reached the house, He ordered all the grieving "commotion" stopped. "She is not dead but asleep," He said, which evoked laughter. Jesus took the girl's hand and said, "My child, get up!" Luke noted, "Her spirit returned and at once she stood up" (Luke 8:55).

2. In the story of the funeral procession outside Nain, Jesus demonstrated His power over the *dead*. The deceased, a young man, the only son of a single parent (and therefore her economic security) was being taken to the cemetery. Luke observed, "When the Lord saw her, His heart went out to her and He said, 'Don't cry' " (Luke 7:13). Jesus touched the coffin, stopped the procession and said, " 'Young man, I say to you, get up!' The dead man sat up and began to talk, and Jesus gave him back to his mother" (v. 15).

3. In the story of Lazarus, Jesus demonstrated His power over the *buried*. The sisters, Mary and Martha, had sent a message to Jesus, "Lord, the one You love is sick" (John 11:3). Jesus, however, delayed. Once He arrived in Bethany, He discovered that Lazarus had already been buried four days. John notes that Jesus "was deeply moved in spirit and troubled" (v. 33). When Jesus wept, the mourners concluded, "See how He loved him!" (v. 36) I believe that Jesus wept at the grief of the sisters and the mourning behavior of the Jews. Eventually, Jesus stood in front of the grave and commanded, "Lazarus, come out!" and Lazarus did just that!

Matthew offered a glimpse into Jesus' grief after the death of His cousin John the Baptist. "When Jesus heard what had happened, He withdrew by boat privately to a solitary place" (Matt. 14:13).

4. Jesus anticipated His own death. Matthew notes that Jesus "began to be sorrowful and troubled." In fact, He said to His three closest friends, "My soul is overwhelmed with sorrow to the point of death." This single adult, facing death, did not want to be alone. "Stay here and keep watch with Me" (26:38).

5. Jesus prayed to be excused from death. "My Father, if it is possible, may this cup be taken from Me" (26:39). His next two rounds of prayer were worded differently, "My Father, if it is not possible for this cup to be taken away unless I drink it, may Your will be done" (vv. 42,

44). His prayer is a model for us.

Isaiah had prophesied that Jesus would be "despised and rejected by men, a man of sorrows, and familiar with suffering" (53:3). The author of Hebrews declared, "He had to be made like His brothers in every way, in order that He might become a merciful and faithful high priest in service to God" (Heb. 2:17). Jesus' struggle with death should make it easier for single adults to "approach the throne of grace with confidence," not only to find mercy, but also "grace to help us in our time of need" (4:16).

The author of Hebrews portrayed Jesus' reluctance to die and declared, "He too shared in their humanity so that by His death He might destroy him who holds the power of death—that is, the devil—and free those who all their lives were held in slavery by their fear of death" (2:14).

6. Writing to the Thessalonians, Paul detailed the Christian's hope of resurrection. "Therefore encourage each other with these words" (1 Thes. 4:18). John declared that Jesus holds the keys of death and Hades. He predicted a day when God "will wipe every tear from their eyes." Moreover, in that day, "there will be no more death or mourning or crying or pain" (Rev. 21:4).

Behavioral Perspective on Death

• Death tied to aging. A remarkable shift in population has influenced death attitudes. Since 1900, there has been a 36 percent increase in the percentage of children under ten, and a 257 percent growth in the elderly.[7] As a result of falling mortality rates among children, there are more young adults who have not personally experienced the death of someone close, other than maybe a grandparent. "Death is becoming more closely associated with advanced age."[8] Experiences influence attitudes. Ruth Stein touched this sensitive issue: "We've established that it's O.K. to be single when you're young and everybody else is in the same boat, and we're finding that we can handle it in middle age. But, whether or not we admit it, we're terrified of growing old on our own"[9] because that means dying alone.

• Change in causes of death. The three primary causes of death among young adult males are accidents, homicides, and suicides; among young adult females, accidents, homicides, malignancies, and complications from childbirth. However, among senior adults, male and female, the leading causes are heart disease, malignancies, and strokes. This leads to the conclusion that the young "tend not to approach the point of death gradually, with conscious opportunities for preparation."[10] Simply, the young are not expected to die.

237

Further, the death toll from AIDS has now topped 100,000; one-third of the fatalities occurring in 1990 alone. This disease and cause of death was for all practical purposes unknown at the start of the 1980s. The Centers for Disease Control estimate that as many as 215,000 Americans will die of AIDS in the next three years, 75 percent of them between the ages of twenty-five and forty-four.[11] By 1989, AIDS had become the second leading cause of death among men in this same age group; by the end of 1991, AIDS ranked in the top five killers of young women.[12] This is the first time in recent medical history that sexuality and death have been linked together.

In addition, suicide is now responsible for the death of one American every twenty minutes, and is a significant health threat to young men. The suicide rate for young males rose 30 percent between 1970–1980.[13]

More than 430,000 Americans died in 1988 of deaths related to tobacco, an 11 percent increase over 1985.

Thousands will die through automobile or vehicle accidents, at least 20,000 attributed to drunk drivers.[14]

Cultural Perspective on Death

• Changes in death protocol. In 1900, 70 to 80 percent of deaths occurred in the home; today, that same percentage of death occurs in hospitals, nursing homes, and hospices. In the former, the family was in charge; in the latter, the medical community controls the dying process. Moreover the decision-making passes into the professional's hands.[15] Spiritual care may be limited by sedatives, tranquilizers, and painkilling drugs, which may lead medicine and ministry into conflict.[16]

Once death occurs, the funeral director is in charge. Where once the remains were taken back to the family residence, friends now visit a funeral home. In many instances, the funeral is conducted in the funeral chapel rather than the church. Indeed, the service may be called a "memorial" service rather than a funeral. The body is buried in a memorial park rather than a cemetery. Americans are good at coining words to further intensify the taboo. A young adult will be "lost" or be said to be "gone" rather than dead.

• Changes in definitions of death. Incredible advances in medical science — no doubt encouraged by an equally incredible fear of death — have resulted in new definitions of death such as "brain death." Thus single adults like Nancy Cruzan and Christine Busalacchi become "sound bites" on network news as the state and federal governments, religious community, medical establishment, politicians, activists, and family debate over

238

when to pull "the plug" to the medical technology that keeps these people breathing. In Nancy Cruzan's case, her parents had to go all the way to the U.S. Supreme Court in their quest to "allow Nancy the dignity of death" after a 1983 auto accident left her "a vegetable."[17]

However, she was allowed to die only after three witnesses related conversations they had had with Nancy before her accident, that led them to assume she would not want to "live" in such a state. Moreover, the issue became clouded when activists from the National Right to Life Committee challenged the parents' right to discontinue treatment.

One clear result of the medical-legal fracas was that thousands of Americans "evesdropping" on the battle resolved to avoid the same fate.

Time phrased the question accurately in asking, "In an era of untamed medical technology, how are patients and families to decide whether to halt treatment or even to help death along?"[18] The new source of anxiety for many Christians is how/when to discontinue treatment.

Moreover, the issue is intensified by the enormous medical costs in battling and postponing death, costs that a growing number of health insurance companies are not willing to absorb. In a day of shrinking health care resources and spiraling health care costs, who will live and who will die?

• Increasing acceptance of suicide. More than 25,000 individuals commit suicide each year and another 50,000 to 200,000 attempt it.[19] Not surprisingly, certain groups have higher suicide rates. One study found four times more suicide attempts among lesbians and seven times more attempts among gays than among heterosexuals.[20] Indeed, the United Methodist Interagency Task Force on AIDS Ministry heard testimony that suicidal "self-deliverance" "can be a dignified alternative to agonizing death."[21] Indeed, some medical personnel facilitate suicide by giving the terminally ill extra painkillers to store up for a deliberate but perceived-as-accidental overdose. This becomes an "acceptable" suicide.

• Media-arts-drama perspective. Given the impact of drug/AIDS-related deaths in Hollywood and among the arts community, death is becoming a frequent theme in movies. Movies definitely mold public opinion. *Ghost*, starring Patrick Swayze and Demi Moore, has earned $214 million and five Academy Award nominations. Swayze's character returns from the dead to warn his live-in that his best friend killed him and is positioned to harm her.[22] *Long-Time Companion* ends with a rebirth sequence, in a world post-AIDS. *Flatliners* chronicles five medical students' experiments in induced death and return.

A universalism persists in the media, and sometimes even in the church, "that we all serve the same God" and therefore "are all going to the same place." Thus death is less harsh and final.

Because of changes in our culture, Americans are more likely to encounter violent death and at an earlier age. Moreover, media exposure through the news makes what once would have been obscure localized deaths lead stories on CNN and major network newscasts. One example is the rape/death of a single woman, Jennifer Logan, in New York's Central Park; also, the death of a young black killed by a group of angry white youth in New York's Bensonhurst neighborhood.[23]

• New Age "answers" to death. Given the growing potential of violent death, the New Age movement offers to detraumatize death and lessen its finality through reincarnation. Once dismissed by religious authorities, reincarnation has attraction for many. Russell Chandler, religion editor for the *Los Angeles Times* and a major student of the New Age, suggests that 30 million American adults believe in reincarnation. Actress Shirley MacLaine has become a best-selling "prophetess" for the movement.[24] Widespread reports of near-death experiences underscore the growing acceptance of New Age philosophies. These are in clear contradiction to Paul's declaration, "Man is destined to die *once,* and after that to face judgment" (Heb. 9:27).

Singleness and Death

W.M. Clements has written that "each person who is dying is involved in an unusual set of circumstances that will never be repeated." Therefore, "one must be prepared to facilitate the death of another human being on that person's terms" and within their context of understanding.[25] "A crucial element in the psychological health of the single person is his or her acceptance of the state of singleness."[26] Has he/she lived "on hold" waiting for an elusive Prince Charming? Research at the University of California has concluded that marriage is a key to the longevity of middle-aged men; males from forty-five to sixty-four who lived with spouses were only half as likely to die within the next ten years as men who lived alone or with someone other than a wife.[27]

Historically, single life in a marriage-oriented world and in a marriage-centric church places pressures on single adults to marry. Some have made the church their family; others have become "lifelong isolates."[28]

Conclusions

All of us are going to die. The only questions are about details: How? When? Where? Under what conditions? Single adults must come to

240

terms with their own deaths as well as the deaths of siblings, parents, and significant others. In a singles subculture that emphasizes, "Eat, drink, and be merry," we must never forget what Jesus reminded His listeners: "This very night your life will be demanded from you" (Luke 12:20). I have concluded that single adults have troubling questions about death which they have a right to ask and to expect biblically sound responses. When they are adequately enlightened, single adults will be more responsive/responsible than when misinformed or underinformed. Even when facing death, they can appreciate and anticipate the life eternal.

In a recently published study of 600 single adult leaders, surveyers asked, "What is the most frustrating aspect of being a leader in singles ministry?" The number five response was, "Lack of interest in spiritual growth among singles."[29]

> One cannot grow spiritually until he/she has faced the inevitability of death. How one views life, its point and its purpose, will share one's approach to death; what one views as a good life will determine what one takes to be a good death. And how one actually deals with death when it comes will often reveal and clarify what one has all along believed about life.[30]

Dr. Francis Schaeffer asked, "How then shall we live?" The pertinent question for single adults today is, "How then shall we die?"

Harold Ivan Smith,
Author and Speaker
P.O. Box 24688
Kansas City, Missouri 64131

Notes

1. Sidney B. Simon, *Getting Unstuck: Breaking Through Your Barriers to Change* (New York: Warner, 1988), 29–30.

2. Jerry Gerber, *LifeTrends: The Future of Baby Boomers and Other Aging Americans* (New York: Macmillan, 1989), 247.

3. Larry Richards, *Death and the Caring Community* (Portland: Multnomah Press, 1980), 47.

4. Thomas C. Oden, *Pastoral Theology: Essentials of Ministry* (San Francisco: Harper and Row, 1983), 300.

5. Vance Havner, *Though I Walk Through the Valley* (Old Tappan, New Jersey: Fleming H. Revell, 1974), 26.

6. Henry Koster, "Death (In the Bible)," *New Catholic Encyclopedia,* vol. 4 (New York: McGraw-Hill, 1967), 685–86.

7. W.M. Clements, "Pastoral Care of the Dying," in *Dictionary of Pastoral Care and Counseling,* ed. Rodney J. Hunter (Nashville: Abingdon, 1960), 322.

8. Ibid.

9. Ruth Stein, *The Art of Single Living* (New York: Shapolsky Publishers, 1990), 247.

10. Clements, 322.

11. "More Than 100,000 Have Died of AIDS in U.S. Since 1981," *Lexington* [Kentucky] *Herald-Leader,* 25 January 1991, A14.

12. Ibid.

13. Jon B. Ellis and Lillian M. Range, "Characteristics of Suicidal Individuals: A Review," *Death Studies,* 13 (1989), 485, 487; "Suicide Rate for Young Men Rose 50% Between 1970-80," *Jacksonville* [Florida] *Times-Union,* 21 June 1985, A5.

14. National Safety Council, *Accident Facts: 1990 Edition* (Chicago: National Safety Council, 1990), 4.

15. G.W. Davidson, "Moral Dilemmas in Dying," *Dictionary of Pastoral Care and Counseling,* ed. Rodney J. Hunter (Nashville: Abingdon, 1960), 321.

16. Oden, 304.

17. Jill Smolewe, "Bringing an End to Limbo," *Time,* 24 December 1990, 64; Nancy Gibbs, "Love and Let Die," *Time,* 19 March 1990, 62–68.

18. Gibbs, 62.

19. Ellis and Range, 485.

20. Judith M. Saunders and S.M. Valenter, "Suicide Risk among Gay Men and Lesbians: A Review," *Death Studies* 11 (1987), 3.

21. Ray Waddle, "Minister Says AIDS Victims May Prefer 'Self-Deliverance,' " *Nashville Tennessean,* 2 February 1991, 5-B.

22. "Money Talk," *Kansas City Star,* 15 February 1991, H3.

23. "The Preppie Killer Cops a Plea," *Time,* 4 April 1988, 22; "A Surprise Finish to 'Preppie' Trial," *Newsweek,* 4 April 1988, 27.

24. Russell Chandler, *Understanding the New Age* (Waco, Texas: Word, 1988), 20–21.

25. Clements, 322.

26. D.L. Schuurman, "Singleness," *Baker Encyclopedia of Psychology,* ed. David G. Benner (Grand Rapids: Baker Book House, 1985), 1085–1086.

27. "Middle-Aged Men: Marry and Live Longer," *Medical Aspects of Human Sexuality,* January 1991, 15.

28. Schuurman, 1086.
29. "The Ten Biggest Frustrations of Singles Ministry Leaders," *Single Adult Ministry Journal*, 8 (January 1991), 1.
30. Wennberg, 224.

A COMPARATIVE STUDY OF SINGLE ADULT MINISTRIES IN MAJOR CHRISTIAN CHURCHES IN THE UNITED STATES

ASSEMBLIES OF GOD

Over 1,600 churches affiliated with the General Council of the Assemblies of God have active singles ministries. The denomination's Sunday School Department in Springfield, Missouri helps individual churches by providing support and training to leaders of single adults. According to William P. Campbell, the Department's Adult Ministries Consultant, much progress has been made over the past ten years in the area of single adult ministry. Denominational leaders have conducted research and begun to develop a base of resources helpful for local congregations. Among the newest of these resources, Campbell lists the Sunday School Department's *Single Adult Ministries Leader's Guide* (1445 Booneville Ave., Springfield, MO 65807), and Fagerstrom's *Singles Ministry Handbook* (Victor Books).

The Department has also begun training singles leaders. The North American Sunday School Convention and the Single Adult Ministry Leadership Training Conference, both of which offer seminars for leaders of singles, are "held every few years."

On the local level, singles are finding acceptance in Assemblies of God churches. Mike Jackson, singles pastor at Bethel Temple in Fort Worth, says about 80 singles of all ages are active in his congregation of 500, and another 50 are on the church's mailing list. He leads a Singles Alive group, consisting of persons ages 18 to 40. Another group, the Single Life, is open to older persons. Singles participate in fall and spring retreats for fellowship, recreation, and spiritual growth. Their Sunday

School department offers three classes: college age, young single adults, and older single adults.

Single adult leaders at Bethel Temple must be committed to the Lord and to the program. They should be willing to participate actively in all phases of the church and be open to training as they grow in their leadership skills. Most important, says Jackson, is "a willingness to submit their plans to the larger picture. A leader who wants to go off on a tangent without regard to the church as a whole is not right for our group."

A unique aspect of the ministry at Bethel Temple is its Monday evening single adult gathering. Jackson describes this "hyped-up service" as an opportunity for worship, praise, preaching, and fellowship on a weekly basis, designed specifically for single adults. A group of talented instrumentalists plays a central role in the Monday meetings. Although these gatherings parallel the structure of their churchwide Sunday services, single adults do not neglect Sunday activities in favor of Monday; they attend both each week. In addition, active single adults from other nearby Assemblies attend Bethel Temple on Monday to be a part of this fellowship.

One benefit of the Monday service, Jackson notes, is that it provides a worship outlet for single adults who serve on Sunday mornings in other capacities, such as nursery or children's workers. It also offers fellowship among singles and strengthens their bonds with one another and with the church.

Jackson has discovered that single adults thrive when they feel ownership of the group. His work as headmaster of the church's day school, besides helping to pastor the church, stretches his schedule almost to the breaking point. Thus, he gives the reins of planning to the single adults. The Singles Alive Council, headed by a ministry president, makes decisions concerning the direction of activities. If, for example, a member hears about a new community project and wants to involve the single adult group, he/she presents the idea to the council, which will consider the project and likely place him/her as chair of the new committee.

Jackson summarizes this ownership concept: "Singles take the initiative in planning and implementing their work. If they want something done, *they* do it! I'm too busy to do it all myself, and I'm glad they're willing to take charge." A new project in which Bethel Temple single adults have become involved is an outreach program in Fort Worth's downtown apartments, working in conjunction with the local Housing and Urban Development and city police. Besides planning and conducting ministry to their own members and follow-up work among visitors to the singles programs, single adults also plan fellowship activities and prepare a monthly newsletter with articles and a calendar of events.

Preparations are underway to expand Bethel Temple's ministry to single adults. Jackson is currently involved in training a group of singles as counselors who can help with spiritual, social, or other matters. A few single adults from the church are attending Southwestern Baptist Theological Seminary in Fort Worth to develop leadership and ministry skills which they can use within their own congregation or as they go on to other Assemblies. The group is also looking for other avenues of social ministry, besides the apartment ministry mentioned above. They are eager to be involved in the life of the church as well as the life of their community.

Bethel Temple is not alone in its work with single adults. Dwayne Betsill, associate pastor to young adults at Bethesda Community Church in Fort Worth, says his 175 adult singles are "always doing things together." Approximately 60 of them meet each Thursday in Betsill's home for a time of worship, prayer, ministry, and fellowship. Once a month, they break into groups of 6 to 8 persons for discussion of a particular topic such as "Christian relationships."

Bethesda single adults participate in retreats, some segregated by sex and others which combine men and women. They are involved in canoe trips, holiday socials, mission trips, and sporting events. They also conduct social action projects: ministering to children at a downtown housing project, visiting hospitals and nursing homes, reaching the poor and needy through the Breadbasket project, and helping youth through Teen Challenge. Some of the church's single adults are considering the possibility of "adopting" an AIDS patient and ministering to that person on a regular basis.

In addition to the active participation of single adults in local churches such as Bethel Temple and Bethesda, there is a loosely organized voluntary association of single adults among Assemblies of God in the Dallas/Fort Worth metroplex. The group gathers for social and sporting events; they also take winter ski trips together and participate in other activities to foster fellowship among singles.

Resources

Mike Jackson, Bethel Temple Assembly of God, 6801 Meadowbrook Dr., Fort Worth, TX 76112. Phone: (817) 457-1111.

Dwayne Betsill, Bethesda Community Church, 4700 North Beech St., Fort Worth, TX 76021. Phone: (817) 281-6350.

SOUTHERN BAPTIST

Southern Baptists have a comprehensive program of ministry to and with single adults of all categories. Resources to help with adult singles ministry within this denomination are varied. The Baptist Sunday School Board in Nashville has several specialists in the area of Single Adult Ministry—persons who work specifically in Sunday School, outreach, and Bible study resources; leadership development; and enrichment.

Each state convention has a person assigned to single adult ministry whose job is to plan and implement retreats, seminars, and training events throughout the state. When a church wishes to begin a single adult ministry, a state worker is available to offer assistance and advice.

Locally, associations of Southern Baptists also provide resource persons. They, like their state counterparts, give assistance to new single adult ministry in churches, and they coordinate activities in which churches within the association may participate. Many associations across the country offer training opportunities for single adult coordinators and councils, joint missions projects, and encouragement to churches beginning single adult ministries.

Individual Southern Baptist churches with single adult ministries offer a variety of activities, depending on their attendance and interest. Medium-size churches, such as Field Street Baptist in Cleburne, Texas, have discovered that since the turnover rate of single adults is fairly quick, *their activities must adapt from year to year according to the changing needs of the group.* Joe Martin, director of the singles department at Field Street, says they have done monthly potluck luncheons, recreational activities, and Singles Celebrations with entertainment, snacks, and table games. Occasionally, Martin invites a musical group from a single adult ministries group of another church, or a drama troupe from nearby Southwestern Baptist Theological Seminary, to supplement the entertainment.

Even Southern Baptist missionaries are becoming involved with single adult ministry. An article in the June/July 1991 issue of *Commission* (published by the Foreign Mission Board of the Southern Baptist Convention) describes missionary Rick Dill's work with single adults in Germany. He has organized a group of singles from several Baptist churches, and they plan retreats, training seminars, and promotional activities throughout the German Baptist Union. The group also publishes a magazine for German Christian singles, *Leben als Single,* which is currently underwritten by the Baptist Union but should be self-supporting within three years as circulation increases.

The Sunday School Board (127 Ninth Avenue North, Nashville, TN 37234) provides a variety of printed materials to assist churches with singles ministries.

Cliff Allbritton, who works with the Single Adult Unit of the Family Ministry Department of the Baptist Sunday School Board, recommends these steps for churches beginning a singles ministry.

• First, present the ministry for church approval. This includes the choosing of a single adult coordinator and a single adult council. The coordinator must, according to Southern Baptist standards, possess certain qualities. Foremost is the requirement that he/she have had a personal conversion experience. Other characteristics include being consistent, openminded, decisive, democratic, appreciative, objective, motivated, helpful, tactful, and communicative (Smith, *How to Start a Single Adult Ministry,* pp. 16–18).

Allbritton's book *Single Adult Ministry in Your Church* explains the single adult council as "an official body of the church with representation from and to each area of the total church program in which single adults are involved" (p. 72). Its function is to ensure that all single adults in the church have opportunities to be involved in a comprehensive, balanced program.

• The second step is a survey conducted by the coordinator and council to determine the number and needs of singles in the congregation. Allbritton suggests enlisting and training interviewers to conduct the survey rather than using mass mailings.

• Third, determine a direction for the single adult ministry based on results of the survey. The coordinator and council may suggest changes or additions to the organizational structure, along with content materials for new programs.

Throughout this process, and even after the single adult ministry has been established, leaders and potential leaders should be trained. An annual training conference is offered by the Sunday School Board, along with special seminars in Nashville throughout the year. In addition, most states schedule at least one retreat per year for leaders of single adults. Associations may sponsor retreats and seminars, as well.

Conferences and events are also available for singles themselves, for training, growth, and fellowship. Allbritton (p. 98) and Hayner (*Growing Together: Singles and Churches*, p. 111) list national events such as ski conferences, single adult cruises, Spring University of Single Living, Memorial Day Marriage Readiness Conference, and Labor Day conferences at Ridgecrest (N.C.) and Glorieta (N.M.).

Southern Baptists, like many other religious groups, realize that singles need more than an organization ministering to them. They need and want the opportunity to serve others. Southern Baptist churches encourage single adults to become involved in serving in various ways: working with the church's food pantry, tutoring students, ministering to internationals (Allbritton, p. 63), helping to improve living conditions for the poor in the community, visiting persons in jail, assisting blind, deaf, and elderly persons (Hayner, pp. 59ff).

Because each Southern Baptist church is autonomous, no standard is dictated by the Sunday School Board to govern the local congregation's acceptance of single adults. Thus, churches differ widely. While one church may allow a single adult to serve as deacon, Sunday School teacher, minister of youth, or even pastor, another church may strongly prefer married persons for every leadership position. Large churches in the South, with more traditional mind-sets, generally choose married persons to fill the major offices of leadership, while smaller churches, especially those in pioneer areas of the North, will accept a single pastor or other staff member more readily.

Resources

Dr. Jim Walter, Associate Professor of Adult Education, Southwestern Baptist Theological Seminary, 2001 W. Seminary, Fort Worth, TX 76122. Phone: (817) 923-1921.

Dr. Joe Martin, Field Street Baptist Church, 201 N. Field, Cleburne, TX 76031. Phone: (817) 645-4376.

CATHOLIC

Like many other religious groups, the Catholic Church finds itself battling a traditional mind-set in the midst of society's changing family structures. Deacon Ron Aziere of Fort Worth is one person interested in reaching out to singles in his diocese, which encompasses approximately 1 million Catholics. He heads a loosely organized group of persons whose goal is to assist in "setting up a ministry base within local churches" for reaching single young adults.

At this writing, the group has begun working through approaches and ideas on a trial-and-error basis, since most of its participants have little background or practical experience with single adult ministry. Aziere and the others hope eventually to form a board which serves the entire diocese and provides a resource base for all Catholic churches in the area.

One of their goals is to become aware of other agencies that can supplement the churches' ministries with single adults. "Catholics realize there are vast needs within the single adult arena," says Aziere. "Specific issues require specific attention, such as the needs of women, the handicapped, sexual minorities, college students, and career people. We'd like to become collaborators with other agencies to provide a well-rounded service for singles." Already the leadership group is recommending existing programs to local Catholic churches whose single members need specific assistance.

From this, churches may cooperate in developing support groups for adult singles. Aziere hopes that one day such groups will become loving, caring fellowships, similar to many Protestant denominations' Sunday School classes. He also envisions a future with "pastoral facilitators," individuals who will be trained to offer guidance and leadership to single adult groups. Moreover, he hopes to see participants reaching out to single friends, relatives, and neighbors—whether Catholic or not—and including them in these groups.

The Catholic Church has only recently begun to take responsibility for work with adult singles. Its Association of Single Adult Ministry Leaders holds an annual summer conference. The Family Life Conference in New Orleans is also well accepted among Catholics who work with adult singles. Other regional and national conferences for leaders are held throughout the year, with the goal of training future single adult leaders to serve in local churches. One example is the North American Conference for Separated and Divorced, organized by Father Jim Young of Washington, D.C. He, along with a national board of divorced lay Catholics, hosts a four-day annual conference for separated and divorced people at Notre Dame.

Except for these, which focus generally on leadership, few national events are available for single adults themselves. However, participation on the diocesan level is increasing rapidly. Mary Morris, administrator at the Catholic Center for Separated and Divorced, states that 65 percent of all dioceses in the United States now have formalized ministries to the separated and divorced:

> Counseling, support and education groups are available for parents and for children. Education of religious clergy and parish staff continues. Training for the divorced to participate in the ministry is sponsored by the North American Conference for Separated and Divorced, also by many diocesan offices. Socializing, an important step in healing for one whose social system has collapsed, is a part of this ministry ("Separation and Divorce from a Catholic Perspective," pp. 155–56, in *Being Single: Resources on Singleness*).

Morris continues by cautioning that leaders of single adults as well as clergy must become aware of their own values, biases, and prejudices regarding divorce. "They need to understand that the permanency of marriage is a value deeply embraced by divorced people even though their own experience is a contradiction to their values and beliefs. They need to tap into the powerful potential that the Church has for supporting people through such a painful life experience."

Except for large parishes, most Catholic churches do not have single adult ministries. Persons wishing to begin a single adult ministry would be wise to consult with other nearby parishes and try a cooperative effort first. Potential leaders may also wish to attend one of the conferences mentioned above and to read literature about single adults written from the Catholic perspective.

Within the local parish, ministry opportunities are limited for single adults. Aziere says that "enough older priests (age 60 and up) are still around who believe they have to do it all because they're the pastor. They're preventing laypersons, including single adults, from taking leadership roles." This attitude, of course, stems in part from the Catholic Church's historical theological approach to priestly leadership and also its traditional orientation to the family.

However, some Catholics are relaxing their stance as they realize that every adult may not be meant to marry. "Singles," says Aziere, "shouldn't be made to feel that marriage is an absolute criteria for life." This attitude is slowly growing among members, as they study their own history and discover important contributions made by Catholic single adults. They conclude that today's single adult may also contribute to the life of the church.

Resource

Deacon Ron Aziere, 7708 Carlos, Fort Worth, TX 76108

CHRISTIAN CHURCH (DISCIPLES OF CHRIST)

We're very congregationally oriented," explains Zena McAdams of the Christian Church (Disciples of Christ). "That's why most of our events for singles occur at the local level rather than nationally." McAdams, who serves as Area Associate Minister for the North Texas Area of the Christian Church (Disciples of Christ) in the Southwest, says that some churches in her denomination are interested in cooperating voluntarily for regional events. Others, such as First Christian in Plano, Texas, have gone a step further and spearheaded ecumenical activities for single adults in their city.

Examples of cooperation can be seen as McAdam's area, headquartered in Dallas, joined with the Trinity-Brazos Area from Fort Worth in the spring of 1990 and co-sponsored a singles spiritual retreat. The two groups have agreed to continue this collaboration in the future, with Dallas organizing the spring retreat and Fort Worth the fall retreat each year at the denomination's camp in Athens, Texas. Members of churches from both areas are invited to each. McAdams was pleased with the 90 persons who attended the first retreat, especially because single adults from every age bracket were represented, and because the age span had no detrimental effect on the fellowship or the study sessions.

McAdams' area office is also developing a young adult ministry for persons ages 18–26, most of whom are single. She organized a recent week-long camp for that group, a successful start, in her opinion, for this region. "We're working on a three-year proposal on how to extend this area of ministry, and we anticipate future growth. Our intent is that this regional event will be a steppingstone for us."

Most Disciples congregations are not yet involved in single adult ministry, either on their own or in cooperation with other churches. J. Cy Rowell, associate professor of religious education at Brite Divinity School, Texas Christian University, offers several reasons for this. First,

253

he cites lack of denominational leadership in the field. "Two years ago, because of economic conditions, we eliminated the national young adult director who worked with singles." Since then, the Disciples churches have had no definite direction for single adult ministry. Another factor Rowell lists is the lack of denominational literature written specifically for single adults. Many Disciples congregations use the Methodist curriculum series *Ages and Stages* for their adult singles' Sunday School and study groups.

Rowell also states that in some congregations, younger singles are enlisted to teach Sunday School classes in other age-groups, leaving few members available to attend a singles class. Those few usually prefer to find fellowship elsewhere, which leads to another of Rowell's points: "Because we don't generally have large congregations, and because we have a relatively liberal tradition, our singles feel comfortable attending large, meaningful single adult ministries sponsored by other denominations, such as First Methodist in Fort Worth, which has a dynamic program."

Regardless of such problems, Rowell recognizes that a few "isolated churches" do have active single adult ministries. Some focus on the widowed or the divorced or students. South Hills Christian in Fort Worth, for example, has a well-organized college student program, led by the church's single and married young adults.

In the local church—even one without an official single adult ministry—leadership opportunities abound for single adults. McAdams, herself single for 15 years, is leading a junior high church camp this summer, and she says most of the staff members are also single. Singles among the Disciples may teach, serve as deacons and elders, or be involved in many other positions. According to McAdams, the church is realizing that a person does not have to be married to be complete.

Leaders must guard against letting a single adult ministry be perceived as simply a dating service. As McAdams says, "We are building single adult groups that are fellowship oriented, but there was a time when this was just considered a place to meet a mate." She points out that the dominant need of singles in the church is not necessarily dating, but friendship and fellowship among their peers.

Another word of caution from McAdams concerns work with gay/lesbian members. "Several of our churches are doing good work among the gay population, and I believe there's a place in the life of the church for this ministry." However, she notes that persons outside her denomination tend to misinterpret the work, and she recommends that single adult leaders consider this a part of their ministry and not be discouraged by outside influences.

Rowell adds to McAdams' list of cautions the "problematic single adult class," which he describes as having socially or emotionally dysfunctional members, with personality problems, few friends, and abrasive temperaments. "The mentally healthy single adult is turned off because the class has more of a therapy-group feeling than Bible study and fellowship. He visits once but won't return." Single adult leaders would be wise to plan the Bible study lessons carefully in order to steer such a class away from personal discussions and toward the topic at hand. Otherwise, a few abrasive people will discourage a visitor from returning to the class.

Resources

Zena McAdams, 1221 River Bend, Suite 260, Dallas, TX 75247. Phone: (214) 631-6991.

Jayna Powell, Division of Homeland Ministries, P.O. Box 1986, Indianapolis, IN 46206.

J. Cy Rowell, Associate Professor of Religious Education, Brite Divinity School, Texas Christian University, Box 32923, Fort Worth, TX 76129. Phone: (817) 921-7589.

LUTHERAN CHURCH, MISSOURI SYNOD

Although Lutheran leaders do not have an accurate estimate of the number of affiliated churches with active single adult ministries, that number is growing, as evidenced by the denomination's overall interest in working with single adults. Every three to four years, an International Gathering for single adults and their leaders is held. Also, Missouri Synod districts throughout the country provide periodic singles leadership conferences for persons in their areas.

On the local level, single adult leaders are beginning to develop cooperative committees encompassing several Lutheran churches. One example can be found in the Dallas/Fort Worth area. The Metroplex Singles Coordinating Committee, with representatives from five churches, meets monthly and organizes such things as trips to the symphony, the rodeo, and professional sporting events, along with picnics and retreats. At least one activity is arranged each month.

Within many Lutheran churches, ministries are developing to meet the needs of an increasing number of single adult members. Greg Drose, a youth director who also works with single adults at St. Paul Lutheran in Forth Worth, believes his church's attitude toward single adults is more positive than in years past. "When we started, we laid out our intention: to help single adults grow spiritually and relationally. A few members were skeptical then, but now that we've been involved a while, the church has come to realize that single adult ministry reaches far beyond the dating club some were expecting."

Indeed, St. Paul single adults participate in numerous activities, including a Sunday morning Bible class for ages 22 to 35, with about 50 on the roll. (The approximately 40 older singles attend Sunday School with married persons their age.) The younger group also has fellowship suppers and other social and recreational events, while older single adults hold socials, dinners, and devotional meetings of their own. Although Drose has not yet seen cooperative activities with other Lutheran single adults in the area, his group does participate in social and recreational events with singles from McKinney Bible Church, a large nondenominational congregation in Fort Worth.

In larger Lutheran churches, such as Holy Cross in Dallas, more activities for single adults can be arranged. Tom Couser, director of young adult ministry there, says his single adult group meets each Monday evening for Bible study and fellowship, in addition to the usual Sunday activities. They are also involved in serving the church in many ways, such as sponsoring the children's Easter party each year and sending Care Packages to college students semiannually. Holy Cross Church also hosts a divorce support group which meets twice a month.

Qualifications for single adult leaders among Lutherans vary from one church to another. Some prefer married persons, while others welcome adult singles as leaders. St. Paul's singles Bible class is taught by a married couple who, according to Drose, "are young enough to meet the needs of the persons in the class." Single adult leaders who are married must have a good understanding of the single person, says Drose, who believes that in many cases "a single might be more effective because he can appreciate what his people are going through."

Drose cautions potential leaders to be alert to certain problems which can creep into a single adult ministry: "Some members become a little overdependent on the group to serve all their needs and fulfill them."

256

Such persons think the group should do everything together — go to movies, picnics, concerts, and so on. "What they fail to understand," Drose continues, "is that this isn't the only group that can help them." Along with the overdependency then, is the problem of unrealistic expectations among a few members, who become disappointed when their needs are not met in a short time.

Couser, who has been in youth and young adult ministry for 22 years, recognizes another concern for leaders of single adults. "This is a difficult ministry in that there is a lot of fluidity. Single adults tend to be more mobile with more flexible agendas." Most single adults, Couser notices, are responsible, mature, and dependable, but work schedules, needs of aging parents, and any number of other obligations might keep them from being active in the church. In addition, many are experiencing major life changes. The result, in Couser's words, is "constant turnover" in the population of single adults at church. "You can bring in lots of new people, but the group never seems to get any bigger." Frustrating, to be sure, but Couser's tenure is testimony to the fact that working with single adults can become an enduring joy. "You just have to love people and be interested in them," he says.

Single adults in many Lutheran churches hold positions of leadership, such as Sunday morning Bible class teachers, participation on committees, and in Couser's church, single adults serve as ushers and on boards. Besides these positions, Couser and Drose agree that single adult ministers are being accepted universally in the Lutheran Church.

Resources

Greg Drose, Youth Director, St. Paul Lutheran Church, 1800 W. Freeway, Fort Worth, TX 76102. Phone: (817) 332-2281.

Tom Couser, Director of Youth and Young Adult Ministry, Holy Cross Lutheran Church, 11425 Marsh Lane, Dallas, TX 75229. Phone: (214) 358-4396.

EPISCOPAL

The Episcopal Church has a surprising number of single adults in leadership positions in local parishes, but it has been slow in developing an official ministry and theology of single adults. According to the Rev. M.L. McCauley, rector of the Church of the Holy Apostles in Fort Worth, Episcopalians who work with single adults must still rely on non- or other-denominational resources, such as *Leadership Journal* and the Hollywood *Presbyterian Church Magazine.* The first Episcopal-produced resource book, *Single in the Church: New Ways to Minister to 52 Percent of God's People,* by Kay Collier-Slone, Ph.D., was published by The Alban Institute in 1992.

The Rev. Thomas Blackmon of St. Michael and All Angels in Dallas, Texas agrees, noting, "Given the structure of our church on the national level, I don't expect to see any changes in the near future." Collier-Slone, however, emphasizes the advantage of the diocesan structure of the church, which can be utilized to include smaller congregations as well as large multi-staff churches which are able to finance a singles' ministry program. Her consulting work throughout the church is based in part on this concept, and "a theology of humanity that embraces all people — including singles." An annual lay-designed and led national conference is currently held at Kanuga Conference Center in North Carolina, with plans for expansion into four other geographical areas. At the national convention of the denomination in Phoenix in the summer of 1991, a resolution was passed declaring the intention of the church to evangelize and minister to single adults, and to assess the work being done in its congregations to date.

In spite of lack of resources, McCauley, who works with young adults in his parish, believes that single adult ministries are much needed in the life of today's Episcopalians. He recommends several steps for parishes who wish to begin a single adult ministry. First, a demographic study through the official parish register is necessary for discovering potential members of a single adult group. Then, possible leaders should be identified. McCauley's experience leads him to recommend male leaders, who he believes tend to attract other males to the group. Blackmon and Collier-Slone emphasize the importance of the personal single adult experience as essential to the training and credibility of leaders, regardless of gender.

If the parish is small, leaders may want to follow McCauley's example and start a young adult group without regard to marital status. His "good time gang" is a blend of always single, divorced, widowed, and married persons who enjoy fellowship and other activities. The Church of the Holy Apostles also has events for older single adults, who, like their younger counterparts, are blended with married persons in their age-groups. To foster a wider circle of acquaintances and to eliminate cliques, names of participants are shuffled every four months, and new groups are formed. Collier-Slone advocates "attitude, intentionality from the leadership, inclusive theology and diocesan involvement" for the smaller parish.

In a larger parish such as St. Michael and All Angels, more activities can be done with singles exclusively—which is also true of a diocesan-based group. Blackmon says his 250 singles are involved in numerous events like camping trips, parties, fellowship suppers. They also participate in twice yearly retreats, during Advent and Lent. In a 6,000 member parish, Blackmon can offer several avenues of ministry to singles, such as separate recovery programs for divorce, single parents of teens, and single parents of younger children. St. Michael's has two Sunday School classes for singles, which cover all ages, and from these have developed Bible study groups, support groups, and service to others. The diocesan, cathedral, or parish-based ministry, says Collier-Slone, can likewise sponsor such activities. Members of smaller parishes may drive several hours each week to participate in recovery, study, or fellowship activities.

One interesting trend Blackmon has noticed through single adults in his parish is their time of transition through the program. Some enter the church's single adult ministry as a result of crisis, such as divorce, or death of a spouse. "Once they get their lives established, they eventually move on to more heterogeneous groups. Of course, this is not negative. The single adult program exists to meet needs. When the need is no longer felt, some people move on to other groups." Collier-Slone says, "For some people, single adult programs are a point of entry. For others, it is a support system, a family from which they go into the larger fellowship."

Even in parishes without single adult ministries per se, single adults have held positions of leadership for many years. There are many single persons among the ordained clergy—always single, divorced, widowed—and other offices, such as lector, eucharistic minister, acolyte, and sub-deacon, are often filled by singles, as well. In the Church of the Holy Apostles, St. Michael and All Angels, and Christ Church Cathedral, as well as many other churches across the nation, single adults are represented on the vestry (a nonordained elected board of administrators) and at various times have been responsible for building fund campaigns, teaching Sunday School, and other leadership duties. Whether married or single, members are encouraged to find opportunities to serve and lead within the Episcopal community.

Resources

The Rev. Thomas Blackmon, St. Michael and All Angels Church, P.O. Box 12385, Dallas, TX 75225. Phone: (214) 363-5471.

Kay Collier-Slone, Ph.D., Christ Church Cathedral, Diocese of Lexington, 166 Market St., Lexington, KY 40507. Phone: (606) 252-6527.

The Rev. M.L. McCauley, The Church of the Apostles, 3900 Longvue, Fort Worth, TX 76126. Phone: (817) 244-2752.

UNITED METHODIST

The United Methodist Church has been actively involved in single adult ministries for over fifteen years. According to Karen A. Greenwaldt, who directs Education and Ministries with Young Adults and Single Adults on the General Board of Discipleship in Nashville, Tennessee, Methodists have developed a useful base of resources for leaders of single adults and for singles themselves within the local church.

United Methodists also offer nationwide events for single adults and their leaders. The National Gathering for United Methodist Singles and also the National Meeting for Leaders of Single Adults occur every two years in various locations across the country.

Individual Methodist churches vary in their approaches to single adult ministry, depending on the size of the church. A small congregation, like St. Mark in Cleburne, Texas, has among its members an experienced single adult leader but no program because of "lack of interest among the few singles who belong." By contrast, First Methodist in Fort Worth has an extensive single adult ministry, with five Sunday School classes specifically for single adults, totaling approximately 400 persons on the roll.

Dr. William Longsworth, associate pastor at St. Mark's Church for the past seven years, is the staff liaison to single adults. He states that most smaller Methodist churches are hindered in developing a single adult program because of few participants. And, with only a few participants, problems can emerge as a result of one over-dominant personality. "A good number to begin with," Longsworth believes, "is about 50 singles. Fewer than that would allow an angular person too much domination." Longsworth states that in a large group, one or two overbearing members would be absorbed into the whole and would not have a negative effect on the other participants.

Another consideration in beginning a single adult ministry is finding good leadership. Longsworth recommends that potential leaders be "upbeat, pleasant, and enjoy working with people." He has discovered that the most effective leaders are single adults themselves. An exception to this is found in the Sunday School structure at First Methodist, where teachers of adults come from a pool. Teachers rotate from class to class within the adult division; therefore, those who happen to be single do not necessarily teach in a singles class throughout the year.

With a numerically large single adult program, Longsworth has discovered that retreats and similar activities with other Methodist churches in the area are too difficult to coordinate. Rather, he promotes activities within his church's single adult community. While individual Sunday School classes often make plans for their own events, Longsworth oversees activities for all singles in the church. At first glance, these social activities might seem to appeal mainly to younger singles; however, at First Methodist they draw singles from all age-groups.

Another stand-alone singles program can be found at First Methodist in Dallas, where the number of singles on roll is close to 2,000. Lane Tunnell, Director of Ministry to College and Singles, says all of her groups' activities take place within the church body rather than cooperatively with other Methodist congregations. "We've talked about working with some other churches around here," she says, "but so far nothing's been done about it."

However, the single adult program at First Methodist is open to anyone wishing to attend, regardless of church membership. They conduct retreats, ski trips, fellowship meals, swim parties, divorce recovery workshops, and various support groups which are organized around a specific need, such as handling the sudden loss of employment. Tunnell also directs a "University of the Spirit" twice annually: a series of six nights in the fall and four nights in the spring dealing with a wide range of topics, like relationships, careers, photography, theology.

Resources

William Longsworth, First United Methodist Church, 800 W. Fifth St., Fort Worth, TX 76102. Phone: (817) 332-6266.

Lane Tunnell, First United Methodist Church, 1928 Ross Ave., Dallas,

TX 75201. Phone: (214) 220-2727.

PRESBYTERIAN CHURCH (U.S.A.)

During the last ten years, Presbyterians have developed a program of ministry to and with single adults, and are aiming for a more progressive attitude toward single adults in the future. The Rev. Dr. C. Raymond Trout, Associate for Family and Single Adult Ministries, Education and Congregational Nurture Unit, for the Presbyterian Church (U.S.A.), says they "try to avoid terminology that defines singles in reference to marriage" (such as never-married or formerly-married), in order to affirm single adults as individuals in their own right, rather than according to marital status.

One of the biggest obstacles in single adult ministries across the denomination is, according to Trout, the traditional family orientation of most congregations. He goes so far as to wish the word "single" were omitted from his denomination's vocabulary, because he believes it perpetuates stereotypical images in the minds of persons who use it. Rather, he prefers a holistic perspective when dealing with all persons, regardless of marital status.

While eliminating the word "single" may be difficult to do, Trout and his cohorts within the Presbyterian Church have done much toward improving the image of single adults in other ways.

Presbyterians offer single adults and their leaders an annual Single Adult Conference in Montreat, North Carolina, which is publicized through denominational periodicals such as Sunday School materials. Singles conferences, camps, and retreats are also offered on district, state, and synod levels throughout the country.

Locally, several churches may work cooperatively in singles ministries. The Grace Presbytery, for example, which covers north central Texas and incorporates 203 churches, has recently developed a single adult committee to coordinate retreats and other activities for the area. Churches which participate do so voluntarily, offering their single members more opportunities for fellowship and growth.

However, some churches conduct their own retreats and conferences, with hundreds of participants. Paul Petersen, director of singles ministry at Highland Park, the largest Presbyterian church in Dallas, says his 1,500 active single members are "such a large group that we'd overwhelm them" at a presbytery function. Because of this, Petersen and his workers prefer to plan activities for their church's single adults only. Such activities may include single parenting seminars, divorce recovery ministries, Bible studies, athletic events, and discipleship groups.

Presbyterian single adults are also involved in serving others. The Highland Park group participates in short-term missions activities, both locally and abroad. For instance, they were recently involved with a Habitat for Humanity project in Dallas, and they have traveled to Merida, Mexico to help a Presbyterian church build a seminary.

In the individual Presbyterian church, single adults are welcome to participate as leaders, according to the church's needs. Petersen says singles in his congregation teach Sunday School, sing in the choir, lead in evangelism, and serve as ushers. Some single adults participate as elders and deacons, though Petersen would like to see more single adults represented on the Body of Elders. Overall, Petersen states, the church is "fairly open and receptive to our singles, their ministry and the gifts and abilities they bring to the church."

When looking for leaders among single adults, Petersen advises churches to adopt an informal type of "farm system," in which they look for people already involved in and faithful to other endeavors within the church. "From that," he says, "you can see who is willing to work hard and contribute." A single adult who has served regularly on one of the church's committees for two years might be a good candidate for a leadership position in the single adult ministry.

Petersen recommends that churches beginning a single adult program seek male leadership when possible. "We always try to have an equal if not greater number of men than women leading our single adult ministry. We've discovered that men tend to attract men *and* women, while women usually attract only women to the program." Concerning the marital status of single adult leaders, Petersen says most are single adults. In fact, all leaders within Highland Park's single ministry — except Petersen himself — are single. "It seems to happen naturally; if a single adult leader does marry, the couple will stay with the work a while, then drift into other ministries of the church." While many married persons are excellent single adult leaders, Petersen cautions that they must constantly guard against a condescending attitude toward single adults.

Among Presbyterians, as among any other religious group seeking to minister to and with single adults, problems can arise. Petersen notes that participants' personalities can sometimes clash and stand in the way of ministry, as can a church's traditions. An overall philosophy of a single adult ministry is to let the participants — not the leaders — own the ministry. If leaders do all the planning and scheduling, single adults will not feel a part of the program and will not take part as enthusiastically as they would if they had helped develop the plans. Good leadership, along with active ownership by participants, will result in a successful singles ministry. Says Petersen: "Resign tomorrow as director, and the ministry would continue. That's a good idea for any ministry."

Resources

People:
Dr. C. Raymond Trout, Associate for Family and Single Adult Ministries, Presbyterian Church (U.S.A.), 100 Witherspoon St., Louisville, KY 40202. Phone: (502) 569-5487.

Paul Petersen, Highland Park Presbyterian Church, 3821 University Blvd., Dallas, TX 75205. Phone: (214) 526-7457.

Doug Fagerstrom, Executive Director, National Association of Single Adult Leaders, P.O. Box 1600, Grand Rapids, MI 49501. Phone: (616) 956-9377. (A nondenominational network for leaders.)

Tapes:

"Starting a Singles Ministry" by Doug Fagerstrom

"Keeping a Single Adult Ministry Biblically Focused" by Mary Graves

"How To's of Divorce Recovery" by John Splinter

"Career Singles/Young Adults" by David Boswell and Pam Harper

"Ministry to Single Parent Children" by Barb Schiller

"Preparation for Marriage (Including Remarriage and Blended Families)" by Harold Ivan Smith

"Leadership Development in Single Ministry" by Mary Graves

"Dynamic Outreach to Single Adults: Evangelism and Discipleship" by Rich Hurst

Videos:

"One Is a Whole Number" by Harold Ivan Smith

"The Sexual Puzzle" by Josh McDowell and Dick Day

"God's Call to the Single Adult" by Mike Cavanaugh

"How to Survive a Divorce" by Jim Smoke

"The Ministry of Divorce Recovery" by Bill Flanagan

"Dream Making in a Dream Breaking World" (2 tapes) by Harold Ivan Smith

"Divorce Recovery" (8 sessions) by Andy Morgan

Additional selected resources from the National Association of Single Adult Leaders (P.O. Box 1600, Grand Rapids, MI 49501).

SUMMARY

All denominations surveyed generally defined singles as persons ages 18 to 64 who are not presently married. Classifications included the following: single college students, never-married career singles, divorced singles, separated singles, widowed singles. (Of course, within each of these categories subgroups may be formed, depending on the needs of the congregation and the preferences of the denomination, such as divorced parents and gay/lesbian persons.) Even though the 18 to 64 age designation was theoretically a part of every religious group's statement about single adults, few of those surveyed included persons in the middle years (approximately ages 40 to 60) as a practical aspect of their single adult ministry. Most ministries focused on younger singles.

• Attitudes. In every case, attitudes toward single adults are more open today than twenty or even ten years ago. Religious groups which would not have considered it in the 1970s are welcoming single adults, their leaders, and their ministries in the 1990s. Divorced singles are being accepted into the church "family," and they, along with the always-

265

single, are being placed into leadership positions such as teacher, deacon, trustee, and other offices, depending on denominational standards as well as on local preference of the congregation. Few groups seem to have an abundance of single pastors, yet the persons surveyed among Presbyterians, Methodists, and Lutherans see this trend gaining momentum in the future.

Unfortunately, the average person in the pew does not yet see single adults as whole, viable, contributing adults. Traditionalists in all religious groups look upon single adults as persons to be somewhat pitied until they are married, at which time they may assume full adult status in the congregation. At the opposite end of the spectrum are persons and churches who see enormous potential in single adults and invite them — as they are — to participate as responsible members.

● Resources. While many denominations, including Methodist, Baptist, Presbyterian, and Catholic, have developed an adequate library of resources for singles work, other groups, such as the Disciples of Christ, have no literature whatsoever which uniquely addresses their own single adults. Among persons who recommended books, some mentioned authors' names more than once; Christoff, Landgraff, Murray, Hershey, Parks, and Fagerstrom all seemed to cross denominational lines.

● Events. Not all religious groups surveyed have nationwide seminars, retreats, and conferences for leaders and for singles. Those with the most of such opportunities were Baptists, Methodists, Lutherans, and Presbyterians; however, Assemblies of God and Catholics are beginning to develop national events for training and fellowship. Other groups, such as Episcopalians and Disciples of Christ, are working more at the local level to coordinate events among their congregations.

● Qualifications of Singles Leadership. All persons surveyed who listed qualifications for leaders of single adults chose positive adjectives like "upbeat," "progressive," "committed to the program," "willing to work," "flexible." And, while many did not state a preference of marital status for leaders, those who did preferred single persons leading other singles. Joe Martin of Field Street Baptist, a young widower for several years but recently remarried, mentioned that he had been a more effective leader of singles before his second marriage. He was, as a single adult, more often invited into the homes of other single adults and thus had an easier path to ministry.

266

Most interesting were the comments from leaders of Episcopal and Presbyterian churches, who expressed a definite preference for male leadership over female in single adult programs. Both stated their reasons similarly: Male leaders attract both males and females, while female leaders usually attract only females. The Presbyterian representative defended his position, not on the grounds of a sexist attitude, but based on statistics which substantiated his claims.

• Activities. Nearly all who responded to the survey indicated that single adult activities must include three elements: spiritual, social, and service. While some groups, such as the Assemblies of God, listed numerous service opportunities for their single adults, others seemed to focus on social events at the expense of the spiritual and service. However, an accurate conclusion cannot be drawn here as to the balance of the three elements in all the religious groups surveyed, because relatively few persons were actually surveyed in each group, and because respondents may not have considered all three aspects equally as they answered the survey questions. Several did mention the desire that the "social club/dating service" stigma be removed from their single adult ministry and be replaced with a Bible study/fellowship/service connotation.

• Transition Time. Interestingly, Episcopal, Baptist, and Lutheran singles leaders bemoaned the fact that the turnover rate is high among participants in a church's single adult program. This can cause problems in long-range planning, in the stability of the ministry, and in the numerical growth of the membership, as well as discouragement among leaders. Tom Couser of Holy Cross Lutheran was correct in his assessment: "You can bring in lots of new people, but the group never seems to get any bigger."

• Ownership. One of the best points concerning single adult ministry came from Mike Jackson, Bethel Temple Assembly, and Paul Petersen, Highland Park Presbyterian. Both stated that the most successful way to conduct a single adult ministry was to let the members themselves "own" the program. By this, of course, they meant that the single adults should make the plans, set up the schedules, organize the sports events, investigate and initiate the social action projects, and do all the other things that make the program theirs. In a church where a leader or a small committee dictates all that is to be done among the single adults, little will be done with enthusiasm. By contrast, when participants feel that their opinions count, they are usually more willing to be involved.

Ruth McHaney Danner
101 South Pendell
Cleburne, Texas 76031

FOR FURTHER READING

Balswick, Jack O. and Judith K. *The Family—A Christian Perspective on the Contemporary Home.* Grand Rapids: Baker Book House, 1989.

Barna, George. *The Frog in the Kettle.* Ventura, California: Regal Books, 1990.

Cook, Jerry. *Love, Acceptance, and Forgiveness.* Ventura, California: Regal Books, 1978.

Dahl, Gerald L. *How Can We Keep Christian Marriages from Falling Apart?* Nashville: Thomas Nelson, 1988.

Dycus, Jim and Barbara. *Children of Divorce.* Elgin, Illinois: David C. Cook, 1987.

Fagerstrom, Douglas L., ed. *Singles Ministry Handbook.* Wheaton, Illinois: Victor Books, 1988.

Greenfield, Guy. *We Need Each Other.* Grand Rapids: Baker Book House, 1984.

Harley, Jr., Willard F. *His Needs, Her Needs.* Old Tappan, New Jersey: Fleming H. Revell, 1986.

House, H. Wayne, ed. *Divorce and Remarriage—Four Christian Views.* Downers Grove, Illinois: InterVarsity Press, 1990.

Juroe, David J. and Bonnie B. *Successful Step-Parenting.* Old Tappan, New Jersey: Fleming H. Revell, 1983.

Larson, Ray E. *A Season of Singleness.* Springfield, Missouri: Gospel Publishing House, 1984.

Murren, Doug. *The Baby Boomerang.* Ventura, California: Regal Books, 1990.

Roberts, Wes and H. Norman Wright. *Before You Say I Do*. Eugene, Oregon: Harvest House, 1978.

Smith, Harold Ivan. *I Wish Someone Understood My Divorce*. Minneapolis: Augsburg Publishing House, 1986.

_____. *Positively Single*. Wheaton, Illinois: Victor Books, 1989.

Smoke, Jim. *Growing in Remarriage*. Old Tappan, New Jersey: Fleming H. Revell, 1990.

_____. *Turning Points*. Eugene, Oregon: Harvest House, 1985.

Williams, Pat and Jill. *Rekindled*. Old Tappan, New Jersey: Fleming H. Revell, 1985.

Wright, H. Norman. *Communication*. Ventura, California: Regal Books, 1984.

_____. *Premarital Counseling*. Chicago: Moody Press, 1986.

Wright, Linda Raney. *A Cord of Three Strands*. Old Tappan, New Jersey: Fleming H. Revell, 1987.